The Teams in Action

Fortier heard the flash-bang grenade go off and the apartment door crash open. Fortier stepped into the room. The occupant had gone to the window but now turned to face the K-9 officer, knife still in hand. Without waiting, Fortier ordered Flic to take the man down. The K-9 jumped over a couch, and as he leaped through the air, Fortier saw the man's eyes grow to the size of silver dollars. . . .

FORTIER AND FLIC: Police Officer Ken Fortier's dog was trained to charge into the face of danger. After two years, Flic had a "rep" even among San Diego's toughest gangs. . . .

MILLS AND FARGO: Officer Peter Mills took his bomb-detection dog Fargo to a scene of death and carnage in San Diego. But the killer wasn't done; there were more bombs in the building. . . .

PECORARO AND AJAX: The San Diego cop and his dog were face to face with a gunman. When Ajax attacked, the man fired—and both Pecoraro and his partner were hit. . . .

Women in and around New Bedford, Massachusetts, had begun to turn up dead. It stood to reason that if four or five dead bodies had been discovered, there might be more out there. . . . In five days of searching, Rebmann and Josie located two more victims. With the coming of spring they returned, and Josie found another. . . .

REBMANN AND JOSIE: Vermont police had a killer and a confession. What they needed was a body. Connecticut State Police Trooper Andy Rebmann brought his tracking bloodhound, Josie, to find a victim who had been buried eleven years ago. . . .

ZARRELLA AND HANNIBAL: Rhode Island State Trooper Matthew Zarrella felt so strongly about the value of police dogs that he trained his own dog, a one-hundred-thirty-pound greater Swiss mountain dog, for search and rescue. Hannibal was to prove himself in the field—and at sea. . . .

PAYNE AND INGO: Sergeant Tom Payne's K-9 partner, Ingo, was a headstrong and cocky Schutzhund. But in Calexico, California, Ingo showed his skill—tracking a killer relentlessly over a heat-baked, concrete landscape, a task for which he had never been trained. . . .

The suspect had gone only a few yards when Hooper saw the man's hand—with some object in it—come up to eye level. The officer then heard two pops. Hooper dove below the door sill of his cruiser. But the instant he released Rex to go for his own gun, the dog bolted after the suspect. . . .

HOOPER AND REX: Sergeant Kenneth Hooper began working with the shepherd when he was only a pup. On the streets of Seattle, Rex would earn the nickname "Wonderdog."

EMERICK AND ADAM: In the deserted, commercial Ballard neighborhood of Seattle, Officer Jon Emerick and his red, tall-eared shepherd hunted for a cop shooter—who vowed to strike again.

FULLMAN AND RODY: The one-hundred-five-pound shepherd once saved a baby rabbit from a cat. But on the streets of Newport News, Virginia, he hunted much more dangerous prey with his female handler—a savage murderer.

K-9
COPS

STORIES FROM AMERICA'S
K-9 POLICE UNITS

RICHARD ROSENTHAL

POCKET BOOKS
New York   London   Toronto   Sydney   Tokyo   Singapore

An *Original* Publication of POCKET BOOKS

POCKET BOOKS, a division of Simon & Schuster Inc.
1230 Avenue of the Americas, New York, NY 10020

ISBN: 0-671-00023-3

First Pocket Books printing July 1997

10 9 8 7 6 5 4 3 2 1

POCKET and colophon are registered trademarks of Simon & Schuster Inc.

Front cover photo credits: police officer © Dorothy Littell/PNI; dog © 1995 Bill Keefrey/PNI
Back cover photo: Timothy C. Barmann

Printed in the U.S.A.

Hannibal

February 18, 1990–April 18, 1996

The book is dedicated to the memory of Rhode Island State Police K-9 Hannibal. Hannibal, a one-hundred-thirty-pound greater Swiss mountain dog, died years before his time. He was a wonderful, talented dog who loved people.

In this book there are stories about many fine police service dogs. A number of them have passed on since I wrote about them, and that is very sad. I knew and worked with both Hannibal and his handler-partner, Trooper Matthew Zarrella.

Hannibal did many extraordinary things in his all-too-short law-enforcement career, and, had he lived, there is no doubt he would have accomplished far more. This unique K-9 will be missed by his trooper comrades. He has left behind many saddened people.

With Hannibal's death, Trooper Matthew Zarrella lost one of his best friends.

Acknowledgments

This book could not have been written without the help of many people. The members of the various law-enforcement agencies whom I interviewed and who gave me their time, some of them many hours, have my thanks and gratitude. I have tried to record their stories as accurately as possible. Whatever errors or omissions there may be are my responsibility.

A number of people, while not direct contributors to the book, assisted me greatly. Lieutenant Steve Hinton of the San Diego Police Department put me in touch with Sergeant Tom Payne of that agency's K-9 Unit, and many wonderful interviews followed. Ellen Count, a fellow writer, helped make a connection for me with Hampton, Virginia, Police Officer Glennell Fullman and her dog, Rody, now deceased.

Lieutenant Chris Ball, commanding officer of the San Diego Police Department's K-9 Unit, as well as the various members of the unit, were most gracious to me on my visit to their facility.

My wife, Frauke, my in-house editor, made writing the book far easier. She is foreign-born; thus, her knowledge of English grammar easily surpasses mine.

And finally, there is Chip, formerly referred to as "the puppy from hell." He is the family's K-8—that is, not quite up to K-9 standards. But then, he tries very hard to be a good boy.

Contents

Contents

Contents

Contents

Chapter 1

Rhode Island State Police
K-9 Unit

K-9s Hannibal and Panzer
with Trooper Matthew Zarrella

We Need a K-9 Unit

Rhode Island may be this country's smallest state, but as it is situated in a line between New York City and Boston, its law officers get to deal with their share of serious crimes. The two hundred troopers of the Rhode Island State Police have to handle everything from homicides to finding lost children, and, as has been shown over and over again in other jurisdictions, sometimes there is no greater aid to a search and rescue—or a homicide investigation—than a working police dog. With this agency it took one determined trooper to get the powers that be to set up a police dog unit within the state police.

Matt Zarrella was born in Providence, Rhode Island. A six-year marine veteran, he's a muscular, fire-plug shaped go-getter of a trooper. Back in 1990, when he started with the force, the agency had no search-and-rescue or cadaver-locating working dog capability. When such a resource was needed they'd call in a neighboring agency, either the Connecticut State Police or the Massachusetts State Police, and use their animals. That was fine, and the other agencies were and remain glad to assist, but sometimes these searches can take a good deal of time, and how long can you borrow another agency's resources?

Back when Zarrella first got on the force, there had been a murder in the state. It was a nasty business. One Christopher Hightower had killed an entire family, the Brendells, over a business dispute. The father had been murdered with a crossbow, the wife had been strangled, and their eight-year-old daughter, well, the medical examiner wasn't sure. It was possible she had been drugged and buried alive, dumped in her mother's grave.

Zarrella, frustrated, watched as out-of-state police working dogs searched for the bodies of the three victims. But even a small state covers a lot of territory, and you can only ask so much of neighboring agencies. After some intensive looking the search came to an unsuccessful end.

A woman, while walking her untrained pet dog, purely by chance discovered the family's burial site.

Zarrella, a working road trooper, had followed the search with interest. He had long advocated the use of working police dogs within the Rhode Island State Police. (At the time the agency did have three narcotics-sniffing dogs.) Zarrella felt so strongly about this resource, and the Brendell murders had moved him so deeply, that he went so far as to take his own pet, Hannibal, a hundred-thirty-pound greater Swiss mountain dog, and have him trained, at his own expense, by one of the most experienced people in the business, retired Connecticut State Trooper Andy Rebmann.

During his training with Hannibal, and once the dog learned how to perform air-scent searches, Zarrella sent memo after memo to his superiors. He first informed them of his progress in training the dog, then, once Hannibal was certified, the fact that the resource was now available to the agency for their use.

Zarrella waited for the call, and, as an English monarch once said some four hundred years ago, "Those also serve who only stand and wait."

One day, while off duty and having just come back home from a training session with the dog (at this time Hannibal and Zarrella were not an official K-9 team), the trooper received a telephone call. It was from state police headquarters. A search had been going on for forty-eight hours. A thirteen-year-old boy, possibly suicidal, had disappeared. Although friends and police had looked over the area where the young man was supposed to have wandered off, nobody had been able to locate the missing youth.

The question put to Zarrella from headquarters was, "Do you want to give it a shot?"

Did he ever!

Putting on a set of marine-issue fatigues, he had Hannibal jump into his personal Chevy Blazer and the two headed for the other end of the state. At the police station in the town where the child was missing he received a briefing from the local officers. Zarrella informed them what Hannibal was capable of doing. At the time the dog was trained to trail and air-scent live persons.

At Zarrella's request the pillowcase from the boy's bed was put in a clear plastic bag and brought to the police station. Zarrella learned that blood had been found on the bedsheets from cuts the boy had made to his wrists. Taking the bag, Zarrella and Hannibal drove to the middle school where the young man, dressed in a blue jacket, had last been seen.

The child had been dropped off by school bus two days before. Fellow students told the police that he had wandered off in a particular direction to the rear of the school. They were positive about that.

Zarrella opened the back hatch of the Blazer and fitted Hannibal into his tracking harness. This would permit the animal to move aggressively forward without placing undue strain on his neck. By the front of the school the trooper took out the clear plastic bag that held the pillowcase, opened it up, and let Hannibal sniff inside. With the command, "Find him!" the dog began to search the area. At first, nose close to the ground, the big dog showed no sign of picking up the scent. There was a light breeze, and when Hannibal raised his head and sniffed, Zarrella saw that he had begun to sense the boy's odor. The dog headed off on the trail in precisely the opposite direction from the one in which all the witnesses had indicated they had last seen the child go.

Zarrella didn't hesitate. As Hannibal pulled the trooper along, the words of his trainer, Andy Rebmann, echoed in Zarrella's head, "Listen to the dog." Zarrella knew that dogs don't know how to lie; they don't know how to play practical jokes. He had absolute confidence in his canine partner's abilities. If Hannibal indicated the scent went in a particular direction, so be it.

Calling to the local officer, "Follow me!" Zarrella found himself being pulled along by his hundred-thirty-pound partner. The trail led the team to the far side of the school, down to a small stream. The dog headed upstream. The humans behind had to dodge trees and crash through the brush in order to keep up with the excited dog. After traveling through the woods for several hundred yards Zarrella found they were on a walking path.

Overhead Zarrella could see that a police helicopter had arrived. Unable to keep up with the pace Hannibal was setting, the trooper had to release the lead from the dog's harness. The big animal raced forward, the helicopter now keeping just over the dog. The crew of the aircraft radioed Zarrella that they thought they saw a blue object just ahead and told Zarrella that the dog was heading right for it and to just keep following the dog.

Good idea, thought Zarrella.

Thirty feet farther, Hannibal made a sharp left turn and climbed over a large rock. Zarrella saw a thin arm come up, reach over Hannibal's neck, and hug the dog. The big K-9 stood towering over the child, proudly wagging his tail.

Zarrella knew then that they had found the boy alive. All at once a rush of emotions hit the trooper: relief, elation, happiness, justification of the time, effort, and energy he had put in training his dog, and of course, a bursting pride in what Hannibal had just accomplished. He didn't know it at that moment, but he would be reliving these same feelings many times in the coming months and years. Soon after the find, the Rhode Island State Police authorized him and Hannibal to become an official K-9 team.

Zarrella looked the boy over. He saw that there were shallow slash marks on the child's wrists. He asked the youngster if he could walk. Trembling and on the verge of hypothermia, the child was unable to stand on his own. The trooper, after radioing in that they'd be coming out, picked the seventy-pound youth up and began to carry him back to the school grounds. As he worked his way out of the woods to where an ambulance was now waiting, he thought it unlikely that the youngster could have survived another night out in the elements.

Well before Zarrella came out onto the school grounds a number of people entered the woods, including Emergency

Medical Technicians (EMTs), who took the boy from the trooper's arms. Waiting at the school were other police officers and members of the child's family. The trooper then saw something he considered strange. The boy's stepfather attempted to hug the youth, but Hannibal placed himself between them, refusing to let the man come near the child.

Zarrella is unable to comment on what Hannibal's puzzling reaction to the stepfather meant. In his experience, Zarrella has found that dogs just seem to know certain things. Maybe finding the lost child was just part of the solution to the young man's problems.

The next day the rescue that Hannibal and Zarrella had made was on the front page of virtually every newspaper in the region. What had begun as an afterthought to an unsuccessful forty-eight-hour search had turned into a forty-minute triumph for the use of police working dogs. The publicity, as well as Hannibal's and Zarrella's obvious achievement, also got the attention of the brass at the Rhode Island State Police. They asked Zarrella, "What do you need?" He replied, Hannibal should be trained as a cadaver-search dog.

So, it was off to Andy Rebmann's body-search school for Zarrella and Rhode Island State Police K-9 Hannibal. And the beginning of their adventures.

Plane Down!

Zarrella and Hannibal were only a few weeks out of Andy Rebmann's training program when their next big job came up. A couple, an eighty-year-old man and his wife, had departed from Long Island for Westerly, Rhode Island, in a light plane. They never made it. The night's weather was poor, and in the morning some debris from the aircraft was found by an area resident, who reported his discovery to the authorities. Eventually it was determined that the aircraft had probably gone down a few miles from the shore.

The Coast Guard spent several days looking for the downed craft. Although on the second day of the search they found the wife's body washed up on the shore, they had no luck locating the plane and its pilot. Five days had gone by since the crash, and Zarrella saw on the news that the probe was being suspended.

The trooper knew that Hannibal had been trained to detect the odor of a dead human body even when the corpse was under water. The chemicals that result from a person's death float to the water's surface, and a properly trained dog will alert accordingly. Of course, the only water that had been used when they were in Rebmann's training program had been fresh, from ponds and streams, but Zarrella figured water is water.

The trooper suggested to his lieutenant that perhaps he and Hannibal could help these people. The lieutenant agreed to inquire and made the necessary telephone calls up the chain of command. Down the chain of command came the response, "Offer them our assistance."

Now that Zarrella and Hannibal were an official team, Zarrella had been issued a Rhode Island State Police cruiser. It was the oldest in the fleet, but at least the pair had a car. He and his K-9 drove over to the Westerly Police Department, the Coast Guard having dropped out of the search. The chief of that department was glad to have Zarrella's help. The family of the lost pilot had come over from Long Island, understandably concerned that their loved one was still missing. They had informed the police chief that they wouldn't leave the area until the body was found.

Police chiefs may possess many talents, but divining the location of lost bodies is not one of them. The chief, while sympathetic to the family's wishes, was stymied and somewhat embarrassed. Without the Coast Guard out vigorously searching for the aircraft and body, there was, in truth, little more he could do. Yet the family wanted results and he was caught right in the middle.

Zarrella's offer to help was a godsend.

The trooper rationalized that since the wife had been found on the shore, there was some possibility the husband would wash up there also. So, for the first day of his search the trooper and Hannibal concentrated their efforts there. They found nothing.

Zarrella decided the only chance they had was out on the water. Transportation was arranged to take them to the general area believed to be where the plane had gone down. The Sunday weather was clear and crisp as the K-9 team were placed aboard a twin-engine thirty-foot watercraft operated by the local rescue corps. In tow behind the small vessel was a dinghy.

As they made their way over the water to the search area Zarrella reflected that for them to actually locate the body would be a long shot. Long Island Sound is a big place, the water is deep and the ocean currents are strong. Even if an aircraft's crash site were known (as it most definitely was not in this case), he knew that the possibility of finding the victim and wreckage was slim.

On the sound Zarrella's boat met up with a salvage team from Newport, Coastal Diving Services, who were already out on the water working the site. They had been hired by the insurance company to locate the wreck. The salvage experts explained to the trooper that they had sophisticated equipment on board, including state-of-the-art side scanning sonar, which they were using in their efforts to find the downed aircraft. Although they had been out for two days and had located some bits of debris as well as the plane's propeller, they had had no luck in finding the main body of wreckage.

Zarrella explained to the salvage crew that Hannibal was a cadaver-locating dog and how he would try to find the body. The resulting response, unbridled laughter, was not an encouraging sign. As an afterthought, or perhaps to simply get the trooper out of their hair, the salvage crew asked that Zarrella's boat stay some yards to their rear, so as not to interfere with their sophisticated electronic equipment or endanger the diver who was being towed along below the water's surface by an underwater line.

Backing off from the other vessel, Zarrella told his boat's captain to go to the location where the Coastal Diving Services people had indicated witnesses said they'd seen an oil slick. The trooper decided to do as precise a grid pattern survey of the area as practical. Zarrella and Hannibal got into their dinghy, along with a member of the rescue corps who would operate the small vessel.

Their search pattern, which was into the wind for Hannibal's sake, had them trailing the salvage crew's ship. Twenty minutes into the search Hannibal alerted. He started to scratch at the bottom of the dinghy and became so excited he even attempted to jump into the water. Only Zarrella's physical intervention held him back.

Even Zarrella, who had every confidence in Hannibal's ability, was amazed at how strongly his K-9 had alerted. He turned to the dinghy operator and said, "That's an alert. We've got to tell these salvage crew people to stop."

Someone from the rescue corps tossed a buoy overboard to mark their position. Then they piloted their boat over to the salvage crew's vessel. Once they were alongside Zarrella called over to the other crew that his K-9 had alerted some thirty yards back. The head of the salvage team asked the trooper what he meant by an alert. Zarrella once more explained how the dog was trained to indicate the presence of human scent and suggested the other man should have his diver check the location. The man made it clear that he had grave doubts about the efficacy of using a dog to find what tens-of-thousands-of-dollars-worth of electronic gear couldn't. Reluctantly he agreed to direct his crew member in the water to take a look in that area.

The diver who was in tow behind the salvage vessel was taken to where the K-9 had sensed something. Thirty yards from where Zarrella indicated Hannibal had alerted, and over forty feet below the salt water of Long Island Sound, the diver spotted the unmistakable cross-shaped outline of a light aircraft. Exploring farther he discovered the body of the pilot, still strapped in the cockpit, seated in place behind the control wheel.

The salvage crew couldn't believe it. They had spent two days searching for what it had taken Hannibal twenty minutes to find. Now, instead of laughter from the salvage crew came calls of, "Good dog! Good dog!"

Zarrella was only too happy to have helped bring to closure a tragic chapter in one family's history. But this wouldn't be the last time he and Hannibal would be asked to find a body under water.

Patience by the Pawcatuck River

It was Christmas Eve, around eight o'clock. Zarrella was off duty and heading to his mother's house in Providence for a family gathering, when his pager sounded its annoying high-pitched *beep-beep* tone. Without looking, he reached to his belt and pushed the button to silence the racket, then yanked on the small plastic box and eyed the number. It was the barracks. Uh-oh, Zarrella thought to himself, not a good sign on Christmas Eve.

By this time both Zarrella's and Hannibal's reputations had begun to spread. When investigators around the state needed someone found—whether alive or dead—it was this K-9 team that got the call.

When he got to his mother's he said hi to everyone and quickly made his way to the telephone. Sergeant Rick Quinn picked up the phone on the other end.

Sergeant Quinn started, "Matty, I hate to do this to you," and went on to relate how he had received a call from Department of Environmental Management (DEM) officers. They were looking for the body of a duck hunter who had drowned and were asking for Zarrella and Hannibal to help them in their search the next day, Christmas. The river where it happened bordered on Connecticut. A dive team from that state police agency had already tried all that day to find the body without luck and wouldn't be sending their divers there tomorrow. Rhode Island DEM wanted to continue the search for the sake of the family. The sergeant assured Zarrella that he would put Rhode Island State Police divers on standby should the trooper and Hannibal discover anything.

Zarrella hung up the telephone and explained to his mom why he couldn't stay long at the family's Christmas party.

Her son had to be up bright and early the next day for an unpleasant job that needed to be done at the Pawcatuck River.

Zarrella recalls that the rest of that Christmas Eve was subdued. The trooper soon returned to his empty home so he could get some sleep.

The next morning the K-9 team and members of the Rhode Island DEM met near the river. They filled Zarrella in on what they knew. The day before, two men, Albert Pinterelli, fifty-two, and Thomas Buck, a man in his early thirties, had gone out to do some duck hunting. The weather that day had been nasty, with heavy winds and snow. The temperature had hovered around the twenty-degree mark.

Both men were large, yet they had used a canoe to get out onto the river. Perhaps they had used that type of watercraft before, but it turned out to be an unfortunate choice on that stormy day. The Pawcatuck River had been several feet higher than normal and its water quite rough because of the weather. At around eleven Pinterelli and Buck's canoe swamped in the turbulent current and capsized, putting both men in the ice-cold river.

The rule boaters are taught to follow when their vessel capsizes but remains afloat is, stay with the boat. Which is what Pinterelli, an experienced man, did. Buck successfully swam to shore and, when on dry land, looked over at his friend. Pinterelli was the man who had taught him everything he ever knew about duck hunting, as well as how to deal with difficult situations, and now Buck saw that his friend was clinging to the side of the upside-down canoe floating away in the Pawcatuck River. Pinterelli waved at Buck and called to him that he'd be all right. Seeing that his friend was okay for the moment, albeit being carried rapidly away downstream by the river's current, and since there was nothing more he could do there to aid him anyway, Buck ran to get some help.

The two men had gained entrance to the river via a private farm. Buck scrambled up the river's bank and ran in the direction of the farmer's home. He spotted the man on a tractor, and soon both returned to the river to locate Pinterelli and somehow help him get to shore. Running downstream the two men couldn't find any sign of the other man at first. They kept on looking until they came upon the overturned canoe. Pinterelli was nowhere in sight.

The two men then rushed back to the farmhouse and called the Connecticut State Police, who responded quickly to the scene. Members of that agency's dive team were also called in and a search initiated immediately. It was tough going for all concerned. In addition to the freezing weather and icy water, the divers had to contend with a faster-than-normal river current along with a blowing wind, which came at them and their support vessel from another direction.

On the bank of the river, which was on the Connecticut side, were members of the Rhode Island DEM and the Connecticut Department of Environmental Conservation, as well as the North Stonington Fire Department. Thomas Buck was also on hand, as was Mrs. Pinterelli, the victim's brother, and his two young sons. It seemed it was going to be a lousy Christmas day for a lot of people.

The Rhode Island DEM personnel had a small single-outboard-motor craft for Zarrella and Hannibal's use. Zarrella noticed that there was no propeller attached to the engine. Instead, the vessel, a Boston Whaler, was pushed along by a jet spray of water and was thus far less likely to get tangled up in the vegetation and normal debris found in the kind of shallow water they'd be searching. Along with the K-9 team, one of the DEM people went aboard the eighteen-foot-long craft to work the controls.

Starting their search from where the man had last been seen, Zarrella had their vessel proceed along a methodically determined grid pattern in the rough and choppy water.

As they moved along on the river, the trooper knew they were going to have a real problem locating the body. The extreme cold preserved human remains just as a home freezer keeps produce from deteriorating; with little or no decay taking place there would be virtually no scent for Hannibal to pick up.

Zarrella and Hannibal worked for eight hours that day. The K-9 showed some interest in one area about two hundred yards south from where the canoe had gone down, on the Rhode Island side of the river. But the water was so rough that Zarrella had been unable to tell whether he was seeing Hannibal alert or if the dog had simply lost his footing and pawed at the side of the boat in an attempt to gain better support for himself. Had Hannibal really tried to jump into the water at that spot or was he being thrown about by the heaving of the boat?

Zarrella couldn't be sure.

After the long and tedious search, Zarrella and Hannibal, knowing they'd be working again early the next day, went straight home. The trooper went to bed soon after.

It hadn't exactly been a merry Christmas.

At eight-thirty the next morning the K-9 team, along with the same people that were there the day before, met at the river's edge. The air temperature was a biting twenty degrees, with a strong north wind that pulled at the emergency workers' clothing. The Pawcatuck River's water was at freezing, and a thin layer of ice had formed on its surface overnight. The conditions were less than ideal for a K-9 body search.

Zarrella started out just around where the canoe had been swamped, the same place he had begun the day before. Hannibal reacted with what Zarrella considered mild alerts. The trooper decided to call the Connecticut State Police and have their body-search dog brought in. He wanted a second opinion.

Hannibal had been working hard for six days in a row now, having just finished a four-day search prior to this incident. Zarrella found he was now sufficiently concerned to ask himself if Hannibal was showing fatigue.

Both days that Hannibal had exhibited alerts his signals had been less than enthusiastic. Could it be the extreme cold that was causing his partner to respond in such a wishy-washy fashion? Was the dog just plain tired and giving Zarrella a false alert? Maybe, just maybe, there wasn't anything under the river's surface to be alerting to.

After all, the current was a strong one and the body could be miles away by now. Hadn't the Connecticut State Police divers searched that very area for an entire day and come up with nothing? Maybe it was Zarrella's fault. Maybe he was misreading Hannibal and talking himself into believing his dog was alerting when in fact the K-9 was doing no such thing.

Trooper Tod Lynch, along with K-9 Iris, arrived at the scene around noon. Although Zarrella got into the Boston Whaler with the Connecticut trooper, he was careful not to divulge to the other handler, either in words or body language, where on the river Hannibal had previously shown animation.

When their small craft came to the place where Hannibal had alerted, Iris did the same. Zarrella quietly sighed in relief.

By this time another volunteer had arrived, equipped with a sophisticated underwater camera and its monitoring device. Zarrella asked the operator to check the area where the dogs had alerted. They placed the man and his gear in a DEM boat. In a short time a wristwatch was seen on the monitor's screen, tangled in an underwater tree branch in an area where the river was about twelve feet deep. The victim's wife was on the scene and, when asked to look at the watch on the small video screen, confirmed it was her husband's.

Now with alerts from two K-9s, as well as the camera's location of the man's watch, Zarrella decided it was time to resume the underwater portion of the search. He went to a telephone and spoke to Sergeant Quinn, explaining in detail what they now knew.

The sergeant agreed with his trooper's assessment of the situation, but it was too late to get scuba teams from Connecticut and Rhode Island State Police on location with the few hours of light that remained to make a dive that day worthwhile. The search would resume in the morning.

It was eight in the morning when everyone involved in the quest to locate Al Pinterelli's body met on the banks of the Pawcatuck River. The early-morning temperature was eighteen degrees with a northerly wind. Zarrella unhappily noted how much the ice had thickened on the water's surface in less than twenty-four hours.

Hannibal and Zarrella were once again put out onto the water. The Connecticut divers felt strongly that by this time the swollen river's fast-moving current had carried the body along. They believed the victim had been washed over the rim of the dam and out to sea.

Zarrella decided it would be wise to explore the remainder of the river out to where it ended, four miles further south, at the man-made dam. During the entire circuit Hannibal stood by the bow showing no interest, until, on the way back to the shoreline, the big K-9 alerted where he had before, now for three days in a row. This time his human partner didn't doubt what his canine companion was telling him. Somewhere close below them, under that cold and inhospitable river's surface, lay the body of the lost hunter.

Trooper Lynch and his partner, Iris, also took to the boat. The results were the same. Both troopers were convinced that to retrieve the victim the divers had only to search in that general area.

Both Connecticut and Rhode Island divers—this was the very first field dive the brand-new Rhode Island team had been involved in—went into the water. Nine divers were involved in total. They found two small bags snagged on some brush, which belonged to each of the duck hunters, but they were unable to locate the missing man. On the Connecticut side of the river's bottom a large bag of animal bones, probably from one of the local farms, was also discovered.

The Connecticut divers thought the dogs were alerting on that bag of old bones. They also thought that the extremely cold temperatures weren't helping matters.

Zarrella shook his head. He was the youngest trooper on the scene, in truth not all that sure of himself, but he was certain of one thing: Andy Rebmann hadn't trained Hannibal to find old animal bones. All the artifacts, the hunters' two bags and the watch, had been found on the Rhode

Island side of the river. Hannibal and Iris had repeatedly alerted on the Rhode Island side of the river. Those damn animal bones had been found on the Connecticut side.

Zarrella wasn't about to get into a public debate with the Connecticut State Police divers, a highly experienced team. News media people on the scene interviewed the Connecticut divers. With the Pinterelli family looking on, the head of that dive team stated that based on their searching for two full days, it was their opinion that the body of Mr. Pinterelli had drifted downstream and had been lost over the rim of the dam. The search for the missing man had therefore been concluded.

Zarrella stood by and kept his mouth shut.

The next day's newspapers reported as fact what was said at the impromptu news conference.

Zarrella was now truly concerned about just how fatigued Hannibal had become. For the last seven days his dog had worked under truly harsh conditions. Hannibal was tired. Zarrella could tell because he had observed that his partner had difficulty paying attention to what he was doing. At times he seemed more interested in what the horses and cows on the riverbanks were up to than with the task at hand. The dog needed some rest.

Before leaving the river, Zarrella quietly spoke with Mrs. Pinterelli as well as with the Rhode Island DEM people. The trooper put it bluntly: he didn't believe Mr. Pinterelli's body had been washed away. He wanted to return in a few days, after Hannibal had a suitable rest, and again try to locate the body.

When Zarrella got back to the barracks he spoke with Sergeant Quinn. He laid out the problem of the conflicting opinions between the Connecticut State Police dive team and his own observations. To further complicate matters, it was that dive team who had originally handled the situation and who had now called the search off.

Zarrella told his sergeant that he believed Mr. Pinterelli's body was still there and asked his supervisor's permission to return as soon as Hannibal was up to it.

Sergeant Quinn could have said no. It was Connecticut's

search and if they said it was over, then it was over. But he didn't say that. He believed in Zarrella's and Hannibal's abilities. He told his trooper to go for it. Quinn also called Mrs. Pinterelli and told her the same thing.

Mrs. Pinterelli thanked the sergeant for okaying the additional search as well as for his persistence.

A couple of days later Zarrella and Hannibal returned to the Pawcatuck River. This time they had an old friend along, retired Connecticut State Police trooper and master K-9 trainer, Andy Rebmann. Rebmann had brought along one of his German shepherds, Marianne, as well as a human associate, Alice Krugerman, who had her Newfoundland, Juno.

The night before, Zarrella and Rebmann had had a long discussion about the situation. Rebmann assured Zarrella that from what the trooper had told him Rebmann was confident Pinterelli's body was where Hannibal had alerted. The retired trooper agreed to come out and give Zarrella a hand.

Hannibal went onto the river first. This time out the temperature had climbed into the forties, the river had receded to its normal height, and a gentle breeze blew, conditions much more conducive to a successful K-9 body search. In the sensitive area the K-9 showed his interest by pacing back and forth, whining, pawing and swiping at the side of the boat. Finally he lay down in his alert position. Zarrella was confident Hannibal was showing him where the body lay. He dropped a marker buoy into the water. It was on the Rhode Island side of the river, near where the lost man's belongings and watch had been found.

The new K-9s also tried the same area and both alerted there as well.

The man with the underwater camera was also present. Rebmann thought about the layout of the river and suggested that the man start not from where the three K-9s had alerted, but from where they first left the shore, and head for the hot area. The retired trooper just had a hunch, one developed after working well over a thousand body searches.

The underwater camera went in the river, and the craft slowly moved out in the direction where the K-9s alerted. Fifteen minutes later an image came onto the monitor screen. It was a man's boot. The camera was manipulated and the body of Al Pinterelli came into view.

A gentle drizzle started soon afterward.

Zarrella went to a telephone and called for his police dive team to respond. By the time the team got there it was pouring rain. An altogether somber setting for a somber event.

The next day the same newspapers that had reported Mr. Pinterelli had been washed into the sea now wrote of the discovery of the body. One of the Connecticut State Police dive team members later called Rebmann and asked where the drowned man had been found. Rebmann, never one to mince words, replied, "Right where you left him."

Three Pointless Deaths

Individuals sometimes make mistakes in life. Most often, even if these errors in judgment are serious in nature, people still manage to move on. In one of Zarrella and Hannibal's cases, however, such was not to be.

Adam and Elena Emery, along with another couple, decided to have a fun night out at the Rocky Point Amusement Park, located in Warwick, Rhode Island. The four people—and particularly the Emerys—had no idea how their lives would be changed during what should have been an innocent evening's excursion.

While parked near the amusement center, enjoying the evening while eating clam cakes in the Emerys' shiny black Ford Thunderbird, another vehicle came up from behind and hit their rear, damaging a taillight. The other driver's inconsiderate operation of his car gave the Emerys and their friends a good jolt and damaged their expensive auto, but to make matters worse, the individual sped out of the parking lot.

Adam Emery was livid. His wife, Elena, encouraged her

husband not to let the driver get away with leaving the scene of an accident in which they were completely blameless. So Adam started up his auto and chased after the other man, who had driven off at high speed. Although at one point he lost sight of the vehicle, Adam Emery soon spotted it again. Or so he thought. He flashed his lights and tried to get the driver to pull over. Instead the other man, Jason Bass, speeded up. Adam then forced Bass's car off the road.

Adam started out of his car but Elena, opening the glove compartment, took out a knife and told him to take it, "Just in case." Adam took the knife. He rushed over to Bass's vehicle and started to argue with the man. Bass, who had no idea what Adam Emery was talking about, and fearful for his own safety, tried to flee once more. He put his car in reverse in an attempt to get away from the crazed Adam and began to back down the street. Adam jumped at the driver through the window and hung on.

What happened next has several versions. Some witnesses say threats were exchanged, others that Adam simply begged Jason Bass to stop the car. One thing is definitely known. Adam Emery took the knife handed to him by his wife and shoved its blade into Jason Bass.

The car crashed to a stop. Bass stumbled from the vehicle and died on the ground. The innocent victim of a hit-and-run driver had taken the life of one innocent Jason Bass. Neither man had a criminal record, and by all accounts both individuals were just normal people trying to lead regular lives.

Adam didn't try to run. When the police arrived he was arrested for homicide and ultimately sent to a correctional holding facility for nearly a year. At his trial Adam claimed self-defense. His attorney argued that while it might be true that Jason Bass wasn't the person Adam had been seeking, nonetheless, at that instant, it was Jason Bass who had put Adam Emery at risk, and thus his stabbing and death had been a justifiable homicide.

The jury disagreed and Adam was convicted of murder.

He was scheduled to be sentenced that same day. Just a few hours prior to sentencing, and over the objection of the prosecutor, Adam was released on $275,000 dollars' bail. It was Adam's thirty-first birthday, and it was clear to him that he faced spending anywhere from the next twenty years to the rest of his life in prison for what he had done.

Adam didn't show up at court later that afternoon for his sentencing. His leased Toyota Camry was found abandoned on the center span of the Newport Bridge (now named the Pell Bridge), two hundred feet above Narragansett Bay. Elena had also disappeared. Police found articles of clothing in the car—some of the same clothing they had worn during various stages of the trial. Also in the car were credit cards and receipts from a nearby department store for work-out clothes, black sweatsuits, for each of the Emerys as well as ankle and wrist weights. From what was learned from the sales people there, the Emerys had done their shopping just three hours prior to driving to the bridge, ninety minutes after Adam had been found guilty of murder.

A trooper had found the car on the bridge and automatically ran the vehicle's license plate. When he realized it belonged to Adam Emery he made the appropriate notifications. The investigators assigned to the Bass homicide case and trial became intensely interested.

Zarrella was working on the night shift (9 PM to 8 AM) when the call for service came in. As luck would have it, Zarrella and his trooper partner were assigned the very patrol area in which the Emery family lived. It was around ten when he and the other trooper were sent to interview whoever was at the Emery house to determine why Adam Emery's car had been abandoned on the Newport Bridge. At that time Zarrella had no idea he'd soon be needing Hannibal's skills.

The sister and brother of Elena made it clear to the troopers—shift commander Lieutenant Doug Badger had by this time arrived at the home—the couple must surely have committed suicide. Such an event had been expected by the family for some time. Elena had been overheard making many comments over the last few months to the effect that she would not live without her husband, and if he was convicted, she might do something drastic. When the verdict was handed down, the family members told the two troopers that they just knew in their hearts that the couple's end would be a dramatic one.

Zarrella and his partner, under the direction of Lieutenant Badger and with the permission of the family, checked around the living quarters of Adam and Elena. Their clothing was undisturbed, as was their luggage, and a goodly amount of cash was found in the house. Not a likely scenario for a couple who might have decided to flee the state.

By six o'clock that evening detectives involved in the investigation were out looking for the Emerys. The law officers were going on the theory that both husband and wife had faked their suicides and were now attempting to evade justice. Zarrella wasn't so sure. He suggested to his captain that it would be prudent for a water search to be conducted by his K-9. The captain gave the trooper the go-ahead to give it a try.

Because the state police assign two troopers to a cruiser during the evening shift, there had been no room for Hannibal in Zarrella's cruiser that night. In any case, Hannibal was not an aggression-trained dog (Hannibal was a lover, not a fighter). Hannibal, who clearly belonged to a better union than Zarrella, was already at the trooper's barracks, comfortably napping in his own Rhode Island State Police issue doghouse.

Zarrella drove back to the barracks and began the task of transferring his gear to his own police vehicle. He put on an orange water-survival suit—a fall into the icy waters around Rhode Island at that time of year, November, could prove fatal in a matter of minutes.

The big dog can read Zarrella's body language. There was no need for the trooper to tell the K-9 he was about to go to work. Hannibal began to whine, wag his tail, and pace back and forth in anticipation of doing the thing he loved the most, working in the field with his partner. Once Zarrella was suited up he put Hannibal in their cruiser.

At eight in the morning, at the base of the bridge, Zarrella and his K-9 met with individuals assigned to the DEM, who had a small boat waiting for the trooper. Zarrella placed Hannibal into the twenty-five-foot-long vessel and, with two DEM people manning the craft, headed for the center span. Although the autumn weather was clear and cool and the current moving at only a few knots, white caps frothed on the water's surface. Fortunately both Zarrella and Hannibal had good sea legs and neither of them suffered from motion sickness.

Starting directly under the bridge where the car had been abandoned, with a water depth of a hundred and thirty-five feet under them, Zarrella gave Hannibal the body-search command, "Look for it!" That first day the team stayed out until six in the evening, remaining in the area of the bridge's center columns.

During the search Hannibal took up a position at the rear of the small vessel. The dog hung his head over the boat's side, his nose close to the water, sniffing. It was while Hannibal was doing this, at about two in the afternoon, that Zarrella saw his dog alert as the boat moved near the east side of the center columns. First he became rigid, then the K-9 threw his head up and placed his paws on the edge of the boat's side, whining. A moment later he leaned toward the water and made a lunge to jump in. He stopped only because Zarrella grabbed on to him.

Using the LORAN (electronic navigation equipment) the exact location where Hannibal had alerted was recorded. Zarrella had the small vessel approach the same spot two other times, from two different angles. Hannibal's response was the same each time.

Although divers were in the water, as was an underwater camera, visibility in Narragansett Bay was zero. Zarrella wasn't sure about Hannibal's results. Could his dog have alerted to decaying seaweed or sewer gas? Maybe the divers had kicked something up and his K-9 had mistaken the odor for that of a dead body. The planes and helicopters circling overhead didn't help either.

Zarrella and Hannibal kept at the search until evening. It was too long. The weather was getting worse, and even in a survival suit, being out on the water was cold, uncomfortable work. While Hannibal didn't seem to mind the elements, it was clear to Zarrella that even his K-9 had started to become weary of their mission. It was time to come to shore and consider what he would tell his bosses.

The trooper had never been on a search of this magnitude before. All eyes were on Hannibal and him. With some trepidation at the responsibility that had fallen on his shoulders, all Zarrella felt comfortable in telling his Rhode Island State Police superiors was that he believed there was a seventy percent chance Hannibal had found evidence of a dead human being under the water's surface. He also used the same percent figure when speaking with the press, something he'd regret soon after. His dilemma was, even if he had said there was a one hundred percent chance that the two bodies were somewhere near where Hannibal had alerted, the water where the divers were searching was opaque; a diver would have to virtually bump into a body to locate it. And because of the extreme pressure found at the over hundred-and-thirty-foot depth, the underwater specialists looking for the Emerys could stay down for only a few minutes at a time.

The search continued for an additional three days on the water, the weather deteriorating as time passed. Sophisticated sonar showed two anomalous human-size objects in the bay, smack in the area where Hannibal had alerted. However, on the last day that had been allotted for the search—even the Rhode Island State Police has a limit to its manpower resources—the water was too rough even to permit the divers to go down to check out the reading.

By this time Zarrella's fellow troopers had decided to have some fun at the expense of their K-9 teammates. Cartoons started cropping up in his barracks. A Xerox of a news photo of Zarrella and Hannibal at work in their small boat had been tacked up on the bulletin board. The aspiring artist supplied his own captions.

From Zarrella came the words, "Come on Hannibal, bail me out. I told the press there is a 70% percent chance their (sic) here. . . ."

Hannibal replied, "Hay (sic) Matt . . . who's the dummy

now! . . . I told you not to sell the plumbing tools yet! . . . [an allusion to Zarrella's former profession]."

Zarrella took it all in good humor, but it irked him that they hadn't yet come up with either of the bodies. As it turned out, neither corpse would surface until quite a while after the initial search.

Eight months later a fishing trawler, dragging on the bay's bottom along the east column of the Newport Bridge—the column where Hannibal had first alerted to the scent of a body—brought a human skull to the surface. The medical examiner determined, positively, it was the partial remains of Elena Emery.

Will Adam Emery ever be found? Zarrella doesn't know for sure. After all, he reasons that the ocean is a big place, with lots of hungry creatures living under its surface. But one thing Zarrella is certain of. When his K-9 partner had alerted on that first chilly November day, Hannibal knew what was down there. It wasn't Hannibal's fault if his human co-workers had been unable to complete the job.

A Drowning Tragedy

What started out as an early fall morning duck-hunting adventure on the Barrington River for three high-school students turned into a sad job for Zarrella. For Hannibal, it would be a test of his patience because of his co-worker's inability to understand what he was trying to communicate.

For Zarrella the job began as a straightforward case. Getting an early morning call from headquarters while assigned to the Hope Valley Barracks, he and his K-9 were to go out and attempt to locate the body of a teenager who had drowned during a duck-hunting accident while on the Barrington River.

The accident had taken place before dawn, still several hours before the start of the school day. Three boys, John Greene, Seamus Muldoon, and Matthew Conway, had gone out duck hunting in a small aluminum flat-bottomed skiff. When the last of the warmly dressed young men got into their boat, the river's water came up to within a few inches of the craft's sides. Clearly the little vessel was overloaded when the trio left the shore, but when you're seventeen such things are of little concern.

At any rate the teens were very athletic. John, by all accounts a popular boy, was on the Barrington High School football team. He truly loved the river, boating, and the outdoors.

Soon after they were out on the river their boat began to take in water. Once the river started to come in over its sides, it took but an instant for the small vessel to nose-dive to the bottom, ten feet below them. A moment later the young men were in the water, trying to stay alive. With nothing to keep them afloat their only option was to head for the shore. They all attempted to swim for land. John, even though he was wearing a thick leather jacket, sweaters, jeans, and heavy insulated rubber boots, called out over and over to his two friends that they should relax. In a calm voice he told them to take it easy, it would be ten minutes before hypothermia set in.

As Muldoon headed for the shore he turned to look back at his friend and saw John's head disappear below the river's surface. Muldoon whirled and dove under to help John. He grabbed hold of his friend, who was sinking quickly in the cold water. Muldoon, barely able to manage by himself and unable to lift the great weight that the water-soaked John Greene had become, was forced to release his friend and kick back to the surface.

He barely made it to shore.

Once on dry land he and Conway screamed for help. People living in the area heard the calls and responded. Soon the rescue squad was on the way, brought in by the Barrington Police Department.

It would be too late for John Greene, who had so loved the river that took his life.

The two surviving boys were taken to a local hospital and treated for hypothermia. Within a few hours they were released and they returned to the scene of the tragedy. Surrounded by friends, the youths fought back tears as they watched the divers look in vain for John's body.

Seventy-five people from eight communities responded to the Barrington River, putting five boats in the water and involving twenty divers. The search began at six in the morning. For three and a half hours the river bottom was thoroughly explored without finding the lost youth. Looking methodically for the victim, the divers marked off the areas already explored with buoys attached to long lines. By the time Zarrella and Hannibal came to the scene, the middle of the river was crisscrossed with the bobbing orange-colored egg-shaped floats.

Zarrella was briefed by the incident commander, Bill Chadwick, of the Swansea, Massachusetts, fire department. The trooper asked that all divers be removed from the water so that he and Hannibal could begin their work.

With a single operator at the controls, Zarrella and his K-9 boarded a rubber dinghy. The big search dog stood proudly up at the bow, facing forward, the wind in his uplifted face. Hannibal was distinctive not only because of his great size and the orange rescue vest he wore, but because of his bearing as well. He was out there doing an important job. Humans depended on him and he knew it.

Zarrella asked the dinghy's operator where the boy's skiff had gone down and where John had last been seen. Taking a reading of the wind's direction, and noting which way the current was running as well as the water's temperature—it was forty degrees, good for Zarrella's purposes—the trooper directed his boat's operator to move ahead.

When satisfied with their location, a position just beyond where the boat had gone down, Zarrella told the man at the helm to head slowly in the direction of the shore, where the boys had come out. He reasoned that the body had to lie somewhere between those two points.

Zarrella had his craft travel against the current, as is customary with any search being conducted for a body lost underwater. Andy Rebmann had taught him that the odors K-9s need to detect generally stay close to the water's surface. His teacher had told him that the best chance for a dog to locate that smell is when a water search is conducted in that fashion.

On the first pass they made, Zarrella noted a mild alert on the part of Hannibal. The big dog had pawed at the side of the dinghy where the boys' skiff went down. Zarrella dropped a buoy to mark the location, praising his partner.

As they came nearer to the shore Hannibal scratched at the bottom of the dinghy and this time lay down. This was a strong alert. Zarrella said, "Good boy," as he cast in another orange float. Moving still closer to the shore Zarrella saw his K-9 alert once more. The trooper tossed a final buoy into the river.

When a deceased human is under water the chemicals released from that corpse, which alert a body-search dog to the victim's presence, rise to the surface. With the flow of water and wind this odor moves about. Zarrella knew that was the most likely reason there had been three alerts from Hannibal.

Their search had only just started and Hannibal had shown Zarrella where he detected the body. Yet the trooper felt uncomfortable in ending his part in the operation just yet. After all, the divers and other searchers had been working hard for nearly four hours looking for the lost youth. In order to be certain Zarrella decided to continue to have Hannibal search the rest of the area around the drowning site. The K-9 team kept at it for nearly four additional hours. Zarrella by this time was becoming worried about Hannibal. The dog had been out on the water for over four hours without a break and badly needed a rest. From Hannibal's body language it had become clear to Zarrella that Hannibal's patience was beginning to wear thin. The trooper had had to remind his dog on several occasions to keep his head over their boat's side when the K-9's attention wandered from his task. His handler could also tell his partner was losing interest in their task when he noted Hannibal paying too much notice to what was taking place on the shore rather than what was under the water around him.

Finally, Zarrella told the dinghy operator, "Bring me back. Let's tell the divers these are the three areas they need to check."

They headed for shore. By this time it was late afternoon and the short winter's day was coming to an end.

When Zarrella told them where Hannibal had indicated the body lay, the divers weren't so certain. They were adamant that they had checked that spot thoroughly and really didn't think it would be productive to look there again. After some discussion, and because the scene commander, Bill Chadwick, believed in what Hannibal had to say, they agreed to give it one more try.

Six divers went into their boat. Four of them entered the water, using lines they had already placed under its surface as a guide, while the other team members operated the vessel. The last thing Zarrella said to them before they went below the river's surface was to ask them again to check the area really carefully. His words almost came out as a plea. What he didn't say was that he should have more carefully read what Hannibal had tried to tell him several hours earlier. They'd probably locate the boy's body right where the dog had told Zarrella it was lying all along.

The divers started at the first buoy. From the shore Zarrella could see their air bubbles rise to the surface as they moved along under the river. They progressed slowly up to the second marker, lingered there for a few minutes and then continued on. Zarrella paced about. He was getting nervous. It was now near dark and he knew there'd be no more searching today after this dive. He also knew that somewhere underwater, along the line of the three buoys he had tossed into the water, was the body of the drowned youth. He badly wanted those divers to find John Greene. He said a little prayer to himself that they wouldn't be too tired and would take a good look by that third marker.

Zarrella wasn't concerned about what was thought of him or of Hannibal's abilities. His K-9 had proven himself time and again in the past and Hannibal didn't owe anybody anything. But it would be a terrible and wasteful thing for the young man's parents and friends to have to do this hurtful thing all over again the next day.

While Zarrella stood off to the side, he watched as the

incident commander, even as his divers were working, began to form up his people for a debriefing. When the other man called out, "Let's wrap it up," and asked someone what the weather conditions for the next day would be and which of the divers would be available, it was clear the search was about to end.

The trooper, standing by himself on the edge of the embankment, now perhaps alone in more ways than one, turned once more to scan the surface of the river. He saw that the divers had come up to the third buoy. There was a splash and one diver popped to the surface, calling out, "We got him! The buoy was right on top of him!"

In relief Zarrella let out a little shout, "Yes!" He and Hannibal had come through once more.

On the way back to their barracks the trooper thought back on what had happened that day. With the clarity of hindsight he reflected that Hannibal had shown him, within only minutes of their getting into the dinghy, where the body was to be found. The K-9 had told Zarrella where the victim was, and still Hannibal had been taken all over the place for hours, to no purpose that he could understand. He had been forced to look for something he knew wasn't anyplace but the spot he had already indicated to Zarrella. It was clear to the trooper now why Hannibal had become frustrated.

Why, Zarrella asked himself, hadn't he recognized the alert for what it was? Had he really been listening to his dog? Or was he more concerned about form and how he might be embarrassed if he ended the search too early, or worse, if after only a couple of minutes of Hannibal and him poking about, he had told the searchers where to find the body and they had not been able to locate anything under the water.

It was a quiet ride back home.

A few days later Zarrella received a letter from the dead boy's mother. She thanked Zarrella for the work he and Hannibal had put in on her family's behalf. The mother wrote that she knew, as soon as she saw Zarrella and Hannibal arrive, that Hannibal would find her son, because her son John loved dogs so very much.

A Dead Man Rises from the Ashes

Trust your dog. Zarrella first learned this lesson from his trainer, Andy Rebmann, and he grew to better understand it as his experience with and understanding of his K-9 partners grew.

But sometimes it can be very difficult to believe your dog when your head and heart tell you something just isn't physically possible. Such as finding the remains of a murder victim whose corpse had been burned in a bonfire for eighteen hours before what little remained of the body had been tossed into a swamp. Six years earlier.

As with so many of the cases Zarrella works, this one started some distance away from Rhode Island and involved a number of local, state, and federal law-enforcement agencies.

What began as a routine car stop up in Ashby, a small town on the Massachusetts–New Hampshire border, ended up as a murder investigation that required the skills only a trained body-search K-9 can provide. David Iacaboni, also known as David Hargraves, along with a female companion, had been stopped for a routine traffic violation. A search of their vehicle revealed a significant quantity— felony level—of drugs inside. Iacaboni offered to make a deal: let his woman friend off and he'd tell the police where a body could be found, the victim of a murder.

The man's story read like the plot from a bad movie. He and another man had an argument with Richard Tuttle, a local twenty-one-year-old, over a drug transaction. There wasn't all that much money or drugs involved. But there was enough. Tuttle was stabbed to death by Iacaboni and his buddy.

The two men panicked. What were they to do with the corpse? Not the brightest bulbs in the chandelier, they decided they'd cremate the remains, presumably figuring that if funeral pyres had worked for the ancient Vikings, then why couldn't one work for them.

The murder had taken place on a remote piece of property, ironically land owned by the uncle of the deceased. The area was mostly wooded and very rural. Iacaboni and his partner first built a large fire, then threw the body on it. For a long time, over eighteen hours, they continued to feed the flames, tossing large chunks of wood on the inferno in an attempt to disintegrate their victim. They finally figured out that the bones, although charred, would simply not go away.

Scooping up what bones remained of Tuttle, they tossed their grisly cargo in the trunk of their car and drove a short distance to a nearby body of water, called Barrett Hill Pond, although it really was more of a swamp. Backing down as close as they could get to the water's soft marshy edge, they opened their car's trunk and threw what was left of their victim out into the quiet, algae-coated water.

The pair drove away and didn't give their act much more thought for the next six years.

Tuttle, a young man from a reputable local family, had been reported missing soon after the homicide. But no one, except his killers, had the slightest idea where he had gone or what had happened to him. Still, fate has a way of catching up with people.

The investigation that was initiated with Iacaboni's admission soon had local, state, and federal agencies involved. Before Zarrella and Hannibal came into the picture, state police divers had scoured the swamp where Tuttle's remains had been tossed, but even after five days of searching they had found no trace of the man. Without locating some actual part of the victim, a successful homicide prosecution would be most difficult to accomplish. It is rare that a case of this magnitude is carried forward solely on the basis of a prisoner's words. Thoughts, which might have been uttered in haste, upon reflection often soon deteriorate into, "They made me say it."

Yes, locating a few bits of Mr. Tuttle's body would be most helpful.

It was the FBI who decided to call Zarrella in on the investigation. The bureau had worked with the trooper on a number of earlier cases. They liked his style, attitude, and perseverance. A special agent briefed Zarrella on the background of the earlier events.

It was nine in the morning, two and a half hours from when he left home, when Zarrella pulled up to the turnoff for Barrett Hill Pond, a densely wooded area. Cars from the various law-enforcement agencies involved were parked wherever there was space. Massachusetts State Police cars were mixed in with local police cruisers as well as unmarked vehicles from the United States attorney's office and the local district attorney's office.

Zarrella pulled his Chevy Suburban in on the dirt lane leading to Barrett Hill Pond, parking about ten yards in from the main road. With him were Hannibal and his newest K-9, Panzer. It had been decided a few months earlier that an additional dog was needed for backup to Hannibal. An anonymous person donated Panzer, a young, good-natured, and energetic female German shepherd. She and Hannibal soon became good friends.

The trooper got out of his vehicle and looked the area over. He could see that Barrett Hill Pond might once have been a true pond, but that had been many years ago. Nature had turned the body of water into what was now a young swamp. Sometime in the future it would become a marsh, then change to soft moist earth, until finally it would become dry land. Such was the natural order of events.

For this microsecond in time Zarrella looked out onto the small body of water the local people had named Barrett Hill Pond. The shape its banks formed was oval, totalling about half an acre in size. Wood debris lay everywhere. Mostly dead branches, there were also the larger parts of trees that had overhung the pond and had fallen in over time.

Zarrella reflected on what he'd be asking of his K-9 partner. Not only would Hannibal have to locate skeletal remains, but the bones he'd be seeking would have been nearly cremated first before having been tossed into a swamp to stew for six years. Hannibal had never been asked to find such material before. In fact, the dog had never been specifically taught to locate human bones, and the trooper wasn't sure how his K-9 would react. The only hope Zarrella held that Hannibal had a chance of finding anything was the fact that Andy Rebmann had assured him on a number of occasions that his K-9 would alert to human skeletal remains.

Hannibal was taken from the car. Zarrella let his K-9 relax—the day was quite warm—and get comfortable with the area. The trooper put on his partner's handsome, thick leather Swiss collar, one with raised brass animal embroidery on it. To Hannibal that meant his job was to locate a dead human. Other collars and his harness—with or without his bright orange rescue vest—meant different things to him.

"Look for it!" Zarrella ordered Hannibal. Those were the words the trooper used for the body-search command.

Hannibal slowly moved along the still water's embankment, his head held close to the ground and swamp to maximize the scent he picked up.

At many of the places where the water came up to the shoreline there was a sharp drop-off—although it was only about four feet deep—into the pond. When Hannibal came to a place along the bank where the shore fell more gradually into the swamp, he waded in chest deep. As Zarrella watched, his K-9 began to circle around in the water with his nose held high. To his handler's eyes what Hannibal was doing was creating his own scent perimeter. The area enclosed in the small circle Hannibal was forming with his movement was where the K-9 believed the odor was coming from.

At the spot Hannibal was indicating, the main body of water narrowed to a thin trickle, which flowed out to a culvert situated under the nearby roadway. The trooper reasoned that the scent Hannibal was picking up was being carried from its source under the nearly still pond—the spot where the bones had been flung by the two killers— and was traveling in a path carried along by the water's flow, then continuing away from the area under the roadway.

Zarrella eyeballed this imaginary line from the place where the murderers' vehicle had been parked and where they most likely had thrown in Tuttle's remains. He figured at that point he had a good idea where the divers would be likely to find what they were seeking.

Nevertheless, Zarrella permitted Hannibal to continue

his search. Not much time passed before Hannibal stopped what he was doing, chest deep in the swampy water, tail wagging. The dog stared at his partner for a moment and then began to bark. Zarrella thinks he knows exactly what Hannibal was saying. His translation of his partner's barking was, "Com'on you stupid idiot, how much longer do you expect me to stand in this water!"

To which Zarrella replied, "Okay, Hannibal, what do you got?"

Hannibal, without further command, immediately came out of the water, scratched the embankment with his paw, and then gave Zarrella a lie-down alert right in the mud. The K-9 was telling his partner that he had found what they had been looking for; no more debate was necessary.

Zarrella sent his dog in for a re-find, to better pinpoint the scent's location. This time Hannibal made his way toward the small stream that led to the culvert, finally stopping at a beaver dam where it ended. Again Hannibal showed an alert, which Zarrella had expected.

When Zarrella took his K-9 to an area of the swamp away from where he had shown interest, the dog gave no indication of any kind. This further reinforced the trooper's observation as to where the scent material lay.

Zarrella decided it would be productive to take Hannibal out on the pond in a boat. The Leominster Civil Defense department provided the team with use of their small rescue boat, a fifteen-foot-long craft with a single engine. As one of the Ashby Fire Department members rowed the trooper and Hannibal around—use of the engine would have stirred things up too much—the big dog attempted to locate the scent.

About fifteen yards from the shore the dog raised his head high, scratched the bottom of the boat, and lay down. Although Zarrella and Hannibal continued to search other parts of the pond from the boat, that first place was the only spot where he showed genuine interest.

Hannibal was praised by Zarrella for his efforts and taken back to their Chevy Suburban wagon. The trooper decided he'd give Panzer a try.

Panzer too had a thick leather search collar, which

Zarrella placed around her neck. Using the word "Cercalo," (cher-car-lo) which means "look for it" in Italian, he sent Panzer out. She ran along the shoreline and upon coming to the area where the killers had backed their car in six years earlier, showed great excitement. Her tail wagged furiously and she began to lick at the water. Like Hannibal earlier, she then followed the slowly flowing water, and upon coming to the beaver dam by the culvert she lay down, indicating to her partner what is referred to as a hard alert. To Zarrella that meant the scent was collecting where the flow of water was impeded by the dam.

It was time to make a recommendation, the toughest time for a K-9 handler. His two dogs had, during the course of the day, told Zarrella that they had detected the odor of a dead human being. Still, it bothered the trooper that the divers, who had been looking diligently for pieces of bone for five days running had been unable to locate anything. Lots of stuff winds up dead and rotting on the bottom of a swamp. Could whatever it was that caused his two K-9s to alert be something other than a dead person? It stands to reason that bones burned in a bonfire for eighteen hours should have no chemical signature left, certainly nothing like bones that had simply been permitted to decompose naturally.

Still, the dogs had said it was there. Zarrella reflected that while they'd both indicated interest soon into their search, there was no reason why that should detract from the validity of what they had to say.

The trooper decided to dispense with the boat for Panzer. It was with some concern that Zarrella gathered everyone together around two in the afternoon and told them to start looking where the dogs had shown interest by the edge of the water.

One diver, dressed in a red wet suit, stepped into the swamp. Less than a half hour after entering the water the diver, waist deep in the pond and only six feet from the shoreline, exclaimed, his eyes wide, "Whoa! I feel something round and smooth!" His hands broke the water's surface; in them he held a human skull, sans lower jaw.

A closer look at the remains by Zarrella showed the bone

to be badly charred. That bonfire must have been hot, he figured.

All the law-enforcement people, the forensic technicians and investigators, who had been on the scene for hours waiting for something to be found, sprang into action. Sticks were pushed into the bottom of the pond around where the first bone was found to mark off the area, and the diver and two others now searched even more vigorously than before for additional remains.

Success breeds success. The three began to find more bones. Two human femurs, one burned in half, were uncovered, as were some vertebrae and the lower jaw. Whatever was left of Mr. Richard Tuttle that could be uncovered was found.

Some members of the Massachusetts State Police Crime Prevention and Control (CPAC) unit (investigators) came up to Zarrella and asked if he'd be willing to have his dogs try to locate where the murder victim's body had been all but cremated six years earlier. Zarrella said no problem, but he added that he promised nothing. Whatever had been there was six years old and should only be residual ash from the burned victim.

The trooper was taken out to the scene of the murder. The Massachusetts troopers told Zarrella that the confessed killer had told them that the ashes that remained after the eighteen hours of burning had been scattered about the site. Zarrella looked around. All he could see before him was a small field, bordered by trees and covered with uncut grass.

Zarrella took Panzer out of the Suburban wagon. He let her loose and Panzer ran over to the tree line, near an ancient, rusted-out milk truck. Near the truck the K-9 lay down, with strong eye contact on her partner, giving Zarrella a firm alert. All the trooper could see was grass. There was no sign there had ever been a fire there, six years earlier or ever.

Zarrella shrugged his shoulders and turned to the two Massachusetts CPAC members, unsure what to tell them. He simply stated that was the only place in the area where his dog showed interest.

They replied, "That's great, that's all we need. That is the area the killer alleged they burned him." They added they needed the confirmation given by Panzer to verify the spot.

What Zarrella found remarkable was that Panzer had alerted on human ash that was six years exposed to the elements, an incredible find.

It had been a good day for Zarrella and his K-9 partners. And it reinforced for the trooper something he should have already known but yet found so hard to do: "Trust your dog!"

As for the two killers, Zarrella later learned that both men were ultimately convicted of murder. They'll both have lots of time to contemplate their actions.

Not a Major Case, but Still a Good One

Not every time Zarrella, Hannibal, and Panzer got called in on a case was a major investigation. Sometimes it was just a routine police matter that required the assistance of a trained K-9 team.

The trooper was working midnight shift out of the Wickford Barracks, in the southern part of Rhode Island. Sergeant Scot Mancini, from the Warwick Police Department, called in to state police headquarters. He explained to the ranking officer in charge, Lieutenant Doug Badger, that a Warwick officer passing near a local Best Eating Donuts establishment had observed a large amount of blood in a nearby telephone booth. The booth in fact had been covered in the stuff; it was all over the phone, the shelf, and on the floor. The officer's dilemma was that no one was now around the bloody telephone booth who was bleeding.

Maybe someone had been the victim of a crime and needed help. Maybe there was another reason why a clearly injured person would try to make a telephone call and then, as the trail of blood showed, disappear into the night. The officer had managed to follow the red drops for several blocks but eventually lost them some distance from where he started. Sergeant Mancini explained to the lieutenant that what was needed was a police K-9, specifically Hannibal, if possible, to attempt to track the injured party.

Now, when Hannibal had initially come aboard at the Rhode Island State Police, the lieutenant had been unsure just how practical the use of K-9s really was in police service. A twenty-five-year veteran of the force, he let it be known that he had never observed a successful find using a trained police-service dog. It wasn't until the Emery investigation, in which just about everyone around Lieutenant Badger felt the couple had fled the country and that their abandoned car found on the bridge had only been a ploy, that the lieutenant changed his mind. On that occasion the only support the lieutenant got for his theory had come from Hannibal, and it sure had been comforting when Elena Emery's skull was dragged up from Narragansett Bay later that spring. It just showed that the lieutenant and Hannibal had been right on the money all along.

So now, when Hannibal was requested, the lieutenant didn't hesitate. He contacted Zarrella by radio, telling him to respond to the scene and assist the Warwick department—with Hannibal, of course.

Zarrella drove back to the barracks to secure the appropriate equipment and get his K-9s ready. When the two dogs saw Zarrella putting on his coveralls and readying their collars and leads, the pair knew what was up. Both tails began to wag furiously, with Hannibal whining, barking, and pacing back and forth while Panzer sprang, over and over, like some overgrown jack-in-the-box, a full five feet into the air with excitement and anticipation.

Finally getting the two happy K-9s into his Suburban wagon, Zarrella headed over to the bloody telephone booth.

At two in the morning the trooper and his partners arrived. Sergeant Mancini was still on the scene, as were other Warwick officers. The sergeant, having worked with police dogs in the past, had been careful to ensure that the telephone booth had not been disturbed or otherwise contaminated by his officers.

The sergeant pointed out to Zarrella how the blood trail led away from the telephone booth. He asked the trooper if Hannibal would be able to follow that track to the location of the bleeding person. Zarrella answered that they'd give it a try. To himself he wondered whether he should have his

K-9 trail the bloodied person's scent, as he would when tracking a living person, or trail the blood proper, as he would when looking for a deceased human.

As he pondered his options the trooper took Hannibal from his vehicle. Zarrella decided he'd use the big dog, because of Hannibal's previous experience, to track on the blood. He put the heavy leather body-search collar on the animal and gave the command, "Look for it!"

Zarrella soon realized he had made a mistake. Hannibal did exactly what his handler had ordered him to do. At each and every spot of blood the K-9 would stop, scratch, and lie down, giving the trooper an alert.

As he walked Hannibal back to the car, Zarrella tried to explain to the now dubious officers who had been watching him work what the nature of the problem was. They, of course, weren't aware that the trouble lay with the handler and not the K-9. Up to that moment the dog had performed exactly as he had been trained to perform.

Zarrella took the body-search collar off Hannibal and put him in his tracking harness, then gave the command, "Find him!" Now, instead of stopping at each speck of blood on the ground, Hannibal lunged forward down the street. He pulled hard on Zarrella as he went first across the main road from the telephone booth and then took the trooper and following officers several blocks, to a residential neighborhood.

After traveling over a quarter mile the blood trail was no longer visible to human eyes. Hannibal continued on his mission, making left and right turns down various streets, following a human track, which by that time was over two hours old, across roads and over sidewalks. The dog's human partners had already given up looking on the ground for any sign of the bleeding person for some time and now were just simply following along.

Hannibal made a left turn on Senator Street, crossed over, and went onto the front lawn of a small residence. Things had taken place so quickly during this track that Zarrella had given up thinking about what his partner was doing. Like everyone else around, the trooper was simply along for the ride.

After walking in circles on the lawn for a few seconds Hannibal then tugged his partner over to the side door of the house. In the nearby driveway the trooper passed by a truck that seemed loaded with a great deal of copper. Then, to Zarrella's momentary concern, he spotted a dish of dog food by the door. The possibility that his K-9 was tracking an animal leapt into Zarrella's head. The trooper didn't have long to consider that likelihood. Near the door Hannibal again began to walk in circles.

Zarrella turned to Mancini and informed the sergeant that this was where Hannibal indicated the trail ended. Without missing a beat the sergeant stepped up to the door and, three-thirty in the morning or not, rapped loudly on its outside. Zarrella silently prayed that Hannibal had taken them to the right place as the sergeant's loud banging reverberated in his ears.

A man came to the door and asked, "Can I help you?"

The sergeant explained that the officers had been following some blood. As the sergeant was speaking to the homeowner, Zarrella couldn't help noticing there was a heavy bandage on the man's right hand.

Mancini noticed the dressing as well. He waved his arm around him and, as if the street were overflowing with the stuff, asked straight out, "Is this your blood?"

"Yeah, that's my blood," came the reply.

The sergeant requested that the gentleman step outside.

To Zarrella's surprise the man was immediately hand-cuffed by the Warwick officers. It seemed that the man's truckload of copper had not been legitimately obtained. The local officers knew the individual to be a thief, one who had been burglarizing abandoned buildings for the expensive copper they contained. They'd been trying to find out who the culprit was for quite a while, and as it turned out, Hannibal's tracking the man to his home, along with finding plenty of evidence in the truck, did the trick.

The story that unfolded was that the burglar had badly cut himself on the hand in one of the buildings he was stealing copper from when he attempted to gain entry to the place by punching in one of the windows. After leaving, and now bleeding, he decided to call his girlfriend from the pay telephone by the donut shop—leaving his truck and illegal cargo safely back at his home—and have her drive him to a hospital.

For whatever reason, he decided not to have his girl give him a ride and ran home to stop the flowing blood.

While Zarrella was still standing around with the Warwick officers, Lieutenant Badger drove by, just in time to see the burglar being placed, securely cuffed, in the rear of a local police car. The lieutenant asked Mancini what was going on. The sergeant enthusiastically replied, "That dog, that dog! He found this guy! We been looking for this guy for months!"

Lieutenant Badger calmly looked over to Zarrella and Hannibal and in a subdued tone said, "Good job. Good job. See you back at the barracks," and drove off. It was obvious to Zarrella that the lieutenant had known all along that Hannibal was up to handling the assignment.

Sometimes It's Nobody's Fault

While Hannibal and Panzer both hung out in their kennel at the rear of the Wickford State Police Barracks, their partner had spent the shift's previous four hours on radio duty. That meant that Zarrella had to sit by a console full of buttons, microphone, and telephones and work as the barracks' dispatcher. It was a job everyone got a turn at performing, but one that few of the law officers enjoyed.

But now the end of Zarrella's thirteen-hour shift had finally arrived. He was looking forward to going home. Thirteen hours made for a long day no matter how enthusiastic a person is about their occupation. The night shift was already in and suited up, and Zarrella was in the process of briefing the trooper set to relieve him at the desk when the telephone rang. For no particular reason Zarrella reached over and picked up the phone, saying, "State Police Wickford, Trooper Zarrella."

After the electronic *beep* sounded that indicated the call was being recorded a woman came on the line. She anxiously told Zarrella that a few hours earlier her husband had chased her from their home at gunpoint. At first Zarrella was uncertain what she was trying to tell him; her voice had a panicked edge to it and she delivered her story in a machine-gun burst of words.

The woman hadn't called in on the emergency line, so her address wasn't displayed automatically on a screen in front of the trooper as it normally would be. Soon realizing there might be a nasty situation in the making, Zarrella's first two questions that he wanted answered were, where was she and where was her husband?

The woman, Avis Cook, told him she was calling from a neighbor's home. As far as she knew, her husband, Wayne, was still in their house on Glen Rock Road in Exeter. Zarrella knew the location to be a large town geographically but one with a small population. It had no police department.

Zarrella continued to work at getting out the whole story from Mrs. Cook. He pieced together the fact that her husband, a man in his late sixties, was quite ill, having suffered a number of recent strokes and heart attacks. He had only a few days earlier discharged himself, against his doctor's strong objection, from Vanderbilt Hospital. Mrs. Cook explained how Mr. Cook's medical condition, and most recently his two latest heart attacks and strokes, had taken a terrible toll on his mental health and stability. That evening they had argued over his accusations that she was plotting to give all their money to her children. To make matters worse, in that day's mail had come stock statements from the family's investments, which had further fueled Wayne Cook's fears. Although his wife showed him the canceled checks that disproved his suspicions, the man would not be dissuaded.

At about five that afternoon, Mrs. Cook said, she had had enough of her husband's abuse. The woman informed Wayne Cook that she was taking all the documents in question to an attorney. She then picked up a plastic bag as well as a metal container, both of which were full of checks and papers. Her husband, who had been seated in his chair in the living room, rose, and while pointing a .22 pistol at her, ordered, "Give me the damn bag." It was at that point that the woman had run from the home, dropping the items she'd just picked up onto the floor.

To further complicate matters for the trooper, Mrs. Cook then added that there were also a number of high-powered rifles along with their ammunition kept in the house. Then in the next breath the woman asked the trooper for help but told him she didn't want her husband arrested or removed from the house. In short she just wanted somebody to do something. What that something was, she wasn't sure. It had, after all, taken her three hours just to decide to call the police.

At that point Zarrella put Mrs. Cook on hold. He called over to Corporal Robert Cruz, the trooper in charge of the barracks' day shift, and told him, "We might have a serious matter here." Zarrella quickly outlined for the corporal what was going on. The trooper also reiterated to his superior what Mrs. Cook had told him, that her husband needed medical care and couldn't be left alone for too long a period of time. The dilemma the troopers faced was a formidable one. They had an armed, physically ill, emotionally disturbed, and unpredictable man, who had just threatened his wife's life, and who had a small arsenal of weapons at his disposal in his home.

After Corporal Cruz spoke with Mrs. Cook to get a better understanding of the predicament, he then contacted the lieutenant in charge of the night shift for the entire state of Rhode Island. Because of budget contraints within the agency the first determination to be made by the ranking member on duty was what to do with the day-shift personnel—hold them or send them home.

It was decided to permit the majority of personnel to go off duty while sending one of the senior day-shift troopers along with two night-shift troopers to where Mrs. Cook was staying. Corporal Cruz and the lieutenant were to follow soon after. Zarrella asked for permission to stay, but he was turned down and told to just make sure his radio relief man knew the background of what was unfolding.

Zarrella did as he was instructed, then got out of uniform, went to the kennel in the rear of the building, and called out to his two buddies patiently waiting for him, "You want to go for a ride?" Their excited response—it never varied when that offer was made—was to run about in circles, wag their tails, and once out of their gated enclosures, bolt for the trooper's car.

The three members of the Rhode Island State Police headed back home for some sleep. Rain pattered against the windshield, making a pleasant rhythm as Zarrella drove along. The thought in Zarrella's mind as he lay down that night was of that end-of-shift phone call he had taken. He wondered if everything would turn out all right.

Meanwhile the drama continued to unfold at the Cook household. The one car in the family was accounted for. Mrs. Cook had driven it over to the neighbor's house. So the question the troopers had to deal with was whether or not Mr. Cook was still in the home, and if so, what to do about it. There was also the question of how to handle the two dogs in the house, a German shepherd named Shep and a rottweiler named Maggie. Mrs. Cook told the troopers that they didn't like strangers and were protective of Mr. Cook.

By ten the troopers interviewing Mrs. Cook decided it would be necessary to put the department's SWAT team on standby.

Shortly before midnight the SWAT members began to arrive, and by two in the morning they had surrounded the Cook residence, a large, natural wood home built on fifteen acres of both pasture and forested land. At four o'clock the highly trained SWAT members entered the home. Mr. Cook was nowhere to be found.

All firearms and ammunition were removed from the home. However, neither the paperwork valued so much by Mr. Cook nor his handgun could be located.

Zarrella and his two K-9s came in for duty at eight in the morning. Before he had a chance to ask about what had happened the previous night he was told by Corporal Cruz that he and his dogs would be needed for a search. The missing Mr. Cook had never turned up, it had rained hard the entire cool April night, and nobody had any idea where the man might be nor what his physical or emotional condition was.

Zarrella changed into his search clothes. A sergeant, the corporal, and he soon headed out to the Cook residence. They drove up the long driveway, past a large barn, and on to the handsome wood home that lay beyond.

It was decided to search the residence one more time, just for the record. The only problem was, there were two upset dogs still in the house. Cruz and the sergeant looked over at Zarrella, who got the message, saying, "Okay, I'll go in."

The trooper noticed that while the dogs were barking viciously at the door, they were also old and upset. Armed with his OC (pepper spray), as he entered he saw that the two animals were backing up. Zarrella decided these were not trained killers. So the trooper holstered his can of chemical spray, relieved that he didn't have to use it on the poor confused dogs, and spoke to the two house pets in a soft and soothing voice. He offered the bewildered and frightened animals some dog biscuits that he found lying about, and from that point on they posed no further problem.

The three men then went through each room in the home but Mr. Cook was not inside.

Outside, as Zarrella stood by his state-police-issued Chevy Suburban, he evaluated the nature of the track technique he'd have to employ. With all the SWAT people running around the outside of the home only hours earlier, whatever scent might have been on the ground had been contaminated. That being the case the trooper concluded that conducting a ground-scent search would prove difficult if not impossible to accomplish successfully. The heavy rain—it was still pouring out—didn't help matters. What he required was a dog who scented from the air, a specialty of Panzer's. Such a technique had the added advantage of being somewhat quicker to conduct than a ground search. With the state of health Mr. Cook was in, time was of the essence. The trooper looked over at his two K-9s eyeing him and made his decision. This would be one game Hannibal would have to sit out on the bench.

Taking out Panzer's blue nylon search collar, he ordered his K-9 from the vehicle and fastened the collar around her neck. Zarrella took the small-boned German shepherd over to one side of a dirt road that cut the rear of the property in half. Methodical as always, he'd have his dog work first the right side of the Cook's fifteen acres, then the left.

The trooper, already in his fatiguelike search uniform, had decided earlier to put on a yellow rain slicker as well. He now realized that had been a wise decision. The downpour showed no signs of letting up. Looking at the long dirt road they would soon start down, Zarrella watched as the heavy rain hit the leaves of the trees, then formed a mist in the forest. If it weren't for the fact that he and Panzer were about to search out an ill and possibly homicidal man, he would have taken the time to enjoy the beauty of the scene.

The search team consisted of Cruz following close behind Zarrella and Panzer. They began to move up the access road and walked through an open field for a few hundred yards. Since a person lying on that ground would be clearly visible, the two men and Panzer moved quickly beyond that point.

They tried to keep moving into the wind, and Zarrella noticed that Panzer showed little interest in the area she had been ordered into. Zarrella kept his K-9 at it, wanting to eliminate one area before beginning work in a new location. There was one reaction from his K-9 he did note. When the wind shifted and came from the direction of the yet unsearched section of the Cook property, Panzer raised her head and began to show excitement.

Finding no one on the right side of the homestead, the team moved away from the first section and onto the second tract of land. Panzer's heightened interest immediately became apparent to her handler. Her tail began to wag to and fro like some crazy metronome, and the trooper could hear his dog begin to take in greater quantities of air through her nostrils until finally Panzer began to move rapidly toward a stone wall up ahead.

Zarrella called out the command, "Vattene," Italian for "off you go." Its use directed Panzer to go faster. The dog broke into a run. When she came up to the wall, Panzer cleared the three-foot-high barrier in a single leap. Zarrella and Corporal Cruz made sure they stayed close behind.

Upon climbing over the other side of the stone wall Zarrella watched as Panzer began to sniff the ground with great intensity, then start to move around in circles. She then raised her head and took in another deep breath. Again, Zarrella gave her the command, "Vattene." The dog headed forward up the logging road they were on. A hundred yards farther through the forest path she stopped, nose pointed straight ahead, acting just like a field dog pointing out birds to her master. But it wasn't a bird that Zarrella saw in the distance. It was the body of the missing Mr. Cook, lying some thirty yards away through the rainy mist. The trooper, who had seen many dead bodies in his career, didn't have to get any closer to know that Mr. Cook was no longer with them.

Zarrella ordered his K-9, "Go ahead!" Panzer ran over to Mr. Cook and nudged his face in a futile effort to rouse the man. Not knowing what to do next, she looked over at Zarrella, then lay down next to the victim, her way of telling Zarrella she'd found the person they were looking for. Panzer had never seen a dead human body before.

Corporal Cruz and Zarrella stepped over to the deceased and looked down at the man. To the trooper it was clear by his skin color that Mr. Cook had been dead for some time. By his side were both the plastic grocery bag and the metal lockbox he had taken from the home, containing all the papers and checks he had valued so highly.

Later the doctors told the trooper that the man had died of a heart attack. It was all rather sad, a bittersweet success, Zarrella thought. From the little the trooper knew of the man's history, the victim had led a productive life, only to become terribly ill and, perhaps most sad of all, to lose his sense of reality and his rational perception of the world around him.

But as a professional, Zarrella still felt pride in the skill his K-9 demonstrated in the search. Panzer had indeed done a fine job of locating the lost man, who had gone much farther into the woods than anyone had suspected.

Still, Zarrella wondered about the whole event, a case that came to an unfortunate conclusion without anyone being at fault.

Hannibal's Last Search

It was Wednesday, April 17, 1996. Zarrella had just come back to the Wickford Barracks from an unsuccessful day of trying to locate the .22 pistol belonging to Mr. Cook. The last thing the troopers needed was to have some child stumble upon the missing handgun and injure him or herself.

Zarrella had just finished cleaning himself up and had changed into his neatly pressed patrol uniform. Making his way down the stairs from the locker room, he was met on the floor below by one of his sergeants. The supervisor informed Zarrella that they had just received a call from the Hope Valley Barracks. Five people, who had last been seen earlier that morning, were missing in the woods. Four of them were young children.

Zarrella stepped over to a telephone to talk to the trooper from the other barracks. There was no time for social amenities. He asked, "What do you have?"

The other trooper quickly explained the situation. A woman had called him, telling him that her husband, Thomas Ware, fifty-four, their two children aged eight and twelve, along with two friends, seven and ten, had left that morning to go on what was supposed to have been a short hike. She did know they were to have started the two-mile trek along a path known as the Blitzkrieg trail, situated in the Arcadia Management Area out in Richmond.

Zarrella glanced at his watch, noting it was already after six in the afternoon, as the other man went on. The trooper on the other end of the line explained that the father was being treated for Parkinson's disease and he should have taken his last dose of medicine hours earlier. To make matters worse, the area they were in was thickly wooded, with dense underbrush and sections of swamp. The hikers had brought little food with them. Further, they were all dressed lightly and the temperature would drop into the mid-forties that night.

Zarrella assured the other trooper he and his dogs would

be out there as soon as possible. As he hung up the telephone he looked over at Corporal Cruz and said, "This is gonna be a night one." He then turned to the stairs and bounded up to the dressing room. It was time to change back into his search clothes.

With Hannibal and Panzer in the back of his car, Zarrella drove as quickly as he could to the place where he'd be meeting other law officers along with the missing family's mother. Even at trooper speed it took him forty-five minutes to travel the back country roads to the command post that had been set up at the Arcadia Management Area.

It was already seven-thirty when he arrived. He met the other law officers—a dozen had been assembled for the search and more were on the way—as well as Mrs. Ware, the missing children's mother, who had brought a pillowcase used by her husband for the K-9s to scent on. Also, Mrs. Ware showed the trooper and the others exactly which marked trail the missing five were supposed to have taken into the woods over ten hours earlier for what was to have been a two-mile walk each way.

A lieutenant from the DEM was in charge of the search operation. Three K-9 handlers would be involved in the rescue effort: one from the DEM, one from the Narragansett Police Department, and Zarrella, representing the Rhode Island State Police.

While waiting for the other two search dogs, Zarrella considered his options and decided he'd use his most experienced animal, Hannibal. He also asked the local trooper to set up roving patrols along the surrounding roads, just in case the five missing people managed to find their way out of the woods.

It was eight-thirty by the time the other two K-9s got to the command post. Armed with a description of what the missing people had been wearing, the DEM lieutenant decided that his agency's dog would start looking from their point of entry, Zarrella and Hannibal would go in from where the people were to have wound up, and the third dog would search a trail just off the primary one about to be searched, just in case they veered off.

Zarrella, along with a DEM officer who would act as his

guide, got into his vehicle and drove off to his assigned spot. Once there he and Hannibal, his big gentle dog now dressed in his orange search-rescue vest, wasted no time in moving down the trail. Even so, it was midnight when, at the midway point, the two search teams met each other. Neither had seen any reaction from their respective K-9s.

Hannibal had worked the search off leash. As Zarrella followed close behind, he noticed in the beam of his flashlight that his K-9 seemed to have a stiff left leg. He'd never seen that in his partner before. He made a mental note that whatever the problem was it would have to be checked out by a vet.

With that part of the operation over, a job that had taken the better part of three hours, everyone climbed into a pair of DEM Chevy Blazers and made it back to the command post. As Zarrella helped lift Hannibal into the truck's heavily loaded back, his dog cried out in pain. Definitely, tomorrow we visit the vet, Zarrella decided.

When they got back to the makeshift command center Zarrella asked another DEM officer to help unload Hannibal from the rear of the vehicle. Even so, when picked up by the trooper and the other man, Hannibal cried out in pain. At that point Zarrella decided his injured K-9 was going back into the Suburban. Panzer would have to take over the search chores for the remainder of the night. Hannibal's vest came off, Zarrella gave him some water, patted him, and left him to rest while the trooper went over to the other search-party members to discuss their options.

The state lands were a maze of hiking trails. That meant that with no success on their first try all the other trails would have to be searched. Zarrella was assigned his area of responsibility and, along with other personnel, he and Panzer checked out the location. No one had any luck this time around either.

Sometime after midnight a new lead came in. A witness claimed to have seen the missing group go into the woods across the road from the trail they were supposed to have taken. The DEM people, familiar with the terrain, informed everyone that the woods in that spot were very dense. A knee-deep swamp was located not far from there as well.

The Narragansett team was assigned to check it out while other trails were investigated.

All searchers returned around two in the morning. The Narragansett officer reported he had attempted to penetrate the woods but they were thick with vegetation and, because he had to keep his dog on a lead, he had only managed to work the area's outer perimeter and roads.

At that point the searchers learned that a Coast Guard helicopter from Otis Air Force Base in Massachusetts was headed their way to join in the search. The machine had both high intensity lighting and a forward looking infrared system (FLIR) aboard. The FLIR would permit the helicopter crew to detect the heat signatures of the lost people, which would show up as recognizable images on a television-like screen aboard their craft.

One of the DEM members opened up a large map of the area. Zarrella suggested that another attempt with K-9s should be made to get into the last spot the eyewitness had indicated the lost people had entered the woods. Other members of the search team dissented, saying that if the Narragansett, K-9 couldn't make it into the place, there was little point in anyone else trying to get in there. Zarrella disagreed. Of all the K-9 team handlers there he probably had the most experience in finding lost people. He put a great deal of weight on the eyewitness sighting and vehemently argued his point.

While this dicussion was going on off to one side, the Rhode Island State Police lieutenant on the scene, Doug Badger, was speaking into his radio. Returning to the group he informed them he had requested the helicopter to first check out the area in question. If they were unable to find anything with their sophisticated equipment, then a ground search of the other areas could be reinitiated.

At two-thirty in the morning, after the military helicopter made its fourth pass over the forest, the crew radioed in that they believed they'd located the group. They were five hundred yards into the woods from where the rescuers were situated.

Although a multimillion-candlepower light was being used by the aircraft, the trees were so thick that only the noise of the machine's turbine engine could be heard in the distance; beyond them was nothing to see but eerie blackness.

The pace of the action picked up rapidly. Now the problem was to get to the victims. A hasty plan was devised. The K-9 teams would attempt to penetrate the woods by Skunk Hill Road, beyond where the group was huddled deep in the woods.

Panzer was taken out of her vehicle. It was so dark that Zarrella attached a red strobe light to her harness. Since his dog would be permitted to search without being attached to a lead, the strobe would allow Zarrella at least a chance of keeping visual track of his K-9. The other K-9 handlers, with dogs who were cross-trained as patrol animals, had to keep their charges on their leashes. Zarrella knew that would place the other K-9 teams at a serious disadvantage in the thick brush they were about to enter.

Once at Skunk Hill Road the teams lined up. Just as they were about to enter the woods Zarrella gave Panzer her search command. The dog immediately entered the forest, Zarrella right behind. While the four-legged Panzer had little trouble making progress through the heavy growth, Zarrella and his DEM partner found they had to fight tenacious wet vines in order to make headway. At times the trooper and DEM officer had to get down on their hands and knees in order to move forward. Soon they were well ahead of the other teams.

As he followed after his dog, Zarrella's flashlight died. Now all he had for guidance was the strobe on Panzer's harness to show him the way. Travel was nearly impossible, but Zarrella could sense that his dog was on the track as he struggled to keep up with the excited K-9.

Thirty minutes into the trek Panzer made it to the five lost people, with Zarrella not far behind.

Zarrella, although in excellent physical condition, was himself exhausted. While catching his breath he took in the scene. The intense white overhead beam of light from the big helicopter made an aura around the four children. They reminded the trooper of little Christmas angels.

Until other rescuers arrived, the immediate area remained

illuminated only by the surreal blinking of Panzer's strobe light and the light from the helicopter overhead. The father and four children huddled together to keep warm but seemed otherwise unhurt to the trooper. They were tired, hungry, and thirsty and appeared to Zarrella to be in shock. But Panzer wouldn't be repressed. She went from child to child, her tail wagging furiously, nudging each one with her nose.

Zarrella asked if anyone was hurt. The little ones shook their heads no, the father stared silently into the light of the helicopter hovering above. The trooper pulled out his first-aid pack and broke it open. Taking out a container of water he asked if anyone was thirsty. Some of the girls said yes and he gave them the canteen. As he was doing so he told them that the dog's name was Panzer, she was a search dog, a friendly dog, and they could pat her.

Soon the children began to giggle and respond to the dog's antics, and they began to play with the K-9. Zarrella gave his jacket to the child who said she was the coldest. Within a few minutes the emergency medical technicians and other searchers arrived.

As things were being sorted out Zarrella stepped over to the father and asked, "How did you guys get here?"

He answered, "I wanted to take a shortcut."

It was quickly decided that attempting to come out of the woods the same way the rescuers had come in would be nearly impossible and possibly dangerous for the five tired people. Fortunately the DEM officers knew where they were in relation to the nearest most accessible road. Using handheld compasses, the group, walking single file, often hand in hand, headed out to the south, where the waiting rescue vehicles were standing by. Zarrella carried one of the tired little girls in his arms.

In considerably less time than it had taken them to make their way into the forest, the group spotted the bright lights of the DEM rescue vehicles which had been turned in their direction. Zarrella handed his tired and hungry bundle over to an EMT and watched as the five people were driven from the area.

In only a few minutes Zarrella found himself once more

at the command post. The trooper began to pack up his gear and prepared to leave. By the time he was ready to drive off he noticed he was the last one at the command post. Silently getting into his Suburban, he drove back with Hannibal and Panzer to the Hope Valley Barracks and watched the rescue on the seven o'clock news.

Hannibal

From Hope Valley Zarrella went straight home. He'd been up for over twenty-four hours and, while pleased with the results of his K-9s' efforts, he was exhausted. But before taking to his bed he called Hannibal's veterinarian. He wanted Hannibal's hip checked out and made an appointment for his partner for later that afternoon. He then went to sleep.

Zarrella got up at one, showered, and put Hannibal and Dozer, his two-hundred-ten-pound pet English mastiff, who was also due for a checkup, in the trailer attached to his Suburban. The trooper was pleased to see that Hannibal's hip didn't seem to bother him as much as it had the night before. The large animal even managed to jump up into the trailer unaided by his master. By three o'clock the trooper and his two big buddies had completed the half-hour ride to the vet's office.

Zarrella had been going to Doctor John Turco, a personal friend, for many years. The doctor knew all the trooper's animals and had taken care of Hannibal from the time he was a puppy.

Hannibal went in first. The doctor watched the K-9 walk, probed the tender spot with his fingers, and decided the hip should be X-rayed. That meant that Hannibal would have to be put under anesthesia, a process that had to be done very carefully, as a big dog like Hannibal can be easily lost when such chemicals are used. In this case, a simple X ray, Doctor Turco decided to use a strong sedative on the dog rather than put Hannibal totally out.

Soon after being injected with the drug, Hannibal began to quiver and lose his ability to stand. Zarrella never liked to see his friend in that condition; it always made him nervous. But in this case it was a necessity.

Zarrella eased the hundred-thirty-pound dog to a lying position on the floor, patted him, and assured him all would be okay. When the sedative had taken its full effect he and Doctor Turco rolled Hannibal onto a stretcher and together hefted the semiconscious dog onto the X-ray table.

Hannibal lay on his back. The doctor was careful not to pull on the animal's rear legs, explaining to Zarrella as he was preparing Hannibal for the X ray that he preferred the legs to remain in their natural position. He did check the joint's range of motion and thought it might be a bit loose, perhaps a bit hyperextended.

The two men stepped away and the doctor took the photo. Once that was done the doctor cleaned Hannibal's teeth, at the same time discussing with Zarrella a food additive the trooper might consider to help with the dog's dry skin and to brighten up his coat.

When the X ray was completed, Hannibal was again placed on the floor and the antidote to the sedative was injected into him. Almost immediately the big dog began to respond.

Soon he was standing by himself. He was just a bit groggy. His hip no longer seemed to hurt him when the doctor touched it. After watching Hannibal for a few more minutes it was time to put him back in the vehicle's trailer.

Taking his partner outside, Zarrella felt great. He'd been quite worried about that hip problem, nothing to take lightly with a large dog. But the X ray showed all was well and it appeared that Hannibal was in fine shape. He was put in the trailer and Dozer was taken out for his session with Doctor Turco.

The other dog's visit to the vet was as uneventful as Hannibal's. As Doctor Turco was a friend of Zarrella's, and was now off duty, the two men decided they'd run over to a nearby restaurant and have a quiet dinner.

Zarrella wouldn't leave Hannibal and Dozer alone at the vet's office, so with the two dogs in tow, they found the Italian restaurant Turco had recommended. As Zarrella was looking for a place to park, Turco suggested he put his car somewhere near where the two of them could watch the dogs.

They finished eating by nine and when they came out of the restaurant they checked on the two animals. Doctor Turco opened the trailer door and took a look at Hannibal. Both dogs seemed fine, quietly content in their trailer, Dozer sitting up and Hannibal lying down. The big dog was his usual, alert self and showed no sign of having any negative reaction to the sedative or its antidote. With that done Zarrella drove the doctor back to the office and headed for home, still tired from the previous day's work.

The half-hour ride back to his house was uneventful. Glancing at his gas gauge he saw that the needle was below empty. He was just too tired to stop at a service station. Tomorrow would be soon enough. In his driveway Zarrella dropped the trailer from its hitch and opened the door. From inside the pitch-dark interior Dozer came bounding out. Zarrella saw that Hannibal was still lying down. He called, "Come on, Hani." The dog didn't move.

Zarrella froze. He reached into the trailer, called, "Come on Hani!" and patted the dog. Hannibal's ears were cool to the touch. Zarrella's heart sank. Looking inside the trailer he saw his partner, lying on his side, eyes open. Hannibal's belly was fully extended. It was a lethal condition called the bloat that could cause a big dog's stomach to twist, cutting off the circulation to his other vital organs.

A cold fear gripped Zarrella. He grabbed Dozer and ran into the house. Yanking up the telephone he dialed the veterinarian service number. An operator answered. While Zarrella tried to explain his emergency and the need to meet the vet at the office right away, the fool on the other end attempted to ask him needless questions. Zarrella slammed the telephone down and dialed Turco's home number directly.

"John, Hannibal is bloating!"

"Bring him down right away! I'll meet you there as soon as I can."

Zarrella ran from his home. As he closed the trailer door

he called out to his friend, "Hani, you better hang on!" It was a prayer rather than a threat. Zarrella raced back to veterinarian's office. During what was normally a forty-five minute ride, but which took him an interminable twenty minutes, he cursed himself for not having taken the time to gas up his truck. As he pulled into the driveway of the veterinary hospital, his vehicle sputtered to a stop. Out of fuel, it would sit there for two days.

Doctor Turco and the vet on duty, Judy Glowicz, were standing by outside. Zarrella yanked open the sides of the trailer and hopped inside. He started to move the hundred-thirty-pound Hannibal toward the opening when Doctor Turco, who weighed no more than the big K-9, grabbed the animal and with virtually no help from anyone else lifted Hannibal out and carried him through the hospital's double doors to the already prepared operating room. Hannibal's still form was placed on the table and Doctor Glowicz, wearing her light blue surgical gown, grabbed a long breathing tube and inserted it down his throat.

Zarrella stepped away. He tried to convince himself that his partner was now in good hands and everything would be all right. He began to pray.

Doctor Glowicz called out, "Matt, you've got to breathe for this dog!"

Zarrella returned to the waist-high table, knelt down, and, taking the end of the tube from Doctor Glowicz, did as he was instructed. For the next forty-five minutes he would breathe for Hannibal.

The two doctors immediately went to work on the dog. Initially they tried getting a tube down his throat to relieve the gas pressure in his stomach. It wouldn't go down. Doctor Glowicz called out to the other vet, "Just cut the stomach!" A moment later Zarrella heard the lethal gas escape from inside Hannibal.

The two doctors continued their attempts to revive the motionless Hannibal. They next injected him with adrenaline. That failed, so they cut into his chest and tried to massage his heart by hand. By that time the reality of what was happening began to sink in for Zarrella. He knew that Hannibal was in major trouble if they had to go into his chest. Yet all the while they performed their surgery Zarrella tried to breathe life into his dog.

But Hannibal was dead. Chances are he had been dead in the trailer when Zarrella first pulled into the hospital driveway. Zarrella was in denial. Doctor Turco quietly told Zarrella, "Matt, he's gone," and that he could stop breathing into the tube. Zarrella wouldn't stop. This was unreal, this wasn't happening. He and Hannibal had too much work yet to do. He couldn't lose his Hannibal now.

Doctor Glowicz gently pushed the sobbing Zarrella away from the table. Doctor Turco had his head bowed, his hands spread apart, holding onto the edge of the operating table. Doctor Glowitcz quietly cried.

Zarrella asked to be alone with Hannibal. The two doctors left the room. The trooper closed his dog's eyes and carefully placed Hannibal's tongue back in his mouth. He spoke to his dog, asking him why he had had to die.

Zarrella slipped the dog's choke collar from around his neck and put it in his pocket. It was over.

Sometimes there's nothing you can do, nothing you can say, that makes it any better. Zarrella and Hannibal had been a team. They loved each other, would have sacrificed their lives for each other.

Why do such things happen? Zarrella asked himself that question for weeks after Hannibal's death. But who knows why? Maybe there's no answer. Or perhaps it's no more complicated than God deciding he needed a really good rescue dog that night.

Epilogue

First there was the agonizing second-guessing between the two men. Zarrella was devastated. Doctor Turco blamed himself; he couldn't believe he hadn't seen some sign of the problem when he had examined Hannibal. Yet the fact was, Hannibal had been with the two people who cared most for him in the whole world. His killer had been silent, deadly, and invisible. There had been nothing for either of the two men to have seen, no warning.

Still, all that didn't make the pain go away.

Hannibal had been known throughout Rhode Island and the surrounding New England area. The big, sweet-tempered dog had been featured on television many times, and he and Zarrella had visited numerous schools. Children loved to play with him. They were a natural pair, the handsome young trooper and his loving, talented, friendly K-9.

Word of Hannibal's death was widely reported on area news. Zarrella began to receive condolence letters, hundreds of them, from all over the country. Many came from children.

A ceremony, to be held at the Rhode Island State Police Headquarters to honor former and deceased members of the organization, had been scheduled for just a month after Hannibal died. The public's interest and concern over the K-9's death did not go unheeded by Colonel Culhane, the head of the state police. Zarrella was invited to speak at the ceremony.

It was an auspicious day. Many high-ranking officials of the state were present. The governor was there, as were the current and former heads of the state police. First those members of the state police who had gone on to their final patrol were honored, then civilian employees. Finally Colonel Culhane spoke about Hannibal and how the search-and-rescue K-9 program came about because of the efforts of one young trooper, Matthew Zarrella. The colonel then called out Zarrella's name. The trooper stepped from his position in the ranks of the men and women standing at attention and marched over to the podium. He gave the colonel a sharp salute, stepped behind the lectern, and read his prepared speech:

Hannibal was a gentle animal who captured the hearts of those who knew him and was welcomed by everyone who needed his service because of what he stood for. He was there to help people.

The motto the state police live by is "In the Service of the State." Hannibal, while in the service of the state, served Humanity well throughout Rhode Island as well as other states and in foreign countries. In performing his duties, he brought honor to the K-9 Unit and the Rhode Island State Police.

After those words were said, the colonel stepped up and presented Zarrella with a large wood plaque to memorialize and honor Hannibal. On its face was a photo of Zarrella, in his utility search uniform, with Hannibal sitting by his side, head held high, proudly wearing his rescue vest. It was a happy photo of the team. That plaque is now hanging at state police headquarters.

Then a sergeant called out an order and a nearby honor guard fired a military salute.

The ceremony was concluded.

There was another plaque, given to Zarrella after the ceremony by the state's K-9 association. An artist then unveiled a large oil painting of Hannibal. The big, amiable dog was shown sitting by the seashore, again in his orange rescue vest.

Memories are fine, but life doesn't stand still. The loss of Hannibal, and Zarrella's plight, became known around the dog-breeding community. Out in Colton, Oregon, a man who raises greater Swiss mountain dogs offered one of his animals to the trooper. Zarrella accepted. He traveled across the country to pick up his new and as yet untrained partner.

Gunner was eighteen months old. He and Zarrella hit it off immediately. When they arrived back at home, the pecking order among everyone in the household had to be reestablished. Zarrella got to keep his place as the alpha male human. The two-hundred-ten-pound Dozer wasted no time in letting Gunner know that Dozer was the alpha male canine. And Panzer—she remains the unchallenged alpha female of the team.

It will take many months of training before Gunner can go on patrol with Zarrella and Panzer. And it will take years before his skills reach the level attained by Hannibal. But so far Zarrella is pleased with his new friend and partner. The trooper senses that Gunner is a smart, self-assertive dog who wants to work.

Perhaps, some time in the not-too-distant future, there will be stories told of Rhode Island State Police Trooper Matthew Zarrella and his big K-9 Gunner, and of the adventures they have shared.

Chapter 2

Connecticut
State Police
K-9 Unit

K-9s Tina, Clem, Rufus, Josie, Lady, and Marianne, with Trooper Andy Rebmann, along with his partner Marcia Koenig and her K-9 Coyote

Over a Thousand Searches

Andy Rebmann started with the Connecticut State Police in 1970. After his first two years he was transferred to the K-9 Unit and hasn't looked back since.

Rebmann has been handler to dozens of various specialty-service dogs and has trained hundreds more. During the many years he has used K-9s in the field Rebmann has seen many unusual sights, performed over a thousand searches, and he and his K-9 partners have made some unique and noteworthy finds.

Rebmann continues in this field servicing numerous local and state law-enforcement agencies around the nation along with his partner, Marcia Koenig. He and Koenig first met over fifteen years ago, when she attended a conference given by the National Association for Search and Rescue at which Rebmann gave a lecture on trailing and air-scent dogs. Impressed by the experienced man's knowledge, she kept in touch with him. As fate would have it, the professional relationship turned into something a bit more serious and now the pair are teamed up running the K-9 Specialty Search Association, in Redmond, Washington, both doing the very same things Rebmann did alone when he was a trooper.

Bloodhounds and Water Searches

It was 1973. Rebmann was a K-9 handler working the Montville Barracks, in the eastern section of the state. At the time he had a K-9 assigned to him, a fine patrol dog. The German shepherd had been trained for handler protection as well as to do tracking jobs. Rebmann and his dog were sent out to Lebanon, Connecticut, where a ten-year-old boy had been reported missing. But it soon became apparent to the young Rebmann that too many fire-department and rescue people had already contaminated the scene with their scents. His K-9 simply didn't have the ability to distinguish the missing child's odor from the myriad smells that bombarded him.

Rebmann decided to try one of his department's newly acquired bloodhounds. Tina and Storm (Storm eventually went to a Florida department) were recent arrivals at the Connecticut State Police, having transferred over from the Massachusetts State Police when that agency disbanded its tracking unit.

Upon being notified they were needed, the bloodhound handlers first had to leave their homes, travel to the state police kennel in Bethany, pick up their dogs, then drive out to the search area. It took them over two hours to arrive.

Before the dogs got there, Rebmann and other law officers interviewed the child's friends. The officers and trooper were told of a play fort built in the woods. That was where the unharmed, sleeping boy was eventually found by the concerned searchers—but without the use of K-9s.

To Rebmann it made little sense to have bloodhounds situated so far from where they were needed. Had the K-9s been more readily available, he knew that much less time would have been spent on the search.

He had an idea. Why not have one of the dogs assigned to him? Rebmann would build a kennel behind his home, where the animal would be available whenever its services were needed. Unfamiliar with the breed, he decided to take a look at the bloodhounds.

Out where the dogs were kept, the trooper stopped by to check them out. Coming up to Tina, who barked and growled at him from her run, Rebmann soon concluded that her forte was not public relations. But he wasn't looking for a pet; he needed a good tracking dog. Anyway, he figured the dog's disposition pretty much matched his own.

Now all Rebmann had to do was convince his superiors at the state police that his idea had merit.

In those days his boss was Bill Smith, a corporal who was also a K-9 trainer. Smith told Rebmann to put his idea on paper and send it up the command ladder. Rebmann did as he was instructed. Within a reasonable amount of time the approval worked its way back down that same bureaucratic ladder, and Rebmann was told to build a kennel behind his house. He was going to get a bloodhound.

Before the official transfer was made, Smith called Rebmann and told him to come on out to where the bloodhounds were kept on Saturday, the trooper's day off. His boss wanted Rebmann to see what it was like to handle the breed before the liaison was officially consummated.

Bright and early, Rebmann met Bill Smith and his twelve-year-old son, Mark, by the state police kennel at Bethany. While Rebmann became acquainted with Tina, the young man was told by his dad to run off a short distance into the nearby woods and hide.

Fifteen minutes after Mark disappeared, Rebmann gave Tina an article of the young man's clothing and ordered her to find him. The eighty-five-pound dog, who was attached to Rebmann's arm by a twelve-foot lead, took off. The trooper was pulled along by the strong animal, and within a few feet of entering the woods, they raced over to the far side of a tree to where Smith's boy was hiding.

Rebmann had never seen a dog track like that in his life. From that moment on he was hooked on bloodhounds.

Bill Smith then told Rebmann they'd run another trail. But the next one would be longer. They'd let it age a while before letting the dog at it. Smith's son ran off and, when he returned to where the two men waited, the three went off to lunch.

After the hour-and-a-half meal the trio arrived back at the kennel. Smith told Rebmann to get Tina and go for it.

Rebmann took the bloodhound from her kennel, commanded the dog to sit, then buckled her leather harness in place. He snapped his twelve-foot lead to the D ring on the harness and showed her the scent article—a shirt—that he had tossed on the ground. With the command, "Find them!" the dog shot off. Rebmann just hung on as best he could and followed behind his new companion.

The weather was warm, so Rebmann was dressed in jeans and T-shirt. He also wore a pair of expensive new sunglasses and was about to learn an expensive lesson on how bloodhounds work.

The track was at first an uneventful hike—a fast hike but still uneventful—through the woods. Then came the swamp. By the indentations the boy's footprints made in the surface, it was clear to Rebmann that Mark had kept his feet dry by jumping from grass hummock to grass hummock. The trooper had no such luck. The water depth immediately reached to his ankles, then soon progressed to his knees. Tina, it turned out, cared not one bit for her handler's comfort. She forged on, full tilt, while Rebmann held on to the lead for dear life. It was somewhere in the first swamp where the trooper figures a whipping tree branch knocked his fashionable sunglasses from his face and into the opaque water, never to be seen again.

Tina kept right on going.

Soon they were out of the swamp and back on dry land. Rebmann pressed on, his feet making squishing sounds as he trudged after his dog. Tina cut back and forth, over and across a paved road, all the while faithfully following the trail made by Mark Smith. Before long she and Rebmann were again in a swamp. Luckily for the trooper this one was only a few inches deep with water.

Finally, Tina's efforts at following the trail had her weave her way over to a tree where Mark was sitting, laughing in delight at Rebmann's plight.

There stood Rebmann—breathing hard, no sunglasses, wet, miserable, and scratched up. Bill Smith walked up to the trooper and asked, "You want to be a bloodhound handler?"

Rebmann's reply was a concise, "Yup!"

That was the beginning of a beautiful friendship.

Rebmann remembers that what really amazed him most about those first two practice tracks he had had with Tina was that this dog, although handicapped with some idiot (Rebmann's word) on the end of her line, someone she had never seen before that morning, a person with no clue what he was doing, had succeeded in tracking another individual through difficult tough terrain.

That day Tina went home with Rebmann.

The two began to train. Or rather, Rebmann trained, Tina kept him company. Soon the trooper developed an affection and respect for bloodhounds that he has to this day. He finds them remarkable animals. They drool a lot, their oily coat has a unique odor, not enhanced by wading through swamps, and they aren't all that obedient. But can they track.

It took time for Rebmann to learn how to work properly with Tina and the other bloodhounds that came to him. Then there were those characteristics of the breed that Rebmann only found out about while operating in the field.

During one search, he and Tina were out in the woods looking for a missing hunter, an older man who had a history of heart problems. The dog started pulling strong right from where the man's truck had been parked. About a mile into the woods, to Rebmann's surprise, Tina suddenly broke off the track, refusing to go forward.

Confused by his dog's actions, the trooper had the good sense to suggest to the other searchers that they look around the area. Less than a hundred fifty feet away, up a nearby slope, lay the body of the deceased man. He had died of a heart attack the previous day.

That was when Rebmann began to learn that bloodhounds don't like to go near dead human beings.

The intensity with which Tina tracked never ceased to fascinate Rebmann. During one search, a ten-year-old had run from his home after his older sister chided him for eating his dad's doughnuts. The sweet-toothed boy had disappeared and police were called in to help find him. Rebmann started Tina from the back door of the boy's house.

With her nose to the ground Tina moved off, going around to the rear of the structure. Never looking up, she then traveled in a straight line until, *thunk,* her head smacked into the side of a police car that had been parked there sometime after the boy had gone off in that very direction. In concentrating on following her quarry's scent she had never even noticed the cruiser.

The dog soon found the young man where he had hid, in the crawl space of a nearby outbuilding, fast asleep.

Back in the early seventies Rebmann recalls that not much thought had been given to tracking dogs and their ability to find people and objects underwater. It took a few tragic finds before Rebmann saw the light himself.

One of the first cases where he observed the phenomenon was during the search for a ten-year-old boy that took place out in Montville. The warm summer evening had started out to be a fun family time. The older brother of the soon-to-be-missing boy was involved in a league baseball game. So, while the family sat and watched one child play ball, their younger son walked off to explore the nearby woods and pond within the park grounds.

Around seven-thirty in the evening the parents noticed they hadn't seen their younger boy for awhile. No amount of calling turned him up. Soon a large search operation was initiated. At eight-thirty Rebmann received a call over at the Montville Barracks. He and one of his bloodhounds (he now had another dog, Clem, who was a new member of his team) were needed at the search site. Taking both K-9s he rushed to the scene.

By the time the trooper and his bloodhounds arrived, a hundred volunteers had already started to comb the surrounding area. It was now dark. Rebmann asked for and received an article of the boy's clothing. Starting with Tina, the more experienced tracking bloodhound at that time, the K-9 team soon found the trail. The big dog took Rebmann down an incline, through some thick brush, and to a small nearby water hole, named Gair's Pond. The bloodhound moved back and forth along the bank, refusing to take the trooper further.

Rebmann tried to figure out what his dog was telling him. Could it be that the boy had been down there, looking for frogs, then had moved on to some other location? The thought that his bloodhound might have taken him to the end of the track wasn't something the trooper wished to think about. After all, nobody likes to find a dead kid.

Rebmann brought Tina back up to the area where the baseball diamonds were laid out and tried to get her interested in other areas. He circled the park, walked along some railroad tracks, then went by a nearby riverbank. Nothing.

Rebmann and his K-9s went home.

Early the next morning the trooper received a wake-up call at home. They'd like him to try again. At six-thirty he and his dogs were back at the ball fields.

This time Rebmann decided he'd try Clem.

Clem had been owned originally by people who showed bloodhounds. Rebmann's first wife had seen the future K-9 at a dog show and, when she asked about the dog, was told he was scheduled to be put down. It seems his conformation wasn't satisfactory. That meant that he didn't fit the aficionados' artificial pattern determined to be ideal for the breed—at least ideal as defined by that group of people who worry about such things.

The dog had "funny looking" back legs—they weren't straight enough for him to be shown—his ears were too short, and on top of that he was sort of cranky. Thus Clem did not qualify as a show dog. Being of no further use to his owners, his life was to be ended.

Rebmann's wife spoke to her husband and suggested he might want to take a look at this bloodhound.

Clem was eventually given to the Rebmanns and became a K-9. Five of Clem's criminal cases would eventually go to the Connecticut Supreme Court, justifying the arrest and conviction of serious violent felons. Three were upheld while the court turned down the remaining two for review.

He found numerous missing people, saving many of their lives, located evidence in criminal cases, and Rebmann believes that during his twelve years of life he made a significant contribution to law enforcement and society.

Clem ultimately received the Cleopatra Big-T Award from the National Police Bloodhound Association, as the Outstanding Man-Trailer in the Field of Law Enforcement. Not bad for a nonstandard bloodhound.

Using the same scent material employed the night before, Clem was soon on the trail, and once more Rebmann found himself on the bank of Gair's Pond. Except this time, after sniffing around the rim of the pond, his bloodhound waded chest deep into the water.

And Rebmann knew that Clem didn't like water.

The trooper took the dog back up to the play field. Still denying what he knew in his heart to be true, Rebmann explained to those in charge of the search that both his dogs had taken him down to the pond and had worked the edge of the water. He offered no further guidance.

Divers went in. Water visibility was near zero. Connecticut Paperboard, the owners of the pond, gave permission to lower its water level.

Later that afternoon they found the boy's body.

Rebmann began to see the light. He started to realize that if a dog was consistent in its work and went to a body of water in search of a person, there was good likelihood that's where the missing party would be found.

Rebmann was learning how to read his dog.

Still, Rebmann didn't give that much thought to the ability.

Less than a year later the trooper would have an opportunity to put his newly acquired knowledge to use.

A woman had been reported missing over in Pomfret, Connecticut. The fifty-four-year-old, who was described as despondent by her husband to the searchers, lived on an estate. It was near midnight by the time Rebmann and his bloodhound teammates arrived at the large property. Clem was started at the door where the missing person had left for her afternoon walk. First, one of the woman's nightgowns was offered to the K-9. Clem sniffed the article of clothing and headed off.

Rebmann found that his dog was taking them along a well-used trail that had been earlier described as the path usually taken by the woman. About a thousand feet behind the house the quickly moving dog veered off, took Rebmann over a bridge above a brook, into the woods, then alongside the stream that ran under it.

Clem stopped and hurriedly moved back and forth looking for the scent. When he found the odor he headed right for the side of the stream, dragging Rebmann into the cold water, then went no further.

Rebmann decided to try starting Clem one more time back at the house. The results were identical; they wound up along the banks of the stream. The trooper then tied his dog to a tree, took his flashlight, and played it along the water's surface. Under an overhang by the bank, the beam of his light revealed the woman's body. It turned out she had drowned after taking an overdose of pills.

Rebmann was getting the idea.

The clincher for Rebmann, as far as using dogs for locating scent under water, took place in Greenwich, Connecticut.

A seventy-year-old gentleman had a habit of visiting a local pub each evening. One night he was dropped off by a few of his long-time drinking buddies at the front entrance to his seven-acre property. He was last seen heading up the driveway in the direction of his large home.

In the morning, when his son realized his father wasn't in the house, the Greenwich police were notified. Soon Rebmann was called out.

By now Tina had been retired. The team of K-9s Rebmann used included Clem, for man tracking, and Rufus, a shepherd, for both tracking and body-recovery work. He was, in fact, the first cadaver-sniffing dog the Connecticut State Police ever had.

On the way over, Rebmann picked up a police lieutenant, a student of his from a local police department. The trooper figured it would be good experience for the man.

After speaking with the son and getting a shoe that belonged to the missing man, Rebmann returned to his unmarked station wagon, took Clem out, and brought the K-9 to the entrance of the large property. After letting the animal scent on the shoe, the trooper followed Clem as the dog headed down the driveway. Just before coming to the big home the dog turned left, went down a hill, and took Rebmann to a two-acre pond.

There was an old and decrepit dock jutting out onto the water. Clem took Rebmann to the dock's end, dipping his nose into the water. Rebmann was, and is, not a man who quickly jumps to conclusions. But on the other hand he doesn't have to be hit on the head all that many times before he figures out that that hurts.

The words, "Oh boy, here we go," popped into his head. Then he spotted a small object floating on the pond. Carefully walking along the dock's support beams—the boards were quite rotten—he recovered the item. It was a wallet that belonged to the missing gentleman. Rebmann figured that was what was called a clue.

Rebmann took Clem back to the station wagon and spoke with his lieutenant K-9 handler student. The trooper told the other man that there was little doubt the missing person was in the pond. But to check further, Rebmann would take out Rufus, the cadaver-search dog, and have him work the surrounding grounds. Just to be sure.

Like his brother K-9, Rufus took Rebmann right to the pond. This time the dog jumped directly into the water and swam in circles ten feet off the end of the dock.

After Rebmann saw that, he figured it was time to call in the divers.

The local dive team arrived, suited up, and went to the water's edge. Rebmann, who didn't get paid by piece work, decided that since it was still early he and his student would watch the body being recovered.

The four divers jumped into the water, and it seemed to the trooper that they were heading in all different directions. Politely inquiring to the man in charge of the search what was going on, he was told that the divers' leader liked them to free search, that is, not use a line in the water to guide them along.

Rebmann, knowing when to keep his mouth shut, shrugged his shoulders and sat back down to watch.

Suddenly a diver popped to the surface, calling out, "We got something!" They had found a car, a mid-fifties Ford. The son explained that well over twenty years earlier, after a night of pub hopping with the boys, his father, the same man who was now missing, had parked his new car by his house and, in the morning, discovered it had been "stolen."

Well, at least one mystery was solved, Rebmann mused.

The divers continued to swim around the two-acre pond. After a few hours they emerged and announced that there was no body in the water.

Rebmann got up, stepped over to the man in charge, and said, "It's Tuesday. Based on my experience with drowning victims this time of the year (it was June) and with the water's temperature, I'd say this guy ought to pop up to the surface around noon on Friday."

With that Rebmann said his good-byes, packed up, and left the property.

Three in the afternoon on Friday, Rebmann's telephone rang. It was his K-9 handler student from that Tuesday's body search. He was all excited. The lieutenant told Rebmann that he had waited until one o'clock but couldn't resist any longer. He had sent one of his patrol officers to check the pond. Floating right off the dock, exactly where Rebmann's dog had circled, was the missing man.

Water search has now become an integral part of Rebmann's training program. With his observations and experience he routinely trains his students—human and canine—on the technique. During the last few years this has resulted in finding hundreds of bodies across the nation that in years past would have gone undetected.

An Innocent Victim

People often get the trouble they ask for. Then again, sometimes they are just the wholly innocent victim of a sick human mind. Rebmann has seen both situations, and this next case was one of the latter kind.

Elaine Noble had been married just over a week. She and her husband, St. John Noble, had just returned from their honeymoon on Cape Cod. They had enjoyed themselves on the water so much that the pair had been unable to resist a bargain and came home with a small sailboat. Their plan was to return to the cape many times during their life together.

Once back in Connecticut they began married life in the nice quiet town of Norwalk. The newlyweds took up residence in a house that they shared with another couple, to save on living costs. It was an older, well-maintained home at Shore Front Park, a neighborhood near Long Island Sound. The place was especially convenient to Elaine, who worked as a medical technician at the Norwalk Group, situated little more than five miles from the house. It was so near, that her habit was to take her lunch at home. One day Elaine had to leave work a bit later than normal for lunch. When over an hour had passed and she hadn't gotten back, her co-workers took notice. Telephone calls were made to her home but there was no answer. Now a bit concerned, a couple of her fellow employees decided to drive over to her house to make sure Elaine was all right.

As they pulled up to the front of the Noble home they noted that Elaine's car was parked out front. Hurrying from their auto they walked up to the front door and knocked. There was no answer and one of her friends grabbed hold of the doorknob, turned, and pushed. The unlocked door swung open. Still unsure of themselves they called out the woman's name and, when no response was forthcoming, stepped inside. At first glance things seemed to be in order. There was an open can of soup sitting on the kitchen counter and in the otherwise neatly ordered kitchen a number of cabinet doors were open. In the living room the television set was on, and a look in the hall closet showed that the woman's raincoat—it was a windy, rainy day—was hung in place and still damp. At the rear of the house they saw that a sliding glass back door was unlocked. As they looked around the home one of Elaine's co-workers noticed that her purse wasn't there.

The real problem, they all agreed, was that Elaine Noble was nowhere to be found.

Her friends telephoned the police.

It wasn't until two days after the woman disappeared, at nine-thirty in the morning, that Rebmann was contacted. A member of the Norwalk Police Department, Inspector Moriarty, called and asked if the trooper could help in their search.

The trooper chose two dogs to come with him on the case: Rufus, his shepherd, and Clem, the eighty-five-pound black and tan veteran of the Rebmann team. The bloodhound was already ten years old when put into service on the Noble case. He had been retired and returned to duty a number of times. According to Rebmann, Clem just hated retirement.

Rebmann decided he'd use both Clem and Rufus on the investigation because their skills complemented one another. Clem was extraordinarily good at finding live people, Rufus at locating cadavers. Like most of Rebmann's male K-9s, the two dogs were friendly rivals. Upon their arrival at a scene, each would want to be the first one let out for the search. They'd get so excited when they knew work was about to be done that each would howl and bay in an attempt to attract Rebmann's attention. Rebmann remembers one time when their noisy tactic failed, at least from the dogs' perspective. The trooper had just pulled up to the home of a missing teenager. It was nighttime and the youngster, who had had a fight with her mother, had run away some hours earlier. When Rebmann opened the rear of his station wagon the two competing dogs, that time it was Clem and his brother Joshua, began to bark and howl. From out of the nearby woods cried a voice, "Don't turn the dogs loose! I'm coming in!"

Case solved. Rebmann wished they'd all be that easy.

Clem and Rufus were loaded aboard Rebmann's old Connecticut State Police blue Ford station wagon, and the trio headed out to the missing woman's home. But first the trooper stopped at the Norwalk police station, where he met Gary Mecozzi, lead investigator on the case, who briefed Rebmann on the circumstances surrounding the investigation.

Just before noon Rebmann, now accompanied by Mecozzi, arrived at the Noble home. The trooper secured an article of the missing woman's undergarments for purposes of scent discrimination. The piece of woman's clothing could only have belonged to the missing person, and Clem would need that specific scent in order to begin looking for Elaine Noble.

In Rebmann's experience there is no better K-9 than a bloodhound for scent-discrimination work. That's not to say that other breeds haven't made remarkable finds. They certainly have. It's just that Rebmann feels if all else is otherwise equal, if you want to find a specific human being, a bloodhound is the way to do it. He's done some things with bloodhounds that a person would think simply couldn't be done with a dog. Clem and other bloodhounds Rebmann has used have routinely located lost individuals two and three days after the trail had been made by the missing person.

Once Clem found a man by following a trail, one fully out in the open and exposed to the elements, that was over eight days old and half a mile long. A truly remarkable feat.

The reason Rebmann took along different animals was because his bloodhounds did not like to search out dead bodies. For reasons that Rebmann can't fully explain, he had observed members of that K-9 breed become upset and actually appear frightened when in the presence of a dead human being. Thus it was important for the trooper to have a cadaver-search dog on hand when he was out in the field.

The trooper started at the rear of the residence, by the sliding glass door that had been found unlocked. First he showed Clem the scent material, then gave the command, "Find him!"

The K-9 worked his way to the driveway, turned around, and sat down. The bloodhound had gone only fifteen feet from the house, and his actions informed Rebmann where the trail ended. The trooper decided to try the dog in the backyard. The dog found no trail. Then Clem was taken to the front of the Noble home, to Elaine's car. The dog started at the driver's door and worked his way to the house.

By his K-9's actions, Rebmann now had a good idea where the victim had been. She'd clearly gotten out of her car and gone into her home, then sometime later left her home via the sliding glass door, entered a car in the driveway, and left.

Rebmann explained his findings to Mecozzi, the Norwalk detective. He kept to himself the thought that in the next stage of this investigation he'd probably need to bring only a cadaver-search dog with him.

Rufus was taken out, and although Rebmann was fairly certain his dog wouldn't find anything in the area, he did a thorough search of the Noble property as well as the surrounding area. As anticipated, Rufus discovered nothing.

Mecozzi informed Rebmann that in the preceding four years four woman had disappeared from the town of Norwalk. A number of the victims had been found in remote areas off exits of a local roadway, the Merritt Parkway. He asked that Rebmann take his dogs to that area and check it out.

Rebmann and Mecozzi drove to where one of the bodies had been uncovered. Rufus was let out and told to "Look for it!" The K-9 headed out to a nearby swamp and promptly located a marijuana plot which contained numerous six- to eight-foot-high plants. The remainder of the area, as well as that of other parkway exits, was searched, but except for the anonymous entrepreneur's agrarian endeavors, nothing more of interest was discovered.

It wasn't until late afternoon that Rebmann's job was done. He was debriefed and returned to the state police barracks.

Norwalk investigators continued working on the case. No one who lived with or near Elaine and her husband were suspects in the crime, nor did the missing woman have any enemies. The Norwalk police, with virtually nothing in the way of leads to work on, decided to make up a list of every person who was known to have ever been at the Noble home.

The couple sharing the home with the Nobles had once placed an ad in the newspaper in an attempt to sell some household item. One of the people who had responded was a man who came from Redding, Connecticut, Christopher Lang. A routine computer check—done for everyone on the list—was run on the man's name. Lang was out on parole for a sexual assault.

A couple of Norwalk investigators thought it might be a good idea to take a ride to Redding and see what this twenty-one-year-old might have to say regarding the missing woman. They knocked on the door to the Lang residence and young Mr. Lang answered. When the officers informed him why they were there he responded, "Talk to my attorney," and shut the door in their faces.

The Norwalk police now had a suspect.

Shortly after the abortive interview with Lang, Rebmann received a call from Mecozzi. How would Rebmann feel about meeting the investigators at the Norwalk police department to help them check out the large wooded area— it was three hundred sixty-five acres in size—behind the Lang house? And by the way, don't forget to bring the dogs.

Rebmann wouldn't forget.

The next day Rebmann met Detective Sergeant Jon Dyer, along with investigators Mark Palmer, and, of course, Gary Mecozzi. Rufus stayed in the back of the station wagon while Rebmann received his briefing. Rebmann hadn't bothered to bring Clem along for this job. The trooper knew all he'd be needing that day was a cadaver-search dog.

The team of investigators and the K-9 officer, driving in their separate cars, headed out to the resident Connecticut State Police trooper's office in Redding. Already waiting there, beside the local trooper, was a representative from the Bridgeport Hydraulics Company, the company that owned the wooded acreage behind the Lang home. Just to be on the safe side the investigators wanted their permission to conduct the search, which was promptly granted.

The three Norwalk investigators and Rebmann drove over to George Hull Hill Road, which abutted the wooded land. From that macadam road they took a short dirt access road that led them to within the property's boundary.

It was just before noon. Rebmann unlatched the rear of his station wagon and let Rufus out. Leaving two of the investigators by the police cars, Rebmann, Mecozzi, and Rufus started off on the search. Rebmann first directed Rufus in the direction of the Lang home, whose property line ran up against the hydraulics company's wooded land. In effect, they would be checking out the area directly behind the Lang home without setting foot on Lang's property.

Fifteen minutes into the search—Rebmann had hardly had the time to figure out how to best conduct their mission—the trooper saw Rufus' head shoot up from ground level, to permit the animal to catch the wind squarely in his face. For an instant the K-9 was rigid with interest, then he bolted away from the two law officers and headed for a large swamp area that was nearby. In a moment he was gone from sight.

A few minutes later the K-9 reappeared from the thick brush, ran up to Rebmann, and aggressively grabbed at the pocket where the reward tennis ball was hidden, then ran off in the same direction he'd just come from. To Rebmann this meant only one thing: Rufus had found something significant.

The trooper and Mecozzi trotted after the K-9, in a vain attempt to keep up. The dog once more disappeared into the thick undergrowth of brush and high grass. The two men fought their way to within sight of Rufus and saw that he was nosing at a green, military-style canvas sack. Rebmann, literally crawling through the nearly impenetrable brush, inched his way closer. It was then that he noticed something odd sticking out of the sack. It was a human foot.

Rebmann called Rufus back, and once they were clear of the vegetation, tossed about the old tennis ball that had been in his pocket and frolicked with his dog in reward for the find. Meanwhile Mecozzi somberly notified his two fellow officers that they now had a crime scene to safeguard.

Fellini would have appreciated the strange scene.

When the State Police Major Crime Squad arrived, Rebmann was relieved from crime-scene guard duty. He and Rufus returned to the barracks, Rebmann to complete his paperwork and Rufus to take a nap. They'd done their job.

The police activity taking place on the property behind his home hadn't gone unnoticed by Christopher Lang. A number of Connecticut State Police cars had zoomed by his street, some with their roof lights flashing. And they all seemed to be headed to one place. Christopher Lang knew all too well where that place was.

Later in the evening the state police received a telephone call from the father of Christopher Lang. He told the police that his son, who had been agitated since he'd seen the police vehicles, had run out of the house. The father was concerned.

A brief search was done in the dark for the young man. The troopers were unable to locate Lang, and it was decided to wait until the first light of morning to resume looking.

Trooper Dave Barger, a K-9 handler and one of Rebmann's partners, was called in to assist. Rebmann would normally have been assigned the chore, but he already was on another assignment.

It didn't take long for Barger and his K-9, Max, to find Lang's body. A suicide note was discovered nearby.

Rebmann figures that the killer had thought that the body was safely hidden where it lay. He was right, except that Lang hadn't counted on Rufus to ferret out his crime. In truth, the victim's body wouldn't have been found had it not been for a sharp-nosed K-9 who loved playing with an old tennis ball.

As for the Elaine Noble murder investigation, it was officially closed. She would have been twenty-eight years old on her next birthday.

A year or so after Elaine's death, her husband, who had

never gotten over his wife's murder, went out sailing. He was lost at sea, his body never found.

Even after Lang's suicide, Rebmann figured you had to add on one more death to the killer's score card.

Murder Will Out

Adults, when they face economic, social, or personal problems are not averse to just taking off. Many so-called missing individuals fall into this category. Often the over-worked missing-persons bureau detectives hesitate to investigate cases in which the party reported as gone is a person who has attained their majority and suffers no extenuating disabilities. In effect, it is not a crime to move and leave no forwarding address.

Then there are the other cases. Here the adult leaves a good job, friends, and perhaps some money in the bank. Especially vexing is the failure to report the person missing by that individual's spouse, and when the missing person's car is found abandoned in a shopping-center parking lot, detectives take notice.

One day Rebmann received a request from the State's Attorney's Office that he and one of his K-9s conduct a body search. It was explained to the trooper that a twenty-eight-year-old married woman, Robin Opel, had been missing for over a month. Her car had recently been discovered parked in a shopping center in Milford, Connecticut, twenty miles from her home. Among the facts that troubled the investigators and their district attorneys was the small matter that her husband, Kent, had not reported his wife gone. Rather, it had been her co-workers at the restaurant where she worked who had notified the police of her sudden disappearance.

To further complicate the issue, she had a boyfriend and so did her husband.

When the police processed the woman's auto for evidence, they came upon a broken-off piece from a plastic owl that had been part of the woman's key ring. This minor bit

83

of apparently insignificant material would prove important later on in the investigation.

Initially the detectives thought they might be dealing with a suicide. Then, after speaking with a number of the woman's friends, they decided that perhaps they should focus on looking for her body in the area where the car had been found, around Milford.

However, shortly before Rebmann left for the parking lot he was notified there had been a change of plans. The trooper was told to head to Monroe, to the Opel residence. An investigator informed Rebmann that a neighbor of the Opels' had told detectives he had heard a cement mixer operating by that home about the time Robin had disappeared. The investigator had information that this coincided with the woman's husband and male friend working on a new patio by the Opel swimming pool.

Kent Opel had given police permission to search his home and grounds. The investigator told Rebmann that he wanted the premises gone over before the man changed his mind.

Rebmann put Rufus in his state police station wagon and the pair headed out to do the search.

The first place Rebmann went to was the local police station. There he was briefed by the investigators on what was known so far in the case. With that done, everyone involved left for the woman's residence.

Pulling up to the Opels' place, the trooper saw that it was located in a quiet middle-class neighborhood. The home was a handsome, raised ranch-style house with a neatly mowed lawn. In the rear of the residence, which was situated on a corner lot, was a swimming pool. The pool was enclosed by a fenced-off area as required by state ordinance for the protection of children. Next to the pool, near its gated entrance and inside a high wood fence, sat a small cabana pool house. The recently built covered patio was set **just** off the cabana and it too was inside the wooden **enc**losure.

Watching Rebmann and Rufus getting ready to conduct the search was a detective from the local department, an investigator from the State's Attorney's Office, and the owner of the property.

The two investigators walked over to Kent Opel and explained that the property would be gone over by a dog. Whether or not such a possibility had even occurred to the man when he had given his consent to the police for them to look around his property is an open question. In any case, with Rebmann and Rufus on the scene, it was too late now.

The trooper started his dog on the well-groomed lawn. As Rufus began his work Rebmann reflected that it might seem strange to people to start off this way. He had his reasons. It was his search technique not to lead the dog to any specific area or transmit any information to the K-9 that the human investigators held regarding where they believed evidence might be found. In Rebmann's experience a false alert was sure to follow once a dog was led down a pathway lined by preconceived notions. In the real world, whatever was being sought was either there or it wasn't. It was Rebmann's opinion that a wise handler will permit his dog to show him the way.

It took some time for Rufus to explore the front, side, and rear of the lawn. Rebmann didn't hurry the animal. He then let the K-9 investigate the back of the home, over to a pile of loam near a small wooded area that stood between that house and its neighbor's. The trooper then slowly permitted the dog to search the far side of the swimming pool. At that point Rufus came up to the wood stockade fence that encompassed the pool and cabana.

Rebmann watched as the K-9 walked along the fence, then lowered his head and stuck his nose into the earth next to the fence, just off the newly laid concrete patio. Rufus's body language was already telling the trooper something when the K-9 began to dig into the soft ground. Rebmann made no sign or outward indication he was remotely interested in what his canine partner was doing. He simply called out to Rufus, "Good boy. Keep looking for it."

The K-9 followed the fence over to where it butted up against the pool house. Rufus's nose went first to the bottom corner of the fence and cabana, then he quickly worked his head up the crack, eventually standing up on his hind legs. Rebmann didn't miss Rufus's excited tail wagging nor his generally animated state.

Rebmann opened the chain-link gate leading to the pool, and he and his K-9 entered the enclosed space. Still following the fence, Rufus tracked his way to the pool house and entered the wood structure. Once inside he began to scratch at its wood floor; to Rebmann's experienced eye the dog's body showed significant interest.

Rebmann encouraged Rufus with a soft continuous verbal patter, "What do you got? Come on, find it. Get to work. Let's look for it." It wasn't the meaning of the words that was important, but rather their tone and sound.

Rufus left the building and worked the concrete patio. Moving over to one edge of the slab, he put his nose down and began to dig into the dirt. To Rebmann that meant only one thing: Rufus was showing him his final alert.

The trooper remained silent, outwardly appearing almost uninterested in his dog's actions. Rebmann methodically completed working the pool area, then took his K-9 out and placed him back in the station wagon.

Walking over to the investigator, Rebmann said, "Okay, I'm all done. I'll see you back at the police station." His tone of voice was neutral, almost to the point of sounding bored.

Rebmann overheard Kent Opel comment, "Well, the dog didn't show you anything."

Rebmann didn't respond. As far as he was concerned no further discussion was necessary.

Once the law officers returned to the police station, they immediately began working on the paperwork required for a search warrant.

The next afternoon, now armed with their warrant, the officers, along with a member of the medical examiner's office and K-9 Rufus, returned to the suspect's house. Opel wasn't home, so the warrant was attached to the garage door. After placing canvas around the patio area to keep their work from prying eyes, the officers took their rented jackhammer (none of the public safety agencies they had asked had one to loan them) and went to work.

It didn't take much time for the jackhammer to break up a three-by-four-foot section of the slab. Removing the four-inch-thick chunks of concrete and setting them off to the side, the men took turns at digging into the earth underneath. The officers noted that the soil was loose, a good sign from an investigator's standpoint.

At a little more than a foot below the surface they uncovered an electrical wire. A sense of foreboding came over the team. The words "Oh shit" were muttered by a few. Could it be that the dog had detected the odor of freshly turned-over dirt and had alerted to that?

Rebmann had more confidence in his K-9 than that. Telling everyone to hold on a moment, he left the site and walked over to his car. Letting Rufus out, he returned with his K-9. No sooner did the trooper let his dog loose than Rufus dived at the freshly uncovered earth and started to excavate. This was no minor alert but rather a full-blown declaration by the dog that this was the spot.

Rufus was tied off and the digging commenced once more. Soon they found a broken piece of plastic. It was part of a little owl, and it matched the piece found sometime earlier in the missing woman's car.

They dug some more.

A few more feet and a hammer was uncovered. A cursory examination by the investigators showed them there was matted red material and hair on the blunt end. The stuff sure looked like dried blood to Rebmann.

At about four feet from the surface they hit lime, then six or eight inches beyond that point they found the body of Robin Opel.

Rebmann still wondered why Rufus had scratched at the wood floor of the cabana if the body was buried under the patio. He soon found out the answer. The day of her murder the victim's husband and his friend had been waiting for her to return home from work. When Robin entered the house, they had killed her using the hammer. Placing the badly broken and bleeding body in a wheelbarrow, the pair had taken it out to the cabana. While there, blood had dripped from the woman and fallen on the floor. The two murderers had been careful to clean it up once they had buried the body, but the sensitive nose of Rufus had still detected the odor.

Both men were found guilty, Kent of murder and his friend of hindering prosecution. Both were sent to jail. With all that effort, the burial and covering the corpse with lime and thick concrete, the two had been unable to hide their crime, and Rebmann was pleased that he and Rufus had done their part to send them away.

Sixteen Years under the Earth

Cadaver-sniffing dogs are talented K-9s. To human watchers it appears that the animals can perform miracles. Finding bodies buried under many feet of earth or submerged in deep ocean waters is beyond our ability to sense, so we see the dogs' actions as somehow incredible.

And then they do something even more extraordinary.

No one is quite sure how old human remains can be and still be located by a body-search K-9. Variables include the type of material surrounding the body, the chemicals that have come into contact with the corpse, and the temperatures the body has been subjected to.

In one of Rebmann's cases he was contacted by the Monmouth County prosecutor's office in New Jersey. The trooper was told a somewhat unusual story.

In the seashore town of Atlantic Highlands there was an abandoned town road, Lower Bayside Drive, situated close by and parallel to the beach. Over the years the area had been permitted to deteriorate and indeed had turned into a refuse heap. A group of citizens had gotten together in an attempt to clean the place up.

During the cleanup one of the people found a lifelike plastic replica of a human skull. For whatever reason, the person took the ivory-colored piece home. After a few weeks of occasionally looking at the skull, the finder had begun to develop a funny feeling about the object. Feeling a bit silly, he nonetheless took it over to the local police station. The sergeant on duty was also impressed with the realistic detail in the man's discovery. The thing was, he pointed out to the citizen who had come in, the skull wasn't plastic.

The medical examiner agreed with the sergeant's opinion. The skull was indeed real. Now the problem was, where was the rest of the body?

A team of investigators from both the prosecutor's office and the local police department went back to where the body part was first found. They searched carefully for a week and a half. Although the area of their exploration measured only two hundred yards by one hundred feet, they had no luck.

Somebody decided it was time to call in an expert with a good body-search K-9. So Rebmann, Josie, and Lady found themselves guests of the Monmouth County prosecutor.

Investigator Tommy Manzo of that office briefed Rebmann at the local police station, along with the chief of police and a group of local officers, on what was already known. They had a human skull, but they couldn't find any additional parts of the body and they would very much like to do just that.

Rebmann's response was simple. He said, "Let's go down to the site and see what the dogs do."

The drive to the crime scene was short and the officers got there around noon. It was a drab, cold, and drizzly day that greeted the law officers at the suspected body site. Perhaps it was uncomfortable, but somehow the weather fit the mood of their task.

Rebmann got out of his station wagon—he had parked his vehicle by a turnaround in the old road—and looked around him. He didn't care for what he saw. The officers who had described the scene as a junk pile hadn't done it justice. Tires lay half buried in sand, as did a few car engines. There were logs and household trash lying over and on top of other bits of debris. Worse, from his point of view, was the fact that there was also some swamp land involved, along with all the odors associated with rotting vegetation and dead animal matter. Rebmann decided it would be a tough area to cover.

He should have had more confidence in his dogs.

The road was at the base of a steep sand dune that ran parallel to the macadam surface. Another roadway ran along its top. It was evident to the trooper that much of the trash around him had been tossed down from above.

Rebmann took Josie, his lead dog at the time, from the car. He made sure that his K-9 saw him put the reward, an old tennis ball, into his jacket pocket. Josie would work her heart out just for a few seconds of playing with Rebmann and that threadbare dirty ball.

Josie always worked without lead or harness. Rebmann looked at the K-9 and gave her the search command, "Look for it."

Without hesitation Josie whirled and started on her quest. Rebmann directed the animal to begin at the base of the dune. He figured that the body might have been dumped from the top. By starting at the bottom of the cliff, he'd have his K-9 cover the entire area in a methodical fashion.

Josie walked up the bank, then down, then up again. She had hardly begun to look when Rebmann noted the dog's body language change. She became more animated, her tail wagged back and forth, and her movements became tense and more deliberate. Hardly more than a few minutes into the search the dog returned to Rebmann, hit the ball in his pocket with her nose, and then returned to the base of the dune and sat down only a few feet away from the trooper. Josie looked over at Rebmann, waiting to be thrown the ball. As far as the K-9 was concerned the exercise was over. To the trooper, what he was seeing was clearly an alert.

Rebmann was skeptical. It was never this easy. Refusing to accept what Josie was telling him, he decided to bring in Lady and have her come in from another angle to see what she had to say about it.

He knew that Josie didn't know how to lie. He threw her the ball and told her she was a good girl. While doing this he eyed the ground where she had alerted. He didn't see anything out of the ordinary.

A professional K-9 handler shoulders a formidable burden. Based on the handler's expertise and opinion of what the dog is telling him, it's the handler's responsibility to give the go-ahead for other law officers to begin to dig. Even a person with years in the business feels compelled to make sure the dog is saying what the handler thinks the dog is saying. And at that moment Rebmann just wasn't sure.

He brought Josie back to the vehicle. Over his shoulder he called out to the watching crowd of investigators that he wanted to "proof" his dog. In other words, Rebmann was seeking a second opinion.

At the truck he took Lady out.

Unlike Josie, Lady had been trained by Rebmann to self-reward. On reflection the trooper knew that had been a mistake. Although Lady was an excellent dog, by permitting her to reward herself for a find, Rebmann lost some control over her actions. Where Josie would do multiple re-finds of a scene, it was difficult to get Lady to do more than one because she was able to go and grab any large stick as her reward. She'd show him once, perhaps twice, what he was seeking. But when Rebmann didn't pick up on what the dog was trying to tell him, she'd become impatient with human ineptitude and run off to find her play stick. Josie, who depended on Rebmann giving her the ball, had to put up with her Homo sapiens' lack of olfactory sensitivity.

Therefore Lady had to be watched closely when on a search or, as the trooper had found out, he could easily miss her alert.

Taking her in from another angle, he gave her the command, "Look for it."

She headed for the same area as Josie had alerted, dropped her nose, looked back at Rebmann, and lowered her nose one more time. Rebmann figured that perhaps the dogs were alerting to body fluids that had drifted down over time from somewhere higher on the steep embankment. He started up the slope, directing Lady ahead of him.

The K-9 went about halfway up the bank, turned around, and returned to the same spot as before. Her nose hit the ground, she looked over at Rebmann and trotted off fifty feet away to tug on a great big piece of buried log.

Lady, clearly, had no doubt about what she had just told her handler.

Rebmann walked over to the spot and still couldn't see anything out of the ordinary besides a half-buried tire and a rusted engine block. The trooper wasn't sure what his dogs were trying to tell him. He headed back to his truck, put Lady away, and took Josie out one more time. This time he started her off several hundred feet away from the alert site.

Working the brush and the bank, they eventually came back to the hot spot. Again Josie became animated and lay down by the same place. Rebmann asked her, "What do you got?"

She rose, trotted over to her handler, and hit the ball, then returned to the site, sat down by the tires and rusty engine block, and drilled Rebmann with her eyes. The K-9 made her thoughts clear to her handler: she really wanted—deserved—that ball.

Rebmann glanced at his watch. The entire search had taken fifteen minutes. With some reservation, he escorted Josie back to the truck and called out to the investigators that the dogs were saying that was the place.

As Rebmann put the dog in the vehicle, one of the investigators bent down and started to move debris from the area. Pushing dirt, leaves, and loose material to the side, he uncovered a bone.

The entire operation was halted as a crime scene was declared and the medical examiner was summoned to the location.

Within a few hours methodical digging was resumed. Between six and twenty-four inches from the ground's cluttered surface the remains of a young woman were uncovered.

The medical examiner reported that it was his opinion that the body had been there for sixteen years. The remains were never identified and no one was ever charged with her murder.

Rebmann had done his job as a professional K-9 handler. He of course was pleased and proud that his K-9s were able to find the victim so quickly. It's just that he finds it troubling to know that, at least up till today, someone has gotten away with murder.

Missing Woman, Eleven Years Gone

For eleven years teacher Judith Leo-Correys hadn't been seen by anyone. At the time of her disappearance she was thirty-three years old. Judith and her male friend were in the process of building a house in Shelburne, Vermont.

She never got a chance to live in it.

Rebmann's office was contacted by the Vermont State Police. That agency didn't have any body-search dogs. They had an eleven-year-old murder investigation to conduct and needed the skills just such a K-9 provides. The Vermont troopers asked if the Connecticut State Police could help them out. Rebmann's boss gave the okay for them to borrow his trooper and dogs, then turned around and told Rebmann he should go, but not to incur any overtime. Which would be quite a trick, as the site Rebmann was to search was on the Canadian border, near Lake Chaplain.

State Police Detective Sergeant Leo Blais, from the Colchester Barracks, had caught the case. He explained to Rebmann that some people, back when the woman first disappeared eleven years earlier, thought they saw the auto that belonged to the male friend of Judith Leo-Correys over at Smugglers Notch, in Mansfield State Forest. Blais was sure they'd find the body there or at the place where the couple had planned to put up their new home.

For eleven years no one positively knew where the woman had gone. Well, perhaps one person did, assuming that she wasn't missing but was a murder victim. And her friend had left Vermont shortly after she'd been reported missing.

Without a body the state police had a problem. Never in the history of that state had there been a prosecution for homicide without a body.

For once the Vermont troopers caught a break. The boyfriend had been located in California, and based on information obtained from him, a warrant for his arrest was issued.

Now all they needed was the victim's remains.

So in June of 1990 Rebmann and Josie found themselves

out in the beautiful Vermont woods, trying to find a corpse that had been buried in that state's rich soil for eleven years. At the request of Blais, the K-9 first searched the former residence, then Smugglers Notch. Josie detected nothing.

And Rebmann knew the problem wasn't with the dog.

The trooper recalled the time he had been called out to help find a lost elderly gentleman who had wandered away from a nursing home. Another state police K-9 handler had already tried to find the man, but because of initial confusion about where the man might have gone, he had been unsuccessful.

The morning after the first attempt, Rebmann along with Josie and Susie (a bloodhound) went out on the case. After speaking with the local police, the trooper went to the nursing home. He pulled into the rear of the facility's parking lot, near a patch of woods. Rebmann had every intention of using the keen nose of Susie for the search but decided to let Josie out first so the dog could relieve herself. After all, there was no telling when Rebmann and the other K-9 would be finished.

Although it was only seven-thirty in the morning, a number of residents were sitting in chairs inside the main entrance while a few others walked about the grounds. It was on one of the chairs inside the home that the missing man had last been seen.

On Rebmann's command Josie hopped from the rear of the trooper's car. The K-9 wandered off into the woods while Rebmann considered where he'd start the bloodhound. With half an eye on Josie he decided they'd begin in the lobby and work their way out from there.

To Rebmann's surprise he noticed that Josie's head had perked up, clearly to better catch the scent in the air, and her nose began to twitch. Almost as an afterthought the trooper asked his K-9, "You got something?"

Josie responded by running off into the woods.

Rebmann was caught by surprise. A minute or so later Josie reappeared and hit the ball hidden in Rebmann's jacket pocket.

Rebmann softly commanded, "Show me."

Josie ran back into the woods, this time with Rebmann

just behind her. Fifty yards into the forest the trooper saw his partner stop on the top of a small gully, turn to look back at Rebmann to ensure that her handler was following, then go out of sight, down the other side of the embankment. Rebmann followed. When he came to the top of the gully he looked down. On that side of the small rise he saw an old abandoned building foundation. Next to it was Josie, standing beside the missing man, who was lying on the ground and talking to the dog while Josie nuzzled him.

Rebmann hurried down to the fallen gentleman and asked, "Are you okay?"

The only reply was the question, "Is it time for breakfast yet?"

"You kind of missed breakfast," Rebmann told him, "but I've got some people coming to help you out."

The man turned out no worse for his night spent in the woods, just a little cold. Searchers on foot had only a short time earlier walked right by him in the dark. The hunt for the missing gentleman, which had gone on for hours before Rebmann and Josie had arrived there, had taken the trooper and his K-9 little more than a minute!

No, Rebmann was sure that when Josie hadn't alerted at Smugglers Notch or by the missing woman's home, it was because there was nothing to be found at those places.

The pair returned to Connecticut.

The boyfriend was eventually brought back to Vermont from the West Coast. Blais interviewed the man and after some time elicited admissions of guilt. The man even told the trooper where he had buried the body of his former significant other, out near the tiny town of Lower Cabot. The problem the state police had was that even with the man's assistance they couldn't find the woman's remains.

The location they were searching was situated a quarter mile between Lower Cabot and Hardwood, Vermont, bounded by three old logging trails. There are no street signs in that hilly forest land, and the best the man was able to do was to estimate the spot where he had buried Judith.

Investigators dug and found nothing.

In November, Rebmann and Josie were asked to return to help the investigators locate the murder victim's corpse. By this time the law officers involved in the search were in the process of excavating a fairly significant piece of ground.

Josie was let out at the site, and she and Rebmann worked the area from several directions. The K-9 came up with a number of solid alerts, and the investigators began at once to concentrate in the place where the dog had shown an interest.

Blais wasn't so sure. He still felt strongly that the man was deliberately misleading the investigators and that the body was to be found either at Smugglers Notch or by their former home. At his insistence Rebmann agreed to try those two places one more time.

The next morning the two law officers and Josie returned to Smugglers Notch. Rebmann sent his K-9 out, but to the disappointment of Blais the dog showed no interest in the area.

Before going over to the house, the three returned to the excavation site. Again, this time with everyone pulled from the site, Josie was sent out by Rebmann. A few minutes after the dog moved back and forth over the ground, Josie alerted strongly once more, at a spot just off from her first place of interest.

As Rebmann watched, his experienced eyes picked up what the problem was. There was no doubt in his mind that the body was there. But it had been put in the ground over eleven years earlier. The decomposition process breaks the human carcass down into basic chemicals which, in their fluid state, wander from the scene because of groundwater and gravity. Josie was right on the money, except that the odor the K-9 was detecting had drifted from the precise location where the body lay.

Rebmann, after sharing his thoughts with the on-site investigators, had to return to Connecticut. The Vermont officers decided to trust both Rebmann's years of experience and Josie's keen sense of smell. They secured a backhoe and, using the K-9's alert spot as the focal point, dug up an area thirty feet in radius around that location.

The body was soon uncovered, three feet under the dark Vermont soil, wrapped in plastic bags.

Rebmann was relieved. Only another K-9 handler can

know the kind of pressure the trooper had been put under. It happens every time a handler is asked by other law officers, "You say there is a body here? Then how come we can't find it? If the dog says a body is here, and we find nothing, then where are we supposed to dig?"

The task of body-search K-9s and their human masters is never easy. Only sometimes it's more difficult than others.

Handlers know their dogs don't lie. It's difficult for the K-9 handler when their dogs indicate one thing but the physical evidence simply isn't there. Yet the animals aren't wrong. It's just hard to explain to a layman that sometimes looking for buried human remains, especially if those remains have been in the ground for half a generation or more, requires a certain amount of art.

Rebmann's Oldest Find

Because his skill had become well known in law-enforcement circles, and his superbly trained K-9s were in demand for working the tough cases, Rebmann frequently found himself on duty outside of his home state. Such a situation arose a few years ago when the Massachusetts city of New Bedford had a string of unsolved killings. Women, many from the seamier sections of the city, had begun to turn up dead. It stood to reason that if four or five dead bodies had been discovered, there might be more out there. So Rebmann, as well as K-9 handlers from the Massachusetts State Police, Maine, New Hampshire, and Connecticut, were enlisted by the local district attorney's office and his CPAC unit to assist in finding out what was out there.

In five days of searching, Rebmann and Josie located two more victims. With the onset of winter Rebmann and the other handlers were sent back to their agencies. With the coming of spring they returned. Rebmann and Josie found another body.

Rebmann was the lead K-9 handler in the investigation, and even as the serial killer was being pursued by investigators (a case never solved, by the way), another job was asked of the experienced trooper.

The district attorney's office had received an unusual letter, postmarked from Canada. It was written by a man who had lived with his family in Dartmouth over twenty years earlier. He wrote that he and his family were strongly religious. Their fundamentalist beliefs were such that they didn't send their children to school, nor did they trust in doctors. The letter went on to explain that twenty-one years earlier the man's wife had given birth to an infant. The baby had been stillborn. He wrote that he had taken his dead child out into the backyard and buried the body there. Now, after all those years, he wished to have the remains put to rest in a more dignified manner.

The man also enclosed a detailed map showing where the body lay.

The CPAC investigators assigned the case asked Rebmann to help them locate the baby's body. They offered the trooper a copy of the father's map, but Rebmann declined. He didn't want to influence his K-9, intentionally or otherwise, when they went out searching for the long-buried body.

It was still early spring. Rebmann remembers the weather was sunny but cool. He followed the CPAC investigators in his Chevy Suburban out to the home where the man claimed to have lived. Arriving at the Cape Cod–style wood-frame residence at about ten-thirty, Rebmann let Josie out of his vehicle to permit his dog to become accustomed to the layout of the place. The people who lived there had already been contacted and had given their permission for the investigators to search the grounds.

Seeing that Josie was comfortable with her surroundings, Rebmann gave his K-9 the search command, "Go look for it!"

Josie started working the backyard. Within a few minutes from when they'd begun, Rebmann saw that his K-9's body language had changed. When the dog had gone by a small shed she stopped and looked over to her handler. She then stepped away from the place but almost immediately returned. Josie then went over to Rebmann and asked for her ball.

Rebmann asked her, "Got anything?" The K-9 returned

to the spot, scratched at the ground, and then lay down in her alert. By that time Rebmann was standing next to his partner. Looking over to the CPAC investigators, the trooper informed them this was the place to dig. He then reached into his pocket, took out the old tennis ball, and started to play fetch with Josie. She'd done her job.

The CPAC members took out the map sent to them by the father. Rebmann let himself take a look at it. Josie had come almost to the spot that had been indicated by the man as the burial place.

The search had lasted little more than twenty minutes.

The next day Massachusetts State Police crime-scene technicians went to the home and dug up where Josie had alerted. They found swaddling clothes and enough chemical identifiers to indicate that indeed the place had been used to bury an infant. As the investigators expected, no bones were found, as a newborn had none that would survive underground for more than a few months before completely decomposing.

The man in Canada was contacted and told of the find. Although he was technically guilty of the misdemeanor of improperly disposing of a dead human being, nothing more was done about the matter.

When Rebmann had first gone out to try and locate the infant's remains, he had quietly wondered whether such a find was even possible for Josie to accomplish. He never mentioned it to the CPAC investigators, but even this highly experienced K-9 handler and master trainer had found it incredible that his K-9 had detected the remains of a baby's virtually disintegrated body after it had lain twenty-one years in the earth.

Murder on a Dare

Rebmann and Marcia Koenig had by this time settled out on the West Coast. That didn't stop the experienced K-9 handler and his wife from continuing his good work.

Young people can make mistakes. Most are reparable and heal over time, while some affect them and others for the remainder of their lives. Marcia Koenig and her K-9, Coyote—a sixty-three-pound, good-natured, tireless, high-drive, sable-colored German shepherd—recently had to deal with one of the latter situations.

Deputy Ron Ryalls, the Washington State King County Search and Rescue coordinator, called Koenig on a case. He told her he needed a K-9 to do a water search, quickly adding that it was for a homicide investigation.

Koenig, along with another K-9 handler, Dick Reininger, an energetic seventy-year-old search-and-rescue volunteer, who brought with him his five-year-old golden retriever, Trippe, met the deputy at the scene. Rebmann stayed home for this search to let other people pick up some field experience without the teacher getting in the way.

Ryalls explained to the handlers what had happened. Three days earlier two teenage couples, one of the boys being a Michael Schuerhoff, had taken a late evening drive to Blythe Park, by the Sammamish Slough, a local river. While there the four met five young men, one of whom was an acquaintance of one of the girls.

While Michael and the five boys went for a walk, the remaining three youngsters stayed back with their car. Sometime later the five boys returned, without Michael. When asked where the other boy was, the group's answers were vague. They replied that they last saw Michael standing atop an abandoned Northern Pacific railroad trestle. The old bridge stood thirty-five feet above the water and was a popular if somewhat dangerous attraction for local youth.

The two young women and their male friend weren't comfortable with the story. They went out in search of Michael but in the dark were unable to locate him. The three speculated that he could have walked over the trestle and for some reason hitched a ride from the highway located at the structure's other end. The three decided to go home.

It wasn't until the next day, when there was still no sign of Michael, that one of the trio called the police. A bloodhound was taken out to the park and trailed the path the young man had taken to the top of the trestle, where it ended. The deputy had also commented that the dog had shown some interest in the water as well.

Search-and-rescue explorers had been requested as well as K-9 units. So while Koenig and Reininger prepared to put their dogs to work, those young men and women also walked the banks of the river for signs of Michael.

Before she and Reininger got into the small boat they had been assigned, Koenig took Coyote down to the water's edge to a spot near the underside of the trestle. To her surprise her K-9 showed definite interest, a positive sign that their mission was likely to produce results. She decided to see what Reininger's dog would do.

Approaching the other handler, but without informing him of the interest her K-9 had shown, she asked that Reininger take Trippe to the river's banks and see what his dog had to say.

Reininger and Trippe walked down to the water's edge, and Trippe began to act excited, pacing back and forth with rapid wagging of the tail. The K-9, an excellent swimmer, jumped into the river without command and paddled his way out toward the middle of the trestle. He got about fifteen feet into the fifty-foot-wide river when the current, with its speed increasing as it passed by the trestle's pillars in the water, forced him to return. It was clear to Reininger, however, that something of serious concern to Trippe was out there.

Their boat, aptly named *The Sheriff,* soon showed up at a nearby landing. The two handlers and their K-9s got aboard. The craft was designed for use by divers and at its front was a hinged piece that could be lowered for use as a diving platform. Both K-9s, of their own volition, stepped onto the now flat platform and set themselves up to best position themselves for the search.

Koenig knew from past experience that both K-9s worked well together. As the boat left the landing she commanded to Coyote, "Find bones!"

With a ten-mile-an-hour wind on their noses the two dogs sought to find the correct scent. Koenig watched both animals intently. When the craft came to within fifty feet of the trestle, she saw that both K-9s became tense, their noses going up in the air. To her experienced eyes it was obvious that the animals were sensing something.

Their boat continued to move slowly toward the old structure, then went under the trestle. At one point Coyote left her position at the front of the boat and, putting her head over the side, moved to the rear of the craft as it made its way forward, showing a definite interest in one specific spot on the water's surface.

The Sheriff went up and back along the river, so that the handlers could try and pinpoint the most specific area their dogs were interested in. Each time the boat came to just south of the trestle both dogs became animated; Coyote would whine and bark, and Trippe tried to jump in the water but, being restrained by his handler, had to settle for whining and pawing the river's surface.

Both Koenig and Reininger decided it was time to find out what was below them. They turned to the three divers already on the boat who had been watching the dogs work, and told them as much. The deputy at *The Sheriff*'s helm returned to the dock, let the two K-9 teams off, and returned to the area under the trestle for the actual search.

The underwater exploration that followed took several hours. During this time Reininger and Trippe left, leaving only Koenig and Coyote on the scene. While walking along the bank of the river the two came under the trestle. Koenig observed that Coyote became most interested in the water near where they stood. Barking, licking at the water, and generally carrying on, Koenig had to restrain her K-9 from entering the water. Finally, Coyote lay down in the river, alerting for her partner.

Koenig then went over to the divers and asked that they perform a particularly thorough search under the trestle. Even as she spoke she was aware that the underwater search would be coming to an end soon. It was already late afternoon, a light rain was falling under an overcast sky, and there wasn't much light getting to the bottom of the thirty-five-foot-deep river for the divers to see by.

The search-and-rescue deputy, Ron Ryalls, came up to Koenig. She assured him that something was there. Based on her opinion, the deputy decided to schedule divers for the next day.

At about ten the next morning Koenig returned to the site. As she headed down to the trestle, one of the local deputies came up to her and said, "Congratulations!" "For what?" Koenig responded. The man went on to explain that she, Reininger, and their dogs had been correct. The five youths had confessed to killing Michael by throwing him off the trestle, so there was indeed a body in the river.

The story he related was that the six youngsters had headed out to the railroad overpass. The five boys who had just met Michael were between sixteen and seventeen years of age, and all were high-school dropouts. They had made a little bet among themselves—the winner would get twenty dollars and some marijuana if he had the nerve to push Michael off the bridge. One of the youths took up the dare, which resulted in the death of Michael Schuerhoff, and eventually all five of the young men were charged with murder.

Koenig stood there, watching the divers work and pondering the unpredictable and savage nature of some human beings, asking herself how such a mindless tragedy could happen. As she stood near some law officers, over their portable radio came the words, "Got him!" One of the members of the dive team reported where they had just located the victim's body. It seemed that the current had carried Michael an additional hundred and fifty feet downstream from the trestle since the evening before.

Is This the Right Body?

The Washington State's King County police had a little problem. They had a body but no head. The story that Detective J. H. "Jim" Doyon of the major crime section told Rebmann and Koenig was that a headless corpse had been found by the home of an emotionally disturbed

Vietnam War veteran. Because of the victim's state of decomposition—it was July, the man had been a recluse, and his body had lain undiscovered for some time—and, because the head was missing, a cause of death had yet to be determined. Doyon needed Rebmann and Koenig's K-9s to assist the police in locating the missing body part.

Rebmann and Koenig went to the scene and had their dogs search the wooded area carefully, but were unable to come up with the man's head or any other human remains.

A bit disappointed at not finding anything, the team went home.

At the end of that summer Rebmann and Koenig received another call from Detective Doyon. Eight miles east of where the headless body had been found, some hikers, who had been out with their pet dog, had come upon a human head. The skull they stumbled upon was complete except that it had no lower jaw.

Doyon told Rebmann and Koenig that at first he figured there couldn't be all that many human heads floating around King County and asked himself, could this skull belong to the deceased veteran of early July? However, the county medical examiner quickly shot down that idea, informing the detective that he now had another body to worry about, because the newly found head wasn't a match to the earlier headless body. At any rate, Doyon went on to explain to the K-9 team that he felt it would be worth a look to see if any more body parts were lying about the second area.

The three made an appointment to meet where the most recent skull had been found.

The patch of woods in which the skull had been discovered was near an upscale housing development. By coincidence it was situated off the same major road as the home of the headless torso some eight miles away. At nine-thirty on the morning of the search, Koenig and Rebmann, with their K-9s Marianne and Coyote, met up with Detective Doyon. The weather was pleasant and mild, the temperature between sixty and sixty-five degrees. The three began their work by entering into the woods in order to get a feel for the locale.

Walking was difficult because of the thick growth of young alder trees as well as the large number of blackberry bushes they encountered. Animal trails could be seen snaking off in various directions. One thing they all agreed on, if there were any human remains hidden in that dense vegetation, they'd be tough to find.

Back at the car Rebmann took out Marianne. Walking along the perimeter of the woods, the dog showed interest, but the thick brush proved impossible to penetrate even for an aggressive working dog.

It was decided to break the area to be searched into sections. Koenig was given the chore of taking Coyote out to where the skull had been found. The spot was marked by a bright ribbon on a wooden stake.

Koenig and her K-9 forced a path through the saplings to her designated spot. Once there Koenig saw that Coyote was on to something. The shepherd's head went up and Koenig watched as the animal sniffed the air excitedly. The K-9, who was not on a line, showed no interest in the place where the skull had been found but instead walked straight ahead into the brush, then dropped her nose. Koenig fought her way to the dog. In front of the animal lay a human vertebrae. Koenig let her eyes adjust to the scene for a moment longer, then spotted objects that appeared to be human ribs.

Koenig wanted to let Rebmann and Doyon, who had both headed back to their cars to pick up some equipment, know what she'd found. At the moment she was unable to formulate a more descriptive alert than by loudly calling out, "Bingo!"

To Coyote she said, "Let's go find some more." The K-9 then headed in the opposite direction. Twenty feet from the skull she again alerted. There Koenig found a human pelvis.

Then Coyote headed off in yet another direction. Following in as close behind her K-9 as possible, Koenig saw that her dog had now found a boot. Nearby was a dark blue sock; off to one side were a couple of leg bones caught between two trees. Although at that point Coyote thought it would be great fun to play with the larger bones, Koenig ordered her K-9 to keep looking. Soon the second boot and sock were uncovered.

Koenig had been so busy watching her partner at work that she had little notion what was around her. Rebmann, who had been under no such pressure, came up to his partner and told her to check out where the various pieces of bone and clothing had been found. It was clearly an animal trail, thus the wide distribution of disembodied material.

Doyon called in the major crime scene unit by cell phone. When they arrived the area was immediately roped off and a crime scene investigation begun.

Koenig assisted in brushing back the area for the investigators. As one spot was being raked back, Coyote, ever on the job, rushed forward and uncovered a finger bone.

On that day all the evidence uncovered had been found by Coyote.

The investigators worked on the site for several more days. Using specially trained explorer scouts, more material was eventually found. A few weeks later a man's shirt was located, as was a sternum. Both contained bullet holes, which showed that the shirt had been worn by the victim when the projectile was fired.

By then the identity of the dead man was known. His name was Robert Neeper, a fifty-five-year-old man. The story was that the victim had been killed by the twenty-six-year-old son of the man's female friend. The three shared a mobile home, and it appeared that all was not sweetness and light within the household. After the deed, which had taken place over the previous Mother's Day weekend, the body had been dumped where it was eventually located. The timing of the murder seemed appropriate since the murderer had told his mother that it was he who had killed her boyfriend. One might speculate that the act may have been a Mother's Day gift in lieu of flowers.

The mother, apparently not wholly appreciative of her son's gesture, informed the police. But without a body they could only investigate the allegation. With the identification of the body parts, the shooter, who was in jail in California on an unrelated matter, was charged with the killing.

And, as to the matter of the initial headless torso that brought them to this investigation, as far as Rebmann and Koenig know, the authorities are still looking for that person's missing skull.

Chapter 3

New Jersey
State Police
K-9 Unit

K-9 Buffy with State Police Detective Sergeant Stephen Makuka

A New Kind of K-9

The New Jersey State Police have had many different varieties of K-9s in their history. But they had never used the services of a body-recovery dog (cadaver dog) until Detective Sergeant Stephen Makuka of their missing persons unit was partnered up with Buffy.

It was 1988 and the two first met when then Connecticut State Trooper Andy Rebmann donated Buffy to the New Jersey State Police. Rebmann also gave Makuka and his new K-9 their needed training. Before that time, when the New Jersey State Police needed a body-recovery K-9 to help search for a dead person, they'd have to call the Connecticut State Police and request Rebmann's services. So, on the theory that, "When you give a man a fish you feed him for a day. When you teach him to fish you feed him for his life," someone in authority decided it was time to cut a little bait.

There seem to be almost as many policies in how police K-9s are authorized to be kept by their handlers as there are departments. Buffy and Makuka have always lived and traveled together. Makuka reflects that she's with him more than he is with his wife and kids. In the morning, when Makuka heads in to the office, Buffy goes along for the ride. And when he's working behind his desk, she's right there next to him.

As a detective sergeant, Makuka's duties encompass both fieldwork and administrative tasks. This includes an entire squad of detectives to supervise. Buffy is an integral part of the team. An enterprising young lady, she knows where every dog biscuit is secreted within every desk of trooper and secretary alike.

Buffy's social life is largely made up of daily visits to her friends in the building whom she knows are good for a dog-biscuit handout. It had all gotten a bit out of hand when Makuka realized his sleek K-9 was putting on unwanted and unneeded pounds. He decided he'd have to curtail Buffy's neighborly visits. One day, upon their arrival at work, he put a sign on her collar with the order, "Don't Feed This Dog!"

He then took his seat behind his desk, thinking nothing more of his act, and started on his paperwork. Soon Buffy walked out of sight. Sometime later Makuka spotted his K-9 heading back to his office. There were over a dozen yellow Post-it notes stuck to her coat. Among the less colorful comments scribbled on them were, "Mean Daddy!" and "Bad Boss."

Buffy continued to gain weight.

Buffy's going on ten years of age. She's still active and continues to go to work with Makuka each day. But time has no heart. So, the trooper would like the world to know what a unique creature his Buffy is and for people to hear about just a few of her deeds.

Under the Boardwalk

Domestic violence is not new, nor, I suspect, on the increase, as social scientists tell us. My personal suspicion is, so long as men and women have had binding relationships there has been a significant amount of violent conflict between them. The only difference is that at this time in our society we openly talk about the problem.

Location, social status, education—these variables seem to have little relationship to intrafamily violence. It's just that, if you have some money and status, you stand a better chance of concealing your acts.

But when you're poor, live in a city, and abuse alcohol and drugs, the world soon knows of your deeds. The Johnson family—the names of those involved have been changed at the request of Makuka, who thought the story too fresh and its ending too painful for the relatives to read—fit that description. The husband, drunk and under the influence of drugs, had a heated fight with his wife. During the argument the man struck Mrs. Johnson, who then threatened to call the Atlantic City police.

Mr. Johnson told her he'd give her a good reason to call the cops. Holding his wife at bay with a knife, he reached over and grabbed their one-year-old son from his crib, tucked the child under his arm like a football, and fled from the apartment. People in the neighborhood who were later interviewed by the police reported that they had seen the baby's head smash against a door jamb and a fire-escape ladder as Mr. Johnson ran off. Some of those who saw what had happened said that the baby seemed to have gone limp in the man's arms.

When neither the baby nor Mr. Johnson returned home that day, the Atlantic County prosecutor's office child-abuse squad was notified.

Mr. Johnson stayed with various friends for a few days until the Atlantic City police finally found him. He did not have his baby with him and claimed he did not know what had happened to the infant. He was placed under arrest for interference with custody. It was a weak charge, but until the baby was found, the authorities wanted some control over him. The longer the child was missing, the greater the authorities' fear that those blows to the head had proven fatal.

When the Atlantic City Police Department called for state police assistance to help them locate a possible dead human body, it was Makuka and his K-9 who were sent. They were, after all, the only game in town.

Makuka and Buffy had completed their course at Rebmann's training school a number of months before. The team had been used in the field a few times prior to the Johnson baby investigation, but this would be their biggest case to date.

First, the still fresh K-9 team checked the apartment complex where the Johnsons lived. Alleys, backyards, nearby abandoned buildings—all areas were searched with no alert forthcoming from Buffy. The exercise had been the Atlantic City Police Department's best guess as to where the baby, now presumed to be dead, might be hidden. And, as with most guesses, this one turned out to be wrong. But with nothing more to go on, there was little else anyone could do to find the missing infant.

Nearly two months later the Atlantic City police came up with some new information. After the authorities had presented the available facts to a grand jury, Mr. Johnson was indicted for kidnapping. If convicted of the crime, he faced a thirty-year prison sentence with no possibility of parole. Mr. Johnson decided to play "Let's Make a Deal." His offer was, if he was kind enough to tell the authorities where his baby's body could be found, would they then offer him a reduced prison sentence? The prosecutor's response was conditional: yes, so long as the autopsy showed the death was accidental and not premeditated. If that were the case, then Mr. Johnson would be permitted to plead guilty to aggravated manslaughter.

So, the good news was, the father had informed the Atlantic City police that he had buried the remains of his baby under their famous boardwalk. Unfortunately, that structure is several miles long, and in the self-induced alcohol-and-drug-generated stupor that the man had been in at the time of the crime, he was uncertain exactly where he had performed the deed. On the other hand, the man had not been so incapacitated on that day that he had neglected to hide the evidence of his crime, but this fact was not given much attention at this time.

One bit of luck the investigators had going for them was that Mr. Johnson told them he remembered seeing a particular monument as he left the boardwalk. Based on that statement the law officers decided to limit the area of their search to the two blocks from which that distinctive structure could be seen.

There still remained a lot of sand in which to bury, and for officers to now try and find, a tiny dead body.

July in Atlantic City is a busy time of the year. People come not only for the casinos along the shoreline but also for the town's attractive beach area as well. So when Makuka and Buffy arrived for their second time to help with the investigation, there was a great deal more activity going on around them.

Once by the boardwalk and at the dig site, Makuka found that not only would he and his K-9 have to contend with food wrappers, sandwich bags, and other debris blown under the long wood structure by the ocean breeze, but there were the sundry odors generated from homeless people who had taken up residence under the boardwalk as well. On top of all that, thirty-five law officers had earlier spent a fruitless day digging up the sand while seeking the missing baby's body. The scene Makuka looked upon when he finally got down under the boardwalk reminded him of the surface of the moon. Even as he scanned the area to be searched, he noticed the incessant hollow noise of feet hitting wood above his head as well as the whooshing sound made by the swiftly passing tires of bicyclists. It made him realize that while the area under the boardwalk might have been cordoned off, people were still traveling freely overhead. Thus the odors from the hoards of boardwalk users were being continually added to the mix of smells where the trooper now stood and where his Buffy would be asked to find the proverbial needle in a haystack.

The situation wasn't going to get any better with Makuka just standing around. He took Buffy's lead and walked her to the position he figured would most likely get results within the guarded space, the furthermost point that faced into the wind.

Makuka took a deep breath. With the other investigators watching him and his dog from a distance, their faces showing a mixture of curiosity and doubt, he gave her the command, "Sit!" As with virtually all working dogs, Buffy does what she is asked to do for a number of complex reasons. First and foremost is her desire to please Makuka. A second element in the equation is the dry dog-biscuit treat she receives whenever she has a successful find.

Now with Buffy at his side the trooper reached down, unsnapped her lead, and asked his dog the rhetorical question, "Do you want to go to work?" quickly adding the encouragement, "Go dig 'um up!" He then released his K-9.

Buffy shot away from Makuka. He tried to stay close behind, but he had to duck the heavy wooden beams supporting the boardwalk structure, which slowed him up. His dog ran fifty feet ahead, nearly up to a cement sea wall, then pivoted to her right and went another fifty or sixty feet, stopped abruptly, whirled about, and started to dig vigorously.

Makuka figured that maybe fifteen seconds had elapsed between the time he released Buffy and when she began burrowing in the sand.

By the time Makuka came over to his partner, she'd stopped. She lay down, as she was trained to do when she found something, and looked over expectantly at her handler. She knew she had just earned herself a dog biscuit.

Makuka knelt down and peered into the hole his dog had just uncovered. Inside was a tan plastic bag. Makuka reached down and touched it. His fingers felt the outline of a baby's hand.

Makuka took a biscuit from his pocket, gave it to his K-9, then began to pat her, all the while telling Buffy what a good girl she was. Even as he was rewarding his dog, the odor of decaying human flesh began to drift up to his nostrils.

Standing up, Makuka called for the lead detectives to come over. Since from the start of Buffy's search they had been waiting some distance away, the other law officers had no idea what Makuka and his dog had located.

Upon hearing from the state trooper that the body had been uncovered, there was general disbelief. After all, hadn't three dozen people worked for an entire day searching for the missing baby? Could this dog have found the body that quickly?

Yeah, she could.

Makuka and Buffy backed away to permit the crime-scene-unit personnel to begin their work. He put the lead on his girl's collar and the two made their way out from under the boardwalk. When they stepped into the bright morning sunlight, the officers standing outside began to applaud.

Both Makuka and Buffy felt good about their well-deserved praise.

Thug in a Rug

One day while at work in the missing person unit office Makuka received a telephone call from the FBI. A bureau agent told him he needed to borrow Buffy for her skills. He went on to explain the reason for the bureau's dilemma to the trooper.

A gentleman had recently come to their attention. Somebody had only a day or so earlier pumped twelve pistol bullets into his four-hundred-pound body. He'd survived and now wished to discuss with the FBI what he knew about various New York City organized-crime members, his former employers. According to the bureau agent, the man—we'll call him Joey—had held a number of positions within the organizational structure of the New York family he had worked for. He informed the agents that one of his talents involved eliminating his employer's business problems. To show his good faith to the government—he wanted to be included in the witness protection program after his former superiors attempted to downsize him from his position—Joey told the bureau agents of a homicide he had helped commit. The victim was John Morrissey, a man who had done business with the organized-crime family for which Joey worked. The arrangement did not quite work out, so Joey's bosses decided to put a few bullets in Mr. Morrissey's head, thereby terminating the relationship.

Joey and another man lured Mr. Morrissey out to a large but abandoned farm in rural New Jersey. After escorting him inside the deserted farmhouse, Joey and his partner shot him dead. John Morrissey, now lying prone and immobile on the floor, then had to be removed. Joey decided to roll the murder victim up in the rug he was conveniently lying on, take him outside, and, using an available backhoe, dig a trench and bury both the man and the makeshift casket he was wrapped in.

This incident, which Joey had just recently related to the bureau agents, had taken place about two years earlier. The farm had since been sold and turned into an upper-middle-class housing development. That wouldn't have been such a problem for the law officers except that the farmhouse in which Mr. Morrissey had been killed, and the spot where he had been buried, could no longer be distinguished from the rest of the now flattened, bulldozed, and prepared acreage.

Thus their need for the services of a body-recovery dog.

Joey explained that the rug they'd used had been twelve feet long. Mr. Morrissey had been placed in its center and the four-foot-deep trench they'd dug had been made a bit deeper at its midpoint to accommodate the bulge and heft of Mr. Morrissey's corpse.

Had Joey been able to go out to the former farm with the agents, their predicament would have been manageable. Unfortunately, as he was still recuperating from his brush with death, Joey was compelled to remain under guard in his hospital room.

Makuka and Buffy eventually received authorization from the state police to assist in the investigation and made their way to the purported homicide scene. Once out there they found that the agents working the case had no idea where exactly Mr. Morrissey's body had been interred. No one had a clue as to the exact spot where they should start to dig.

The investigators knew where the old farmhouse had been; its concrete foundation was still visible. But the scene as described by Joey had been dramatically altered. The recently retired hit man had told the agents he and his partner had stepped from the rear of the house while carrying Mr. Morrissey, taken about fifteen paces, then turned left and dug their long, four-foot-deep trench with the backhoe. As it was nearly two years since Joey had been there, no one realized at first that next to the parcel of ground in which Joey's victim had been put to rest had been a raised driveway, its mass of earth and gravel held in place by a stone wall. When the farmhouse was razed, the stone wall was also demolished. Therefore ten feet of earth and debris from the former driveway now lay over the grave of Mr. Morrissey.

Makuka and Buffy worked with the investigation team for three days. It was a tough search. Each early spring morning they'd leave home, drive an hour and a half to the former farm, and start working at eight-thirty. At first the weather was fine and warm for their mission. Emulating Joey, the agents, using heavy equipment, had four-foot-deep holes dug around where they suspected the body lay. After each dig, Buffy would be placed at the bottom of the new hole and asked by Makuka if she detected anything. Before long the trooper saw that his K-9 was becoming both frustrated and upset by the regimen. He knew that a sensitive creature like Buffy couldn't be turned on and off like a light switch. She was used to doing a methodical search of an area, not conducting these strange spot checks.

At various locations the trooper, using an antique four-foot-long, cast-iron fireplace poker—a gift from a local county prosecutor—worked at poking holes in the surrounding earth. He hoped to bring the odor of decaying corpse up to the surface. But the ground proved too dense and unyielding, the point of the probe going down little more than half an inch. That meant that whatever scent might otherwise have escaped from a decomposing body remained trapped under the tightly packed ground.

On the second day, the agents decided to bring Joey's wife out to the old farm. She too was now in the witness protection program. Upon her arrival all those people who didn't need to know what she looked like were backed off several hundred yards, Makuka and Buffy included. The trooper watched from a distance while the woman took a few of the agents to the location where she believed the body had been buried.

Makuka never did learn how she had come upon this knowledge. He speculated that maybe she, Joey, and the kids had gone out for a Sunday ride and he'd shown his family where daddy worked.

At any rate, after the woman left, the search resumed.

Using heavy earth-moving equipment, the area where the stone wall had collapsed was taken down to grade level. Buffy was brought in and Makuka observed her show what he considered a faint alert in one area. Based on his observation and expert opinion, a twenty-by-twenty-foot section of ground was roped off.

More test holes were dug. Once again, Buffy was asked to jump down into each. She'd then be given the search command by Makuka. Buffy would sniff the ground and, with no other alerts forthcoming, the trooper would inform the agents they'd have to keep on looking.

After performing this ritual a number of times, the trooper quietly began to become concerned. He speculated that perhaps, because of the way his K-9 was being used, she was not detecting the scent. Or, worse yet, maybe he was missing a subtle alert on her part.

Another plan was put into effect. The agents opted to have the ground removed from the surface of the twenty-foot-square area approximately one foot at a time. Now with the scraping of the hard-packed earth, Makuka began to observe faint alerts from Buffy. With each lowering of the ground level the trooper found that his partner's alerts were becoming stronger and more definite. Buffy's nose would go down to the ground, her tail would curl, and she'd paw at the earth's surface.

Four times Buffy showed interest in an area of ever-decreasing size. After each of her tries an additional quantity of surface earth would be removed. After the last excavation Makuka took his K-9 from his Chevy Blazer and had her check the spot. This time she went to the center of the square, dug vigorously at the earth, and lay down. He looked into her eyes and could tell—finally, a hard alert.

The agents took Makuka at his word. They now carefully worked at removing the earth underneath where Buffy indicated she had detected something.

However, it was near the end of the day. Also, the weather had decided it was no longer going to cooperate with the law. Heavy rains were forecast for that night. The backhoe operator was directed to dig a drainage trench around the circumference of the possible grave site, and a large tent was erected over the excavation to further protect what had already been uncovered. A team was left to guard the scene while everyone else left until the next day.

On the third and last day the digging resumed. Once more Buffy was asked to search, and now she was adamant about where the body lay. Makuka strongly suggested that they concentrate on the exact spot his dog was interested in. He was right. After going down an additional three feet below the ground's surface they discovered the rug.

It soon became apparent that Makuka's K-9 had alerted at the exact point where Mr. Morrissey lay.

The bureau agents, using a makeshift plywood stretcher, carefully uncovered the rug and its victim and took them away for proper forensic examination. Later they found that when Joey and his partner had rolled up their murder victim in the rug, the spent casings from their guns had been entombed as well. The agents thought that was most thoughtful of them.

This search had been the longest Makuka and Buffy had ever worked on. It was also one of their most difficult and frustrating finds. The densely packed earth had proved a formidable obstacle even to Buffy. But teamwork among the federal agents and state and local authorities had won the day.

Fox in the Henhouse

The reason police officers most frequently gravitate to their line of work is because of a desire to help people. But in every group there are individuals with other, less noble motives. Arthur Seale was one of the latter.

A former police officer, his first profession appeared not to offer the remuneration he wanted. Arthur Seale then left his law-enforcement job to become a member of the Exxon company's security unit. This multibillion-dollar concern clearly had need for such protection. Its facilities, both in the States and around the world, required constant guarding. Threats were received from everyone from crackpots to terrorist groups, common vandals to sophisticated saboteurs. A single large refinery might hold enough gasoline and other volatile petroleum products that a fire or explosion there could prove to be an environmental and public safety disaster. In addition, many of the company's numerous high-ranking executives also needed protecting. In short, a high-profile company equated to a high-risk environment.

Perhaps it was the lifestyle of the executives whom he had been hired to protect that seduced Arthur Seale to commit his crime. Maybe it was just plain greed. Whatever the motive, Arthur Seale, with the assistance of his wife, Irene Seale, decided he had figured out a way to make all the money they'd need for the rest of their lives. Seale would kidnap and hold for ransom one of the very people he had been hired to protect.

The victim chosen by the couple was Sidney Reso, president of Exxon International. Mr. Reso lived on a large estate in northern New Jersey. Arthur Seale obtained his address while he was a member of the Exxon security staff. Mr. Reso's habit was to leave his home in the morning and drive himself to work. On the day in question, some time after he'd departed for his office, the executive's car was found, still on his property, with the engine running and the driver's side door open. Mr. Reso was missing.

Kidnapping was soon suspected. A massive manhunt was initiated by the Morris County prosecutor's office. Within a very few hours, with no sign of the missing man nor any clue as to what his fate might be, the FBI was called in to the case.

Within some days after the investigation began, a ransom note was received by the Reso family. Eighteen million dollars was demanded for the release of the Exxon executive, ostensibly by a radical environmental group that called itself the Rainbow Warriors.

For several days bureau agents and the kidnappers sparred. The kidnapper made calls from a cellular telephone, making it impossible for the government agents to pinpoint the caller's location.

Then, for reasons the bureau people could only guess at, the calls and communication stopped.

What the federal agents learned later was that when Mr. Reso had been grabbed from his vehicle, he had resisted his kidnappers. During the struggle the man had been shot. The badly injured victim was forced into a coffin-sized wooden box, which sat in the rear of the kidnappers' van.

Driven to a self-storage facility located only a few miles from where he lived, Mr. Reso, still in his wood box, was locked inside one of the metal bins. The kidnapping took place April 29. The sun is quite warm by late April in New Jersey. With virtually no air movement in the box, and the bin a heat trap, the last days of the victim's life were hell. The Seales at first brought him some water and a small quantity of food a few times a day. They tended to his gunshot wound with over-the-counter antibiotics and vitamins. By May 4 he was dead.

Now with a dead victim on their hands the two kidnappers panicked. The first order of business was to get rid of Mr. Reso's corpse. Taking him from the storage facility, the pair drove over eighty miles south, to a part of Jersey far removed from the state's population centers. The place where they chose to rid themselves of the body is known as the Pine Barrens, a wild, heavily forested area noted for its sandy soil. Arthur Seale took the dead man from the van and, while his wife waited by their vehicle, carried the body and a shovel down a sand road.

He returned some time later carrying only the shovel.

Unaware that Mr. Reso was dead, the authorities continued to hunt for the missing victim. Because of Makuka and Buffy's success in finding the Thug in the Rug, the Morris County prosecutor's office and the FBI asked for their assistance in locating Mr. Reso. Time was of the essence. If the man was still alive, they'd have to locate him quickly. The fact that the kidnappers had gone silent wasn't taken as a good sign by the authorities.

The husband-and-wife kidnapping team, weary after the preparation, execution, and botching of their crime, decided to go on vacation. They traveled down to South Carolina, thus the break in their ransom demands.

It's difficult to know whether they would have ever been apprehended for their acts had they not let greed tempt them to try for the ransom money upon their return to New Jersey. Kidnapping a person is a relatively simple task. It's the procuring of the ransom and escaping undetected with it that's complicated. Arthur Seale should have known that. But he must have figured he was very smart.

He just wasn't smart enough. He and his wife were arrested during their attempt to pick up the money.

With dozens of federal and local law officers involved in the investigation, and with the perpetrators of the crime now identified and in custody, numerous search warrants were obtained. The men and women who were assigned to find Mr. Reso still didn't know whether the man was dead or alive. They had to assume the latter and worked around the clock in order to locate him in time to save his life. When Makuka and Buffy came on the scene, they too were thrown into the fray. The K-9 and her handler were given the task of searching the missing man's home and his large estate as well as the surrounding properties.

The pressure on Makuka was tremendous. The victim had been kidnapped a month earlier. Was he secreted in some house? Perhaps he was buried underground in a makeshift prison. The suspects weren't talking—yet. All the law-enforcement personnel, human and canine, could do was search tirelessly for the missing man.

June in New Jersey can sometimes be very warm and humid. So it was during the Reso case. The hot sun and sticky weather made working long hours most difficult for Buffy, who always wore her fur coat regardless of the temperature. Both Makuka and his charge found their fruitless labor physically and mentally draining.

But then came a break.

To love, honor, and cherish might be the traditional wedding vows, however, Irene Seale figured that nobody had said anything about sharing the electric chair with her husband. She decided it was time to go her own way.

She made a deal with the government: in exchange for telling them what she knew, she'd be spared the death sentence and would serve a lesser jail term.

Irene Seale claimed that Mr. Reso had been accidently shot during the initial part of the kidnapping. Since he wasn't around to dispute her version of the story, there was little room left for debate. She told the investigators of the trip she and her husband had taken to the Pine Barrens after the man had died. Although she knew the location where the van had been parked when her husband had taken the body from it, she didn't know the exact place the corpse had been buried.

That would turn out to be Buffy's job.

Makuka and Buffy were asked to find the body. The general location of the suspected gravesite had been cordoned off into two security areas. Only law officers were permitted within the outer perimeter. Access to the inner perimeter was allowed to only a handful of people who had a valid reason to be there.

Getting to the inner perimeter required Makuka to pass through a number of radio checkpoints. Once within its boundary he parked his state police cruiser, got out, and walked over to several bureau forensic experts. From what they told him it quickly became evident to the trooper that the wife's information was of limited value. After all, she'd stayed behind while her husband had disappeared out of sight, down a long, narrow, sandy road, only to return some time later without their victim.

For his K-9 to be successful, Makuka informed the agents, it would be necessary that there be a minimum of fuss and distraction in and around the search area. He requested that the majority of the law officers withdraw to the outer perimeter. Once that was done he took Buffy from their cruiser and walked with her to the area believed nearest the burial site.

Upon receiving her search command, his dog worked quickly. Within a few minutes she showed interest in one particular spot. But it was what Makuka referred to as a mild alert—some inquisitiveness on Buffy's part but really not much else.

Makuka put his K-9 back in the cruiser, took out his four-foot cast-iron probe, and found he could easily push its tip into the sandy soil. After a number of holes were produced in that fashion the trooper returned to his car, had Buffy hop out, and again gave her the search command. This time she raced over to the same area, picked a spot, and began to dig furiously.

Makuka's K-9 was so aggressive in her digging that one of the agents watching cautioned Makuka about the possibility of his dog destroying potential evidence. The trooper ordered Buffy to stop. She lay down in the freshly uncovered hole and looked up at her handler, knowing she had just earned herself a dog biscuit.

Makuka pulled her off the site, gave her her reward, and praised and played with his partner. While he was doing this FBI agents came over and dug down deeper into her hole. They quickly uncovered Mr. Reso's head.

All work at the site stopped. The New Jersey state medical examiner was called to the scene, a man known to Makuka and Buffy from previous cases. When he arrived he immediately ordered that a twenty-foot square around where Buffy had dug be cordoned off and a forensic exhumation of the body begun.

With Buffy now back in their cruiser, the trooper was free to watch the methodical retrieval of the corpse. He wasn't at all surprised to see that the two places Buffy had alerted, first the location where she had shown mild interest, then the spot where she had become aggressive after Makuka had poked some holes, were where the victim's feet and head were buried. They were the two parts of Mr. Reso's body that were closest to the surface.

Arthur Seale received the maximum jail time for his crime. He was sentenced to serve a life sentence in the federal penal system and a subsequent life sentence in some New Jersey jail, a neat trick if he can do it. Irene Seale was sentenced to twenty years in prison. With good behavior she'll probably get out in fourteen. Sidney Reso will be dead forevermore.

Buffy's reputation was enhanced by her latest find. The bureau was so impressed with her skill that the next mission Makuka and his K-9 found themselves involved in entailed a trip to a foreign country.

But that's another story.

Chapter 4

Kentucky
State Police
K-9 Unit

K-9 Bingo with Trooper
Sergeant James "Fred" Davidson

These days, especially since he recently stopped smoking, Fred Davidson will admit that his six-foot-one-inch frame might now weigh a bit more than his normal hundred-eighty lanky pounds. There are also a couple of gray hairs hiding under his Smoky Bear hat. Inside, he insists, he still feels the same as when he first put on the gray uniform of the Kentucky State Police twenty-six years ago.

For the last eight of these years, Trooper Sergeant Davidson has had a K-9 patrol partner. Bingo, a long-bodied, black and tan, ninety-five-pound German shepherd, works the roads with the trooper. Not only can he back up the veteran officer in a pinch, but Bingo has been taught how to track people, as well as how to locate dead human bodies. The pair received their training from Andy Rebmann.

In his twenty-six years as a trooper Davidson has seen many things. Yet, even after giving the matter some thought he figures the most unusual events he has had to deal with have taken place while he and Bingo were out on the road as a team.

Not Enough Bullets

It was the second marriage for Bill McHargue, a young man still in his twenties. And this one was going as badly as had his first. Rhonda McHargue had asked her husband for a divorce. Bill complained to his buddies that his first wife had taken him to the cleaners financially. This time he vowed he wasn't going to spend any more money on his marital problems than he had to.

It was on a September Sunday that Bill asked Rhonda to go for a ride with him. Maybe they'd be able to work out their differences, was what he said to her.

He picked up his wife at her parents' home in Elizabeth Town, a small farming community of fewer than fifteen thousand people located twenty or so miles from Fort Knox. The couple drove off in Bill's small Datsun, just to talk, he had assured her parents.

Rhonda didn't come home that evening. Nor did Bill stop in to explain where his wife had gone. When questioned by Rhonda's relatives, he told them they'd had another spat and she'd gotten out of the car and had refused to get back in, stalking off in the direction of the Blue Grass Parkway. He said that was the last he had seen of her.

The tale had a funny ring to it, especially since Rhonda had a two-year-old child waiting for her at home. The twenty-three-year-old woman had never before left her son for any length of time without first telling her parents or grandparents where she was off to. And the fact that Bill had to be sought out to explain what had happened between the couple gave everyone an uncomfortable feeling. His story was strange enough that Rhonda's relatives immediately sought out police help. They went into town and made out a missing persons report at the local state police post.

They described their daughter to Trooper Detective Bob Foster, telling the investigator she was an attractively slim young woman, about five-five, with strawberry-blond hair. They informed him that when she left the house she had been wearing blue jeans and a white top, and no one had heard a word from the woman since her husband had driven off with her that morning.

After speaking with Rhonda's parents, Foster contacted her husband, Bill. After speaking with the man, the investigator was no more impressed with his story of what had happened than Rhonda's relatives had been.

Davidson was on patrol that Monday evening, working out of the Hazard Post, when a call came in from the Elizabeth Town Post. Foster explained to the other trooper that he was an investigator working out of that barracks and had caught this particular missing persons case. He could use the services of a tracking dog.

The next morning it took Davidson two hours, even in his big-engined gray Ford Crown Vic Kentucky State Police cruiser, to get to the modern brick building that housed the Elizabeth Town Post. The morning was a hot one for September. Neither Davidson nor anyone else had been particularly comfortable the last few days. It hadn't rained in nearly a month, yet the humidity remained uncomfortably high. Careful to park his cruiser under a shade tree so that the engine wouldn't overheat while the air-conditioner was on high for Bingo's sake, he climbed from the state police car and looked up at a dark ominous sky. Ninety degrees and humid. Damn. It wouldn't be much longer before the weather was going to make up for that drought, in spades, the trooper figured as he headed for the post's front entrance.

Inside the building there were several people already waiting for Davidson. Foster was on hand, plus another K-9 handler, Trooper Reed Smith. Smith's K-9, a bloodhound named Flash, had searched for the missing woman the day before. Today it would be Bingo's turn. After all, bloodhounds weren't normally used for seeking out dead human bodies.

The trooper received a thorough briefing from Foster. The woman's husband had told them the approximate location where he claimed his wife had gotten out of the car. Smith's K-9 had worked that site for hours the previous day and had been unable to pick up her trail. Unstated among the three men was the obvious fact that the trooper's bloodhound would certainly have found a scent trail if one was there to be found.

There was one other small matter that had been bothering the investigator. He mentioned his concern to Davidson and Smith. A month earlier Bill McHargue had taken out a hundred-fifty-thousand-dollar life-insurance policy on his wife. Foster also told the other troopers that in a short while Bill McHargue was due to take a polygraph examination over at state police headquarters in Frankfort.

Returning to his cruiser with Smith, Davidson saw that Bingo was lying down comfortably in back on his carpeted platform. As he positioned himself behind the steering wheel, the trooper reflected that the day's hot weather—it was now nearly noon and plenty warm out—was going to use up his K-9's energy quickly. The plan the men had discussed inside was for the three troopers to return to where the missing person's husband had said he'd last seen his wife and start looking from there.

Driving out to the site, the trooper followed a dusty gravel road to where Bill McHargue claimed he'd last had contact with his wife. The trooper looked around and noted that the nearby trees were beginning to turn brown even though it was early September. He figured the unseasonable change resulted from a combination of unusually high temperatures and a lack of water.

Bingo was let out of the cruiser. Although the team worked the area for some time, like the bloodhound the day before, the K-9 was unable to pick up a trail. After a few hours of unsuccessful searching, it became clear to Davidson that there probably was no trail out there for his K-9 to find. By then a light rain had started to fall, and Davidson decided it would make more sense to scout out the general area rather than spend any more of their time at a place where their main suspect wanted them to look.

After Davidson gave a hot and tired Bingo some water, the three members of the Kentucky State Police got back into their cruiser and slowly moved down the road. A quarter mile or so further on Davidson noted another gravel road that forked off into an old field that was covered in waist-high grass. His experienced eye also noted some crushed grass and disturbed gravel that signaled a small vehicle's wheels had recently left the place in a hurry. The trooper calculated that the width of the telltale marks was just about the right size for a Datsun.

He commented to his fellow trooper as he pulled into the field, "Somebody's come out of here in a hurry. Let's go see what was back there."

Once out of the cruiser the two troopers looked at what was nothing more than an illegal dumping ground for local residents. Old car tires, pieces of rusted scrap metal, and other debris lay around the area. The grass was wild and uncut and briar patches grew in abundance.

Davidson let Bingo out of the car, more to give the dog a

break than to work the animal. Just as Davidson and Smith began to poke around the area, Davidson noticed that Bingo's ears had gone up and that his K-9 had turned and looked over at him. Clearly the dog was on to something and, being the highly trained K-9 that he was, was waiting for further direction. The trooper called out the command, "Show me!" and Bingo immediately ran over to the lip of a ravine that lay forty yards farther into the field.

The two troopers ran after Bingo in a vain attempt to keep up with the speedy K-9. In a few moments the dog was standing on the lip of the drop-off. Still several yards from his canine partner, Davidson again called out to Bingo, "Show me!" The big shepherd immediately disappeared from sight.

Davidson and Smith ran to the top of the drop-off and looked down the steep slope. Below them they could see Bingo and, near the dog, concealed by brush, a woman's foot.

Davidson turned to Smith and said, "Might as well call the coroner." Looking closer at the scene below, the trooper was surprised to see Bingo licking the woman's face. Dogs don't lick dead human bodies. He quickly hurried down the treacherously steep bank.

At the bottom he came up to the victim and was amazed to see that she was alive, albeit paralyzed to the point where she couldn't even move her head. The woman had been lying in that position for forty-eight hours. Davidson called up to Smith to get them an ambulance, quickly.

The trooper asked her what her name was. She replied, "Rhonda McHargue." He then asked what the problem was and she answered that she'd been shot. Weak and critically injured, the woman told the trooper her story. Her husband had picked her up and they'd driven to the field that lay above them. The two had talked on the drive over and when they parked had made love in the Datsun.

When they finished, the man got out and walked to the car's trunk, saying, "Honey, come on back here. I've got something to show you."

He took a .22 caliber pistol from the trunk. Upon seeing

the handgun, Rhonda McHargue fled for her life. As she ran through the deep grass she could hear the *pop, pop* sound the little pistol made. Five lead slugs tore into her back, one severing her spine.

Bill, thinking Rhonda was dead, picked up his victim and tossed her, like the other refuse around them, down the ravine.

It took her rescuers some time to remove the nearly lifeless woman from her would-be grave, but once out, she was quickly airlifted to a local hospital.

State Police Trooper Detective Bruce Slack, polygraph specialist, was just about ready to administer the test to Bill McHargue when he received a telephone call. It was from Detective Foster.

Slack listened for a few minutes, then hung up the telephone and walked into the testing room. Bill McHargue was already seated, in preparation for the polygraph exam. Slack looked down at the man and in his best Kentucky drawl said, "I got some good news and some bad. The good news is they've found your wife alive. The bad news is she said you're the SOB who shot her."

According to Slack that was not a happy moment for Bill McHargue. No polygraph test was conducted that day.

McHargue was found guilty of attempted murder and sentenced to seventeen years in prison for the crime. Davidson reports that Rhonda McHargue went through much rehabilitation and lived at home with her son for the remainder of her life, which ended four years after she'd been shot by her husband.

Davidson is just a cop, and cops don't have much to say about how things go after an arrest is made. He finds it hard to see how justice was served, though, when the victim's killer will be out of prison when still only in his mid-forties, only a few years after the woman he shot in cold blood had been buried.

Crime and Justice

The Louisville police department had a vexing case on its hands. Brenda Shaefer, sister of an officer who had been killed in the line of duty some years earlier, had been reported missing. So, as one might expect, the investigators working the case took the matter personally.

The detectives had little to go on. They'd interviewed all the woman's known friends without success. The officers did have some concerns regarding a boyfriend of Shaefer's, Melvin Ignatow. The pair had been going together for about four years. But at that time the investigators had nothing more than a bad feeling about the man.

Fifteen months after Shaefer had been reported missing, Davidson was on patrol within the confines of the Hazard Post when he received a radio call directing him to contact a detective from Louisville. Pulling his big gray cruiser into the first convenient gas station he saw, Davidson parked and stepped over to a telephone booth. He remembers it was eight o'clock on a February evening and the weather was foul—cold, windy, and rainy. So while the trooper had an uncomfortable and chilly conversation on the phone to Louisville, Bingo stayed nice and warm in the cruiser.

The gist of the exchange between the two law officers was that the Louisville investigators had gotten a break on the Shaefer case. Both that department and the FBI special agents working on the investigation had spoken to Maryann Shore, another girlfriend of Ignatow's. She had told them a rather bizarre story. Shore claimed that she had been a witness to the murder of Shaefer, that Ignatow had bound the woman up, beat, sodomized, then strangled her. According to the witness, Ignatow then carried Shaefer's corpse out into woods behind the home, to an already dug grave. She claimed to know where the body was buried.

Based on the woman's statements, as well as on some circumstantial evidence found in the man's home pursuant to a search warrant, Ignatow was arrested. The dilemma the investigators faced was twofold. Number one, they had reservations regarding the veracity of their one witness and, two, without the victim's corpse to demonstrate that a murder had in fact taken place, it would be extremely difficult to prove their case.

The Louisville detective asked if Bingo might be available. And Davidson could come along too, if that was all right.

After ending his call to the detective, Davidson requested and received authorization from state police headquarters in Frankfort to take on the mission. Next morning he, along with his K-9 partner, made their way to Louisville. It was two hundred twenty miles from where the trooper normally worked, but he and Bingo arrived at the meeting spot at nine-thirty. Already there, waiting for their arrival, were both federal agents and local detectives. After a quick round of hellos among the law officers the small convoy headed out to the possible crime scene, situated near Ignatow's home off of Poplar Level Road.

Shore had told the investigators that the body was buried in some woods behind her former boyfriend's home. The police and federal vehicles parked at the far end of a school parking lot that bordered on the woods they were interested in. Davidson looked around and saw that the neighborhood was pleasantly middle class, with a mix of wood and brick single-family homes on its streets. The land they wished to search was situated between homes on one side and the school on the other. The area was clearly designed to act as a visual and noise buffer. Davidson got out of his cruiser and surveyed the area he and Bingo would be expected to cover. He estimated there were around ten acres of land they'd have to search. That was a good amount of property to check out in one day.

Davidson was glad to be dressed in his gray army-fatigue-style work outfit. The weather was no better than the night before, and he was pleased to have brought along a heavy jacket as a cold wind blew against his body and a light rain hit his face.

What was less pleasing to Davidson was the fact that an

unwanted entourage of several dozen area law officers from the commonwealth attorney's office and some television media people with satellite relay trucks were also in the school lot. It was clear to Davidson that he and his K-9 were expected not only to conduct a thorough search, but to do it before everyone present, particularly the civilians—they being used to hour-long television crime shows—became bored. And he'd damn well better find something.

Davidson took Bingo from the rear of the cruiser and started to work. As the K-9 moved to and fro the trooper, using hand signals, directing his dog how far to travel and in what direction. Keeping a tight pattern during the search, the team worked the area for several hours. During that time there was no alert from Bingo.

As hard as he tried it was impossible for Davidson to ignore the fifty pairs of eyes on his back. He was also painfully aware of the fact that he and his partner had been methodically searching for the victim's grave for several hours and had completed checking only a fraction of the ground they would have to cover.

The trooper gave his dog a break and went over to a nearby detective. He suggested that it would save a great deal of time if someone could bring Maryann Shore, who was in FBI custody at that moment, to the scene and have her point out where she remembered the murder victim to have been buried.

A little more than an hour later Shore was brought to the wooded area by FBI agents. She was dressed in pants and a sweatshirt and was wearing a dark blue FBI windbreaker, so the majority of onlookers had no idea who she was or why she was there. Davidson stopped Bingo's work and waited until the woman took the officers to a hundred-yard-square section of woods.

Once that was accomplished Davidson moved his search over to where Shore had indicated the body lay. Within twenty minutes the trooper saw Bingo become agitated. The dog stopped by a small sprouting plant and began to sniff at the little bush excitedly. He then thrust his nose into the nearby earth. To his handler's experienced eye what had happened was obvious. In the fifteen months the body had been underground the chemicals from the disintegrating corpse had migrated into nearby vegetation through the root systems, which is why his dog stopped by the young bush first.

Davidson ordered Bingo, "Show me!" and the K-9 then began to dig furiously at the ground. That was when the trooper knew they had the right spot.

Davidson stooped down next to Bingo and pushed away some leaves. The trooper observed that the earth underneath had recently been disturbed. He pulled his dog off the site and called out to the other law officers and the medical examiner that he had found the place.

Shovels were brought in and the earth carefully removed. Two feet from the surface the body of Brenda Shaefer was uncovered. The medical examiner saw that she had been wrapped carefully in three layers of black plastic garbage bags. The bags had been placed over her body from both her head and feet. The killer had secured them using silver-colored duct tape.

Doctor George Nichols did the autopsy. He reported that the woman had been tied up with rope, gagged, and strangled to death, just as Maryann Shore had said.

The trial of Ignatow took place in December. The case went to the jury less than a week before Christmas. For whatever reason the jury members became deadlocked during deliberations. The trial judge, probably hoping to encourage a verdict, told the jurors that they'd be sitting for as long as it took to get one, even if it meant keeping them in the courthouse through the Christmas holidays.

The jury retired once more and, within a very few minutes, came back with a verdict of not guilty.

The FBI wouldn't let the matter drop. A grand jury action was taken against Ignatow, and because of the perjured responses he had given during that proceeding, he was charged and found guilty in federal court and sentenced to ten years in prison.

Some time later new people moved into the home where the homicide had taken place. While doing some renovating, they stumbled upon a hidden heating duct. Noticing something inside they opened up the grate and found photos of Ignatow in the act of torturing and killing Brenda Shaefer. Maryann Shore had taken the pictures during the murder.

Davidson can only hope those jurors had a very merry Christmas.

Chapter 5

New Hampshire State Police K-9 Unit

K-9 Kaiser with State Trooper Detective Sergeant David Kelley

Kaiser, the regal black-and-tan, ninety-pound German shepherd K-9 partner of Dave Kelley, is going on eleven years of age. Kelley has been on the force for fourteen. The pair have been together for all but six weeks since the dog was born, which was how old Kaiser was when they first met.

The K-9 remains healthy, vigorous, and working, a remarkable feat considering how old he is. Kaiser was originally trained as a patrol dog; then he learned how to track and trail. Finally, when he was two and a half, he and his human partner were sent to Andy Rebmann's school to learn how to be a cadaver-search team.

Kelley finds that his partner is a very curious soul, which is why the New Hampshire State Police sergeant believes he's so good at his job. While Kaiser is a dominant male dog, he is nevertheless excellent with children. Kelley also commented that Kaiser's preference among individuals within the human species seemed to be women.

The trooper plans to keep his K-9 partner out in the field and active for as long as he can comfortably work.

Missing Senior Citizen

James E. Smith, Sr., was a proud, self-reliant, and spry eighty-six-year-old New England yankee. Every day the man, who lived alone, would drive his old car around his property in Conway, keeping an eye on things and making sure all was well with the world.

He was so independent that his family didn't think it particularly strange when they didn't hear from him for several weeks. For some time each member of the family assumed others had spoken to the gentleman. It wasn't until the beginning of June 1989, when the man's daughter started to look for her father in earnest, that people became concerned. Because Smith's pattern of riding around his property was so well established, a search was first begun around his acreage. On the first day the man's medium-size car was found parked at the dead end of an old logging road, a trail so rough that the searchers had used an all-terrain vehicle (ATV) to get there.

Although a serious search was begun that very day by New Hampshire Fish and Game Department personnel— they were the unit responsible for search and rescue in the state's thick woods—the forest was very dense and there was a swamp nearby, and they quickly realized that it was going to take a lot of people a long time to make any progress. The fish and game people had already pieced together the fact that the man hadn't been seen by anyone for nearly a month, and they knew that there was no possibility they were looking for a live person. Still, the family wanted their father found. Then somebody remembered the New Hampshire State Police K-9.

Only a few weeks earlier Kelley and his K-9, fresh out of Rebmann's school, had given a demonstration at headquarters to a group of public safety people of Kaiser's new ability to locate cadavers. Among those who witnessed the presentation was a major from fish and game. He had spoken about what he had seen to others within that agency.

On a beautiful June Monday morning Kelley received a call from fish and game. They told him of their problem and asked if he could bring his K-9 to Conway to help them locate the presumed dead man. Kelley assured them he'd be there in a couple of hours.

As soon as he could, Kelley got his dog and equipment into his state police cruiser. He usually dressed in the road uniform of a trooper: a handsome forest-green shirt adorned with shiny brass buttons, along with so-called military pink (a color more akin to tan) slacks. On the pants were matching forest-green stripes that ran down each leg. For this mission he chose to wear the more appropriate military fatigue outfit used by members of the K-9 unit.

Still, the stylish New Hampshire State Police patch was prominently displayed over his breast pocket.

This was the first time Kelley and Kaiser went out by themselves looking for a dead human. The pair had worked on the New Bedford, Massachusetts, serial killer case only a short time earlier, but so had a dozen other K-9 teams, including their trainer, Andy Rebmann. Now the two were out there by themselves, either sinking or swimming on their own merit.

To make matters worse, Kelley was aware that fish and game had used trained dogs in the past with mixed results. On other occasions civilian volunteers, well-intentioned folks who possessed varying degrees of experience and training, had tried to help the agency locate missing people. The results had, on occasion, been less than successful.

The reason fish and game wanted Kelley and Kaiser there was perhaps more to cover their butts—"Yes, we used a dog but he couldn't find anything either"—rather than because they had confidence in the team.

Kelley drove to the scene quickly in his state-issue Ford Crown Victoria. The bottom half of that vehicle was the same forest-green color as his road uniform—clearly someone in authority really liked that color. The K-9 team arrived in Conway around ten in the morning. Driving directly to the area where the search was being conducted, he met the state trooper from the local Tamworth Barracks who was handling the case, Peter Gould. It was Gould who had made the initial call to Kelley. Also present were members from fish and game as well as civilian volunteers.

Gould took Kelley to the side and gave him a short briefing on what was going on. The missing man's car was where it had first been found. The trail was so rough that the searchers were traveling in and out using a four-wheel open-back ATV. How Smith could have driven his car back there was anybody's guess. It was just another indication that the man had been a truly independent person.

Lieutenant Richard Estes from fish and game was in charge of the search effort. He informed Kelley that the previous day three of his people, along with three local

Conway officers, had gone over the area around where the Smith car was parked. They had found nothing.

With little more to talk about, Kelley and Kaiser climbed onto the bed of the fat-wheeled ATV and were driven through the woods and out to the car. Ten minutes later they came onto the rough logging road. Kelley spotted the small vehicle and silently wondered how Smith could have managed to drive it out there. It gave the trooper a hint as to the older man's determined personality, a useful bit of information to have for the search ahead.

The pleasantly warm air was calm; small insects hovered about like miniature helicopters. The trooper looked around at the primal forest setting they were in. He was surrounded by trees and nature, and had Kelley been involved in any other activity, it would have been a magnificent day. In such a dense growth of woods, however, the air is still and doesn't carry scent nearly as well as a light breeze. And he and Kaiser weren't there to admire the forest.

Kelley turned to the poker-faced people around him. He figured they all expected to see him and his K-9 perform a magic trick. As tactfully as possible he explained their situation and how a K-9 team worked. First, there were a lot of woods out there and only one dog. Second, too many people chasing after Kaiser would only confuse the animal and might well throw him off. Finally, if a couple of the experienced fish and game, search-and-rescue trained folks would accompany Kelley into the forest, that would be helpful. Would the other people please remain either where they were or back out on the main road?

As the group started off to their respective places, Kelley turned to Kaiser and softly whispered, "I'll have to leave it up to you."

Kelley began by letting Kaiser run around the immediate area, just to get him warmed up to his task. He then sat his partner down, rubbed his handsome chest and, bending down to Kaiser's ear, softly asked, "Do you wanna do some work?"

Kaiser began to whine in excitement and anticipation.

Immediately Kelley stepped a few paces away from Kaiser and ordered, "Look for it!" then snapped a finger.

To the K-9 that meant only one thing. He was to search for and locate a deceased human being. The dog ran into the woods.

Kelley and the two fish and game officers followed behind the prancing Kaiser, trying to stay between twenty-five and fifty yards from the animal. While Kelley moved through the forest he had another task, which was to watch for his partner's alert signal. Each trained K-9 is unique. When Kelley and Kaiser were trained at Rebmann's school, the dog got into the habit of looking up when he sensed he was near his quarry, even if the scent was below him. Kelley knew he would have to observe his dog carefully for such a signal. Rebmann's continuous refrain of, "Watch your dog! Watch your dog!" repeated itself over and over in his head.

As he pushed through the undergrowth it was almost as if his trainer were behind him.

The team moved deep into the woods. The ground opened into a copse of pine trees, then turned into a swamp.

Kelley pushed on but wondered how the eighty-six-year-old Smith could have gone this far. And would he have walked into a swamp?

By that time the team had traveled close to a half mile from the abandoned car. The three men began to speculate. The fish and game officers asked Kelley if his K-9 could be following after a game animal? After all, he was a dog.

Kelley found he was asking himself the same question.

All the while Kaiser continued to forge ahead. Kelley did note that his dog flipped his head up, took in a whiff of air, and seemed to be proceeding in a meaningful way. A gentle wind began to move in Kaiser's direction, a good sign to Kelley.

Still, an eighty-six-year-old man walking this far?

The questions from the fish and game officers became more insistent. "Do you think he has anything? How will you know when he has something?"

Kelley replied, "I'll know," and could only hope that Kaiser was going in the right direction.

The dog had moved out well in advance of the men. Kelley saw Kaiser look up at the trees as he bounded along, a clear indication he had sensed something.

The trooper called out, "What do you got? Show me! Good boy!" The words were intended to reinforce and support his K-9's behavior.

More questions started to come from the two fish and game officers: "What do you think he has? Do you think he's going in the right direction?"

As they slogged through six inches of swamp muck that pulled at their boots, Kelley said aloud what everyone there was thinking, "Boy, I just can't see an old man coming out here. It just doesn't make sense to me."

Kelley lost sight of his K-9 but could hear him about twenty-five yards to his left. He began to call out for Kaiser to come. The dog normally returned on the first yell, but Kelley found himself calling his K-9's name over and over.

Kelley headed for the hidden rustling sounds that could only be his K-9 moving about in the woods. With the fish and game officers still twenty yards behind him, Kelley pulled back a bush and came upon Kaiser, who was prancing around the base of a tree.

Kelley, seeing that his dog was excited, asked, "What do you got?"

Kaiser ran over to Kelley and demanded his ball. Again the trooper asked his partner, "Well, what do you got? Show me! Show me!"

Kaiser ran back in the direction he had come, Kelley close behind. The dog was on some high ground in the swamp, and although Kelley's eyes poured over the terrain before him, he was unable to see anything out of the ordinary.

Then, when only a few feet away from Kaiser, who continued to dance around the base of the tree, the trooper looked off to the side. He softly uttered the words, "Oh my God." His K-9 wasn't hovering around a tree, but was moving about the remains of the missing man's body.

Smith had disintegrated to the point where little more than bones and clothing remained. Kelley—and anyone else for that matter—would have walked right by the corpse had Kaiser not been there to point out where it lay.

Kelley was beside himself with pride in his dog. He gave Kaiser his ball and told him what a good boy he was, a gross understatement under the circumstances. But Kelley couldn't devote the time he wanted to his talented partner for he knew there was work yet to be done.

He called out to the fish and game officers in his best professional, what's-the-fuss-all-about voice, "Hey, guys, it's right over here."

Now running and splashing through the swamp water, one of the fish and game officers called out in disbelief, "You're kidding me!"

As they came up to the dry land and saw Smith's remains, the two officers were effusive in their congratulations and praise of Kaiser. Both kept repeating, "Good dog! Good boy!"

As Kaiser, ball in his mouth, ran about the men and played, the two dumbfounded officers could only say over and over that the find was unbelievable. It would have taken them months, using the assistance of dozens of volunteer and public safety searchers, to locate the body where it lay. In fact, under the circumstances, and given the nature of the terrain, even then the remains might not have been possible to find.

Kelley glanced at his watch. They'd been at the search for well under a half hour.

The three men and the dog worked their way back to the car. One of the fish and game officers had called in by radio to have the hearse come to the scene, so the rest of the mission was anticlimactic.

At Smith's car Kelley and Kaiser once more jumped aboard the back of the ATV. When they came out onto the macadam road so soon after first going in, Trooper Gould asked, "No luck?"

Kelley casually replied, "Yeah, we're all done for today."

Unsure what Kelley meant, the other trooper asked, "Did you find him?"

Kelley explained what had happened to a disbelieving Gould. It had all been so simple.

A Lovers' Quarrel

Hopkinton, New Hampshire, is a very nice town. The community is situated only twenty miles from the state capital, Concord, and is filled with lovely white buildings, including a classic New England town hall adorned with Greek-style columns out front. By all accounts it's a pleasant place to live.

So when something is amiss in such a place—such as when a nineteen-year-old woman disappears—the police take notice.

Detective Kevin Sullivan of the Concord Police Department was assigned the case of Melanie Derosia-Waters. A troubled, perhaps rebellious young woman, she chose to experiment with drugs and keep company with others of like mind. Most people grow out of such stages. Melanie never got that chance.

On the 5th of April, 1991, Kelley received a call from Sullivan. The Concord detective explained that he'd been working on the case since January 19. Friends and family of Melanie, aware that she was one month pregnant, had become concerned when the young woman vanished. They reported her as missing, telling the detective that such behavior was out of character for the girl.

Sullivan had some thoughts on what might have happened to Melanie, but they were based on little more than his cop's intuition. The detective explained that he had had a number of interviews with Shayne Pitts, Melanie's eighteen-year-old boyfriend. The investigator hadn't been comfortable with the results. Pitts had told Sullivan that the last time he'd seen Melanie was when he had driven her over to Manchester airport, where she was to have taken a flight back to West Virginia—the young woman had relatives in both New Hampshire and West Virginia. It seems that Melanie had been pregnant and she wanted to go home to her mother. The boy was the last person to have seen the woman. No one in either of the two states had heard from her since January.

Pitts had stated to Sullivan that he and Melanie had been dating for several weeks. They had argued over whether or not she should have an abortion, and she decided to leave for her home state to have her baby, as well as to better deal with her drug problem.

According to what the detective told the trooper, Pitts, too, came from a less than idyllic family situation. He lived in a large, expensive home in Hopkinton that was situated on a sizable piece of property, and his father (adoptive) had recently divorced his stepmother. There had been some dispute over who would get the home, but the father had recently prevailed and once more taken control over the property.

And there was one last thing. The Pitts home on Hedgerows Lane was so large it required the services of a caretaker. Victor and Ilene McAllister had been hired by the father to clean up the home and take care of it. When interviewed by Sullivan, they volunteered that a number of rounds, both spent and live, of .32 caliber pistol ammunition had been found by them in the basement bedroom of Shayne Pitts, as well as an empty box for a small, two-shot handgun of that caliber. Victor McAllister had kept what he'd found and had turned it over to the police.

The detective also spoke to Shayne Pitts's father, Francis, who gave the law officer permission to search the home—which is why Sullivan needed the services of Kelley and Kaiser. But the detective was quick to let the trooper know that while the boy's story didn't make sense, Sullivan had no reason to believe they'd find Melanie's body at the home. It was just something that he believed, as a thorough investigator, he should do.

The detective left the trooper with one last bit of hope. If the girl was in fact dead, and somebody tried to bury her in January, they certainly wouldn't have been able to get very far down in that frozen New Hampshire soil.

On April 12 Kelley, working as an investigator (troop detective) out of Troop A, along with his K-9 partner, Kaiser, drove to the Concord police station in their unmarked gray Ford LTD. Parking in a shaded spot behind the modern police headquarters, Kelley made sure the vehicle's windows were open so that Kaiser received plenty of fresh air. The outside temperature was around sixty degrees. Had it been much higher he would have turned on the car's air-conditioning—his dog liked it cool.

Kelley stepped up to the building's front door. Wearing neatly pressed military fatigue pants and a forest-green golf shirt with the New Hampshire State Police emblem on his chest, and military lace-up boots, he was dressed for work.

The officer at the desk directed the trooper up to the detectives' offices on the second floor. Having previously served as a road trooper in the area, Kelley already knew where to go. He thanked the officer and continued on his way.

At the top of the stairs he walked over to the large, open office space where the department's detectives labored. Seeing the tall, blond-haired Sullivan working at his desk, the trooper strode over to the fellow law officer, said his hellos, then took a seat.

Sullivan passed over to the trooper a photo of the missing woman. Kelley looked at it. Melanie was—had been?—an attractive young woman. The detective took the time to fill Kelley in on all the information he had on the case. He reminded the trooper that the girl had now been missing for four months. He was concerned about how that might affect their use of the dog. Kelley assured him that wouldn't be a problem.

The pair discussed the layout of the property. The home was situated on a ten- to twelve-acre piece of land. Because the area was privately owned, the detective believed that if someone had hidden a body in the woods behind the home, it was unlikely that anyone would stumble on it by chance.

Sullivan was interested in the section of woods behind the house and asked that Kelley concentrate on that area.

The trooper followed Sullivan out to the Hopkinton residence. Going through a gated fence, he traveled along a winding driveway until coming upon the sprawling brick house with its attached garage. It was a lot more house than a trooper could ever afford.

At the home, Sullivan took the opportunity to give Kelley some background on Shayne Pitts. The boy was a local youth who had had his run-ins with the law. The detective figured that many of the young man's problems stemmed from alcohol and drug abuse. It wasn't a story that Kelley hadn't heard before.

As the two men stood outside the home and spoke, Chief Ira Migdale of the Hopkinton Police Department arrived. No introductions were required. Since Kelley had previously been assigned to the area, he had worked with the chief in the past.

The trooper verified with the two men that their paperwork was in order for the search of the grounds. Although the three agreed it was unlikely they'd be coming up with anything, an unauthorized—a so-called illegal—search would have destroyed the prosecutorial value of whatever it was that they might uncover. Sullivan and the chief reassured Kelley all was in order.

Sullivan wanted the back woods checked out first. He felt that if anything was to be found, it would be out there. Kelley told him he understood. After explaining his need to work the area only with Kaiser, the trooper informed the other officers that he had some orange carpenter's tape with him, so if he came upon a suspicious site he'd mark the spot, return to them, and at that point they could all discuss how to best proceed further.

With nothing more to discuss, Kelley and Kaiser left the other officers standing on the driveway while they walked to the back. Kelley let Kaiser run about to loosen up for a few minutes, then called him over and put his leash on. He gave him the command to sit, and, as was his custom, rubbed his chest, at the same time asking his partner if he wanted to go to work. He then unleashed the now excited K-9 and ordered him to, "Look for it!" With a snap of the trooper's fingers, the dog was off into the woods.

The team began their task at around ten o'clock. Kelley made sure that Kaiser methodically examined the large piece of ground, even permitting his dog to go beyond the property's border, on the theory that a person might want to dispose of a body at a site other than where they lived.

They worked the area for over an hour. The tree growth wasn't dense, so the K-9 was able to accomplish his assigned duty quickly. Kaiser never showed his handler the slightest indication he was interested in the wooded area during this time.

Kelley returned with Kaiser to the two officers. He explained that there was nothing in the back of the property. A disappointed Sullivan asked him if he was sure. Kelley told him he was, but decided that in order to put the detective's concern to rest, he'd best do a test of Kaiser.

The trooper returned to his vehicle, put Kaiser inside to rest for a moment and, popping open the trunk of the car, removed his training case. Placing a minute amount of the chemical Cadaverine (to simulate the odor of a human cadaver) on a cotton ball, he then placed that in an empty coffee can and strolled back to the woods. Sticking the can up on a tree branch, he walked back to his cruiser, called over to the two officers to watch what would happen next, and let Kaiser out.

Using the same commands as before, the trooper released his dog. Kaiser began to work the area, soon alerted, and headed to the tree that held the can of Cadaverine. The K-9's distinctive response, first looking up at the tree, then back over to Kelley, then getting up on his hind legs and stretching out his nearly six-foot length so that his paws were pressed high above the ground against the side of the tree, was so clear that the two law officers could only say, "Wow," to the result. Now they knew what was meant by a K-9 alerting.

If Kaiser said there was no dead body hidden in those woods, you could put money on it.

Kaiser was returned to the cruiser and the three men talked over their options. Kelley asked about the house. Sullivan told him that the house had been searched thoroughly but nothing had been found. He had even queried the caretaker about the likely places to hide a body in the place, and the other man hadn't been able to come up with any promising suggestions.

Kelley asked to speak to the caretaker, Victor McAllister. McAllister was laid back, long-haired, bearded, and fiftyish. Kelley asked him about the home. The man's attitude to the officer's questions was indifferent.

Even as he spoke to the caretaker, Kelley couldn't help reflecting that if their missing person had in fact been dead for the previous four months and hidden in the residence, somebody would have smelled it by now.

McAllister went over in detail with the trooper how the house was set up, where the closets were located as well as the number of rooms it had. By the end of that part of the conversation, Kelley was certain that Sullivan and the chief had gone over the place as meticulously as it was possible to do.

McAllister then went on to tell the officers about the root cellar, a small room situated under the garage. Kelley asked to see it.

With Kaiser remaining in the car, the four men stepped to the rear of the garage. At floor level a narrow wooden stairway led them to a below-ground space. Inside, illuminated by a single, low-watt light bulb, the officers saw a low-ceilinged, twenty-by-ten-foot room containing gardening implements and a stack of scrap plywood. Although its walls were cement, the floor was dirt.

Kelley detected a musty odor, which he concluded was normal in such an airless, underground place. He turned to Sullivan and said, "It wouldn't hurt to bring the dog down here. Let's see what he does."

Kaiser was taken from the state police cruiser, given his let's-go-to-work pep talk, and released. Kelley started the K-9 at the driveway. He walked the animal through the open garage door, went on to the rear, and stood with Kaiser over the open entrance to the root cellar. The K-9 peered into the dimly lit space below. Kelley gave the find command and the K-9 padded down the stairway. The dog seemed at first to sniff at the base of the wall on the opposite side of the woodpile. Kelley thought that might be significant. In his experience of building searches, a person's scent often follows along a wall, so a K-9 will sometimes detect a person's odor opposite the place they are hidden.

Kelley began to pinpoint different parts of the earth floor, asking, "Is it here?"

Going from square of ground to square of ground, the trooper slowly worked his way to the woodpile. There

Kaiser smelled the base of the stack and climbed onto the top. Kelley, concerned that an unseen nail would harm his partner, pulled Kaiser off and returned him to the car. He told Sullivan that the stockpile of wood in the cellar would have to be moved, and the two men returned to do the job.

Once that was done, Kelley took Kaiser from the car, gave him his command, and let the dog go. Without further direction the K-9 bolted through the garage door and headed down the root-cellar stairs. He made a beeline to the place where the woodpile had been.

Kelley noticed that the earth under the pile was softer than in other parts of the room. Retrieving a shovel from the garage, he pushed its tip into the yielding soil. Kaiser began to dig alongside Kelley. Clearly, something there was making the dog curious about that spot.

Kaiser was encouraged by Kelley to find it. After a few minutes the trooper pulled his dog off and went upstairs. Telling Sullivan to watch, he said to Kaiser, "Show me!" The dog ran back downstairs and resumed his excavation of the cellar floor.

Sullivan asked Kelley what he thought. The trooper replied that the area had best be checked out further. Bringing the dog back by the cruiser, he fastened Kaiser's leash to the door handle and put out a bowl of water for the K-9. Then he and Sullivan went back down into the cellar room.

The two men carefully began to remove soil from the hole Kaiser had started. When they got down six inches they uncovered a PVC pipe. Kelley voiced a thought that had jumped into both men's minds. A leak in a waste pipe, which carried raw sewage, could conceivably result in the type of odor a cadaver-sniffing dog would be interested in. They stopped working and called out to the caretaker. He confirmed the fact that the pipe led from the house to a septic field out back.

The two officers discussed their options. They decided to keep on digging a bit farther. Soon a wool ski hat was uncovered. They kept on digging. When they were just about ready to call it quits, they hit a piece of flat wood. Making the hole wider they removed the three-foot plywood square. Wondering how that could have gotten there, Kelley noted that the material was not decayed, an indication it hadn't been there very long. He then looked over at the pile of wood scrap they'd moved earlier. The plywood piece in their hands was of the same sort as several other sections that lay in that heap.

They resumed removing earth. Kelley was beginning to get excited. The men knew that neither the plywood nor the ski hat had any business being in that hole. Still careful about how they went about excavating the site, they found they almost had to force themselves to control their expectation. Kelley reminded himself that he was a professional, a police officer, let's not get too excited here. The trooper wasn't privy to what thoughts were going through Sullivan's head at the time, but they were probably very similar.

At about a foot under the cellar floor Kelley uncovered some cloth. It was a blanket. He brushed and tugged at the material. A moment later the unmistakable sight of greenish decaying human flesh was visible. Then came the odor.

Both men stopped what they were doing. They called for the chief to step to the cellar entrance, and the other man peered down into the room. In truth it wasn't necessary for him to come further. By that time the smell of rotting flesh had moved up to the cellar's entrance. He walked down to the men, looked down, and said, "That's flesh."

"That's flesh," parroted Kelley.

The chief stood up and said, "Don't do another thing!"

The admonition was unnecessary. Both investigators knew better than to continue to disturb the body. Once discovered, a homicide victim and the surrounding area must be safeguarded. Technical experts have to be called in to process the site so as to ensure retrieval of the available forensic evidence, as well as to ensure there is no tainting of that evidence that might endanger a successful prosecution.

They all agreed that the major crime unit should immediately be notified. A minute later both local officers were on their respective cell phones. Not long after, other officers from the towns involved arrived at the home. Kelley stood off to the side. He and Kaiser had accomplished the task for which they'd been sent.

Kelley's boss, State Police Sergeant (now lieutenant) Arthur Wiggin drove up. He looked at the activity around them and simply commented, "The dog did it again, huh?"

Kelley looked over to his cruiser, where Kaiser was sitting by his bowl of water, and just nodded his head in the affirmative.

The lieutenant told the trooper, "Go buy that dog a steak. Good job."

Kelley walked over to Kaiser. He couldn't contain himself any longer. Calling out, "Good dog, great dog!" the trooper grabbed hold of the animal and rubbed and fussed over his talented partner. Kelley didn't want there to be any doubt in Kaiser's mind that he'd just done something very special.

After a while the trooper looked at his partner and said, "Our job is done. Let's go get a steak."

Shayne Pitts was arrested two days after Melanie's body was uncovered and went on trial for the homicide. His defense was that Melanie had slipped him LSD, and, in this involuntary, drug-induced state he had shot her. The young man found it hard to convince a jury of that theory, especially when they learned that the weapon used to kill the woman was a two-shot derringer and Pitts had had to reload to finish her off. He was found guilty of first-degree murder, which means he'll spend the remainder of his life behind bars.

Kelley was told by the investigators that the case would have never been resolved without his K-9. The trooper gives full credit to Kaiser for the successful outcome of the case. What Kelley doesn't mention is that he and his dog are a team. What would have been the result if he had not suggested they check out the root cellar? What if he hadn't wanted to bother moving that pile of wood? What if he had decided not to dig beyond the PVC pipe?

Yes, it's true that the body would not have been discovered without Kaiser. But it is equally accurate that without Kelley's presence at the scene, Shayne Pitts would still be a free man and Melanie Derosia-Waters's murder would have gone undetected.

A Very Smart K-9

Steven Roy really knew computers and how to program them. He was so adept in the field that by the early 1990s this very bright man had created a small but successful company with clients all around the country. The business employed half a dozen people and was situated in the town of Freemont, New Hampshire.

Steven Roy was an entrepreneur, a good businessman possessing a strong personality. He had lived in a number of states before coming to the Northeast. For a time he had lived in Florida. There Steven Roy met Maria Zarate, whom he hired as a baby-sitter for his two children from a previous failed relationship. The two became lovers, and the woman accompanied Steven Roy as he traveled and eventually bore him two children.

Some time after leaving Florida the couple, along with the two children Steven Roy had from the previous relationship, moved to Alexandria, Virginia. While working as a consultant there he met Joanna Kozak. The woman soon fell in love with the tall, dark, and confident Steven Roy. Before long she left her employment and came to live with him and Maria, serving as a sort of live-in nanny. What Steven Roy saw in Joanna was a computer-literate businesswoman, intelligent and capable, as well as a useful addition to his household group.

For some time the unconventional family lived together in Virginia. But then trouble struck. The authorities had received reports of child abuse within the Steven Roy home circle. There were allegations of sexual assault against Steven Roy's four-year-old daughter. An investigation was initiated. Rather than wait around for the results, the assemblage of adults and children moved to New Hampshire. But not before a federal warrant had been issued for the arrest of Joanna.

The Freemont home where the group moved was situated down a long drive, sitting at the rear of a dead-end road.

Steven Roy expanded the already large structure with an extensive addition he put on to accommodate his computer software business plus the half-dozen employees he had recently brought on board.

The house in Freemont had an expansive lawn. There were many chores involved in maintaining the house and grounds. Steven Roy decided he needed to hire a handyman. He advertised the position and was contacted by Charles J. Kelly, someone who came from the Boston area, a man with a checkered criminal past. Kelly was interviewed by Steven Roy and Joanna, who was his office manager. The man was eventually hired, quickly becoming an integral part of the group. Among his jobs he acted as bodyguard to Steven Roy and eventually became involved in the computer business itself.

Still, all was not going well within the Steven Roy extended-family household. Maria was becoming increasingly jealous and upset with the man's continued relationship with Joanna. The second woman was not only a lover of Steven Roy's, but she seemed to be playing an increasing role in his business life.

Joanna, too, had problems. She had begun to miss her family in Pennsylvania. Since becoming a fugitive from justice she had been unable to communicate with them. This lack of contact with her relatives and friends had begun to weigh heavily on her.

So, although Joanna was given money and had a home and ample travel opportunity, in June of 1992 she informed Steven Roy that she wanted to surrender to the authorities. Joanna told him she thought she'd only be sentenced to probation. Once that was over she could get on with her life. That idea held no appeal to her lover. He assured her that everything would be fine and that he'd take care of her problems. He also implied he would marry her.

Perhaps his words eased her concerns for the moment. But it would appear that Joanna knew things that made her boyfriend very nervous. She should have been wiser than to trust Steven Roy's pledges of protection.

One of Steven Roy's hobbies was to ride his off-road motorcycle in the neighboring woods around his home. A favorite place he liked to visit was a rundown, abandoned boy's camp, formerly called Camp Se-Sa-Ma-Ca. The out-of-the-way facility was laid out on many wooded and open acres of land. The place hadn't been used for over thirty years, and its buildings had fallen into disrepair. Most of the structures had simply become run down; a few had been burned to the ground by vandals.

Among the spots of interest on the overgrown property was an old family cemetery. It dated back to the Revolutionary War and was situated in a remote section of the place. The wrought-iron gate at its entrance stood rusted and frozen in place. A slab stone fence surrounded the fifty-by-fifty-foot burial ground, which had last been used for its intended purpose in the 1920s. A section of one of the cemetery's walls had either collapsed or vandals had pushed the stones over. A number of the moss-covered tombstones lay on their sides, whether because of the heaving and sinking of the New Hampshire soil or because of the mischief of vandals was difficult to tell.

The lonely place gave Steven Roy an idea.

Freemont is only an hour's drive north of Boston, thus fugitives from federal warrants who live in Freemont are the responsibility of the Boston FBI office.

For the bureau office in Massachusetts the story began when Joanne was declared a fugitive. Special agents assigned to the Violent Fugitive Task Force were assigned to seek out the woman. One of their first stops was to visit the Steven Roy home in New Hampshire.

Steven Roy and the other members of the household told the investigators that they had no idea where Joanna had gone but assured the agents that if they found out where she was hiding, they'd let them know.

The agents suspected that Joanna was hiding right there, and they were correct. The woman was an integral part of the Steven Roy business, traveling around the county under a fictitious name and functioning in many roles within the organization.

But how much time could agents devote to searching for one fugitive among the hundreds they had been given the task to find?

In November 1992, Kelley had been promoted, and he was now serving as a corporal with his agency's major crime unit. He was the only investigator in the history of his state police to have a K-9 assigned to work with him. The logic of that decision was simple. The New Hampshire State Police had only one Kaiser, and he and Kelley worked together as a team.

Kelley's new role was to investigate serious felonies and murders, which was right up Kaiser's alley. The team had only been there a month when a call came in from the trooper detective from Troop A Barracks. The detective needed the services of a cadaver-search dog. He began to relate what he knew of the complex story involving the Steven Roy–Joanna–Maria triangle to Kelley.

The trooper informed Kelley that the FBI had received an anonymous telephone call. The woman at the other end of the line alleged that Joanne had been murdered by Steven Roy and that her body lay buried in an old cemetery.

According to the other trooper, bureau agents had done some investigating. Using that agency's resources, they determined that the call had been made by Maria. The woman was eventually contacted by special agents down in Florida, and she told them she knew that Joanna had been murdered by Steven Roy. It seems that Joanna had mysteriously disappeared during the early part of that summer. Steven Roy's story to Maria and the other employees who worked in the house in Freemont was that he and the other woman had had a disagreement and both agreed to go their separate ways. And the best of luck to her, was what Steven Roy had told everyone.

The strange relationships within the household probably explained why there were so few questions regarding the sudden departure of Joanna. No one questioned the fact that the woman had left behind all her belongings, which included not only clothing and personal items but family heirlooms as well.

No one asked Steven Roy about what had happened except Maria. She remained curious about how the breakup had taken place and why the woman had never telephoned anyone, not even to make arrangements to get her things.

Rhode Island State Police trooper Matthew Zarrella with K-9 Hannibal during a search they conducted for human remains that had been tossed into a swamp. *Arthur Brown*

K-9 Hannibal is shown here conferring with the author in regard to a number of his adventures. *Richard Rosenthal*

Trooper Matthew Zarrella holds the plaque presented to him by Colonel Culhane, head of the Rhode Island State Police. The commendation is in remembrance for the fine work done by K-9 Hannibal. *Richard Rosenthal*

Trooper Zarrella with his K-9, Panzer, next to Andy Rebmann and Marianne. The pair were searching a New England town's cemetery for the remains of victims of a serial killer. *Richard Rosenthal*

Andy Rebmann and his K-9, Marianne. *Richard Rosenthal*

New Jersey State Police Detective Sergeant Stephen Makuka and Buffy. This photo was taken just after Buffy's successful find of an infant whose body had been buried under the Atlantic City boardwalk. *Detective Bill Hamilton*

San Diego police officer Gene Oliver with his newest K-9, Roy. Here the officer is pointing to the electronic device kept on his duty belt that is used to open his cruiser's rear door to release his K-9 for action. *Richard Rosenthal*

San Diego police officer Peter Mills with his current K-9, Barry, in front of the K-9 unit's headquarters building. *Richard Rosenthal*

San Diego police officer Ken Fortier puts K-9 Flic through his paces at the department's training facility. *Richard Rosenthal*

San Diego police officer Frank Pecoraro and his K-9, Ajax (Ax). Here Ax's attention is on one of the handlers, who is showing him a toy. The dog is quite sweet-natured and loves being petted and fussed over by people. *Richard Rosenthal*

Seattle police K-9 Rex is seen here taking a break from training. *Ken Hooper*

Seattle police K-9 Topper coming at you. His handler, Officer Gary Kuenzi, can be seen just on the other side of the four-foot-high window. *C. Roberts*

Seattle police officer Gary Kuenzi pries open a board behind which is hidden a pound of cocaine. His K-9, Pounder, was alerted to those drugs as well as to a bag that contained $15,000 and which was hidden fifteen feet away in another part of the wall. This find eventually resulted in a multi-kilo seizure, as well as the confiscation of more illicit money and a number of additional arrests. *Lieutenant Kevin Esping*

Seattle police officer Jon Emerick with his current K-9, Deiter.
Jon Emerick

Seattle police K-9 Adam with Jon Emerick's daughter, Lindsay.
Jon Emerick

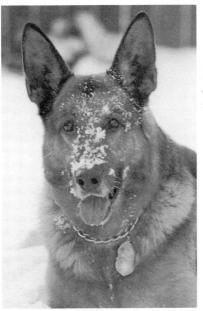

K-9 Adam after exploring some Seattle snow. *Jon Emerick*

Hampton, Virginia, police K-9 Rody. *Glennel Fullman*

Massachusetts state trooper Kathy Barrett with her K-9, Dan. On the day this photo was taken the pair were involved in the search for a woman missing for several months.
Richard Rosenthal

Trooper Barrett and Dan are seen here searching a small pond for a missing woman. The trooper was up to her knees in water during most of the search.
Richard Rosenthal

Massachusetts state police K-9 Dan standing by for a command from his handler, Kathy Barrett.
Richard Rosenthal

Maria went on to explain to the authorities that one summer day Steven Roy had taken her out for a motorcycle ride to a small secluded cemetery. Once they got off the bike, he walked with her over to one of the graveyard's stone walls and asked her if she wanted to know where Joanna was, would she like to say good-bye to the other woman? When she asked him what he was talking about, he told her that she was standing right over the other woman's head. As he said this, he was urinating on her grave.

While she stood before her lover in silent disbelief, Maria claimed, the man told her the entire story. He asked her to recall the time, during one Saturday in July, when he told her and Charles Kelly to take the kids out for the afternoon. His explanation had been that he wanted to have some quality time alone with Joanna.

Steven Roy had taken Joanna for a motorcycle ride. Arriving at the old cemetery, they had dismounted and Steven Roy suggested to the woman that they have sex. To heighten the intensity of the moment, he pulled out a pair of handcuffs. She agreed to his proposition. Steven Roy related to Maria how he had then handcuffed Joanna's hands behind her back, laid her down on her stomach, and, taking a metal weight bar, had bashed the woman's skull in.

He assured Maria that the other woman never saw it coming.

Steven Roy then told Maria that he had tried to bury the woman but soon became tired. He returned to the house, telling his handyman that the motorcycle had broken down and directing Charles Kelly to come with him. Kelly and Steven Roy then left with shovels, which they tossed in the back of the family station wagon. Once they got out to the scene of the crime, he told the other man, who was out on parole, that they were in this together. For whatever reason Charles Kelly appeared to believe that he was now implicated in the murder of Joanna. The two men removed her clothing, wrapped her in a brightly decorated sheet, and buried the woman where Steven Roy and Maria now stood.

Maria was now aware that the only three people who knew of Joanna's murder were Charles Kelly, Steven Roy, and herself. She didn't like the feeling. In the late fall of that year, when Steven Roy was out traveling on a business trip, Maria took the child to whom she had given birth by the man and flew back to Florida.

Just before she left for Florida she made her anonymous call to the Epping, New Hampshire, police department. They in turn notified the FBI in Boston.

The words she used to describe to the police where the body lay initially caused some confusion. She told the Epping police to go to the Scribner cemetery in Raymond and look behind the wall. The problem was, nobody at that department recognized the name Scribner. It took some investigation—mainly speaking to old-timers in neighboring towns—before the location of the cemetery was pinpointed.

Putting what pieces of the puzzle they now had together, the agents suspected there might well be a body out at that cemetery. An agent and the state police detective from Troop A went out to the abandoned camp. They saw they were dealing with a large piece of wild and unkempt property and decided they needed the services of a good cadaver-search dog.

On a cold November 23rd, Kelley and Kaiser traveled down to the Troop A Barracks and met the bureau agents and detective trooper assigned to the case. From that location a small convoy of police and state and federal law officers, each in their respective vehicles, made their way out to Camp Se-Sa-Ma-Ca. An iron gate with heavy stones set on either side blocked the long driveway leading into the property, forcing the men to leave their vehicles and walk the winding mile and a half road that took them to the camp itself.

Kelley eyed the crumbling buildings, the expansive grounds overgrown with vegetation, as well as the several large mounds of sand and earth that lay around the area. It was obvious to him that if a body were hidden anywhere around them, it would take a considerable effort to locate it. He asked the men in the group where the cemetery was located. The state police detective led the way.

First Kelley tied Kaiser off at a nearby tree. His K-9

partner began to whine and cry. It would have been difficult to explain to Kaiser that his partner simply wanted to survey the area, check for obvious signs of disturbed soil, and try to develop a plan for a search. Kelley would also have liked to be able to explain to his K-9 that he wanted to make sure there were no hazards there that might cause harm to Kaiser. But all the trooper could do was tell his dog he'd return for him soon.

The small cemetery showed no sign of disarray beyond that caused by nature and the local vandals. Maria's words to the police were that the woman was buried behind a wall. Well, there were four walls facing Kelley; which was the one she meant? And did she mean twenty feet behind the wall? Ten feet? Fifty?

The thought that he and Kaiser were being asked to look for the proverbial needle in a haystack sprang to Kelley's mind.

He turned to the law officers around him and told them that he would start with the obvious and search the cemetery. Their response was the predictable, "If your dog can't find a body in a cemetery, what good is he?"

Kelley had heard that joke on a number of occasions. It hadn't improved with age.

As he walked over to Kaiser, he wondered how the body could have been buried anywhere near the outside of the cemetery's wall. The trees that had grown up over the years around the area were large and old, with well-developed, far-reaching root systems. It would have been a tough job getting past them, not to mention leaving obvious signs of digging that the officers and agents would now see.

Kelley was also concerned over the number of people who would be watching him and Kaiser work. He knew that when too many people were around, the dog became excited and distracted. What the trooper didn't consider was that he was also under pressure from having four curious and anxious men, from two different law-enforcement agencies, watching his every move.

Kelley gave Kaiser his usual pep talk, then let the animal run loose. Kelley had a notion what Maria had meant when she told the police that the body was buried next to the cemetery wall. He directed Kaiser over to that area. However, Kaiser first jumped over the cemetery wall and began to circle around. That wasn't the place Kelley had in mind. He called his dog out and told him to look over at the place Kelley wanted him to look. The K-9 showed no interest in the spot. For the remainder of the day the dog showed virtually no interest in any of the areas he nosed around.

With no alert showing, Kelley called an end to the use of the K-9. The men decided to poke around the area a bit more. No one had thought to bring shovels, so, using sticks, they scratched at the hard, cold ground around the outside of the cemetery's walls. Nothing of interest was found.

Kelley and Kaiser went home. It was clear to the trooper that Kaiser had shown no response during the search. Was the information bogus?

A few days later the group assembled once again at the camp. It was a beautiful fall day. The remote area surrounded the officers with an almost palpable silence. The stillness of the place made the noise of leaves crackling underfoot sound almost loud to their ears as the men walked onto the property. This time Kelley decided to start his dog well away from the cemetery. He let his partner go and Kaiser again entered the walls of the graveyard. He sniffed about, showing some interest in one of the walls. For a second Kelley saw his dog look up into the branches of a nearby tree. That meant something to Kelley. But whatever the dog had sensed, it hadn't been enough to keep his attention. He continued on, walked out of the confines of the cemetery, and went on searching.

Kelley walked into the cemetery and eyed it more closely. Looking as hard as he could on the ground before him, he couldn't see any sign of disturbance. Peering over the wall to the other side only showed the trooper the extensive root structure of the large trees. Nothing could have gotten through those without showing.

Kelley called the investigators over so they could discuss the situation. The trooper explained that he thought he'd seen Kaiser alert inside the cemetery, but it hadn't been a strong alert. He could have his dog check the area out again but was afraid that to do so would invite a false alert, that is, the animal would alert in a misguided effort to please his handler.

Everyone decided that they wouldn't search the area again until more information was obtained.

Over the next few weeks the results of the two cemetery searches nagged at Kelley. At home he shared his thoughts with his wife, Lee Ann. He told her that he believed he had seen Kaiser alert, albeit briefly, inside the cemetery. The information received from Maria certainly seemed to have been genuine. What were the chances he just had missed it?

Lee Ann reminded her husband that Kaiser had never let him down. She also reminded him of what he'd learned during training with the words, "You should always believe your dog; he'll never let you down. Remember what Andy Rebmann said?"

Kelley replied with a weak, "Yeah, but . . ."

Lee Ann hushed him, told him that late the next day, December 10, the weather people were calling for the first major snowstorm of the season. After that happened there'd be no searching until the spring thaw, regardless of any new information they might obtain. She told her husband, "You should go back tomorrow. Something tells me something's not right. Go back one more time before we get this snow. Just to satisfy yourself."

The next morning Kelley and Kaiser headed out to the camp. Before going he notified both the FBI in Boston and the detective from Troop A of his intent, but he made it clear to them that it would be only him and his K-9 this time.

Now armed with a key to the lock of the iron gate at the front entrance, the trooper and his partner had the luxury of driving onto the property. He shut off the big Ford's engine, and the silence of the lonely place struck Kelley once again. Looking up, he saw the threatening gray clouds hovering above him. The cold air carried with it the feeling of snow, and the trooper knew he didn't have all that much time before the storm hit.

He left Kaiser in the warm car and walked over to the cemetery alone. He wanted his dog to think this was a training exercise. Once he stood within the four slab stone walls, he said quietly, "If you're here, tell me you're here. Give me some signs. Tell my dog."

Going back to the car, he let Kaiser out. The dog bounded from the cruiser, anticipating a swell game of hide and seek. This was fine with Kelley, who wanted his dog to think of it as just a fun day.

Shovel in hand, Kelley followed behind his dog. Kaiser once again bounded over the cemetery wall, to the very same place he had shown interest in weeks earlier, a spot near the rotted iron gate.

"What have you got? Show me. You got something? Show me." Kelley called to his partner, taking the chance that he might be pushing him too hard. He then pulled the excited Kaiser from the cemetery and had him do a re-find. The dog returned to the same place.

Kelley walked into the graveyard and, with Kaiser standing alongside him, he said, "Okay, let's take a look," and began to dig. His heart pounded in anticipation as the shovel bit into the cold, hard earth. Slowly the hole grew larger. As Kelley progressed, he noticed that his dog was lying down two feet away, Kaiser's beautiful amber eyes fixed on him, quietly and intently watching what his master was doing.

By the time Kelley dug down two feet he was beginning to feel let down by his K-9. Nothing was there but hard-packed earth. He stopped, looked up at his dog, and in frustration blurted out, "Kaiser, well what have you got? Show me."

Kaiser stood up, looked down, and began to scratch at the surface right where he had lain.

Kelley said to him, "All right. Look, out of the way, out of the way." He dug at the spot where his dog had just scraped with his paws. At ten inches he spotted a section of a colored bedsheet. With his gloved hand he began to scrape away at the dirt that covered the cloth.

"Oh my God, there's that multicolored sheet!" Kelley exclaimed, asking himself, could this be true?

He dug some more so he could pull up on the sheet. Kelley exposed flesh. The body lay less than a foot from where he had made his first hole.

The air was still around him. The import of his discovery

had so stunned the trooper that for a moment he had to think carefully about what his next actions should be. He wanted to avoid having too many people come to the crime scene, so whatever he radioed in would have to be worded carefully. Perhaps he should use a telephone. On the other hand, he couldn't leave the scene now that the body was exposed, so if he was going to communicate, radio was the only way he could do it.

He started to head back to the cruiser with Kaiser. First he began by telling his K-9 what a good boy he had been. Before he knew it, he was in a dead run along with Kaiser, loudly calling out to his dog what a super K-9 he was.

Over the air he contacted headquarters and let it be known that he needed someone out at his location. Soon the detective from the Troop A Barracks came in, then other law officers arrived. Before long, half of New Hampshire law enforcement had shown up. And with the officers came the snow.

By that evening, hampered by the driving snow and forced to work under the glare of floodlights, the evidence team uncovered the body. The news media were held at bay by the camp's gate.

Kelley was soon receiving much praise. He tried to explain that the credit should go to Kaiser and Lee Ann: the former found the body and the latter got him and his K-9 out there in the first place.

The next day, back at the major crime unit office, he briefed his boss, Lieutenant John Barthelmes, on what had transpired. Now that it was a homicide investigation rather than a missing person case, Kelley was outlining for the lieutenant what steps might be taken to further pursue the matter.

Barthelmes paused for a moment, then said, "Well, I'll tell you what. It's your case."

Such a high-profile case wasn't normally assigned to a junior member of the team. Kelley, the newest trooper in the unit, was stunned into silence.

His lieutenant continued, "Nope, you've brought it this far; there's no reason why you shouldn't take it all the way." There was a pause, then, "Don't you think you can do it?"

Now able to speak, Kelley replied, "Of course I can do it!"

"Well then, get to it!"

It was a year later that Steven Roy was convicted of first-degree murder. He is currently serving a life sentence with no possibility of parole at New Hampshire State Prison.

And all because of a stubborn, concerned trooper, a supportive wife, and a fine K-9.

Chapter 6

San Diego
Police Department
K-9 Unit

K-9s Argus and Ingo
with Sergeant Tom Payne

Two Burglars

Sergeant Tom Payne sat in his patrol car and fidgeted uncomfortably as he and his partner, an eighty-pound German shepherd police service dog named Argus, drove through downtown San Diego. Payne wasn't having a whole lot of fun this particular day tour. The late-summer weather was fine as usual, but he reflected that the neat-looking heavy black utility uniform, which the other K-9 officers had lobbied him so heavily for, was not particularly comfortable when the temperature climbed into the high eighties. His bullet-resistant vest didn't help the situation, and he found he needed his car's air conditioner turned on full blast just to stay reasonably comfortable.

Moving slowly down the street, the city's downtown buildings towered over him. Back when he first put on the uniform of the San Diego Police Department, what was now the urban sprawl of two million citizens had been little more than a collection of small communities of people who worked in the assorted military bases that surrounded the area.

Perhaps the city had had a population of two hundred thousand in those early days of his career, probably less. Back then there was only a single tall building in San Diego, a hotel-restaurant called the El Cortez. There was also a hell of a lot less crime.

Sitting in the back of the patrol car was his newest K-9 partner. Payne was confident that, while Argus might be little more than a raw recruit (it was August of 1991 when this incident took place), he would turn into a good partner to have. A young but highly trained member of the force, the dog was one of forty-six police service dogs that served with the department.

Sergeant Tom Payne, as the person in charge of the unit, was responsible for them all. While people commonly used the expression K-9 for these skilled, intelligent dogs, Payne was aware that that name was a vestige from the United States military's use of the animals. Payne's personal preference was the far more accurate term "police service dog." After all, that was the function of these animals, service, both to the public and to the members of the department.

Back in 1984, when Payne was first given the task of setting the unit up, its purpose was to put search dogs on the street. Within a few years it was determined that K-9s could serve the department, and the community, in other ways. Back then, when an officer came into contact with a dangerous criminal who resisted arrest, there were few alternatives to the use of force, deadly or otherwise. With no other options available, it was often necessary for members of the department to resort to their firearms to protect themselves from deadly physical attacks. That wasn't necessarily a good thing for officers or the city. And as the population of San Diego increased, so did the city's crime rate. The use-of-force numbers kept creeping up. Top management in the department felt that something had to be tried to stop this escalation of violence. The mission of the K-9 unit was altered so as to emphasize the reduction in both civilian and police casualties. And it had fallen to Payne to put together the unit in a way that might accomplish this.

As it turned out, the bosses were right. The number of fatal police-perpetrator contacts took a dramatic drop when the K-9s—police service dogs—hit the streets.

Coming to a red light, Payne smiled and reflected how little he had known about working police dogs in those days. With quiet satisfaction he figured he knew a heck of a lot more about the subject now.

A report came over the police radio that brought Payne's attention back to business. Two burglary suspects had been seen exiting a house situated in the northern part of the Balboa Park area, about two miles from where Payne now patrolled. The officer casually turned his cruiser in the direction of the action, just in case. Hearing other cruisers starting for the location, along with a transmission indicating that the two burglars now seemed headed across a freeway and toward the park, Payne decided it was time for Argus and him to enter the fray. He reached down and flicked the necessary switches to activate his lights and siren, picked up the cruiser's microphone and notified communications that he was about two miles away, and headed for the scene. Another K-9 patrol unit—he recognized the call numbers of Officer Dean Davison and his service dog partner, Al—also reported they were responding. From what Davison said, it was clear to Payne that the other unit was already a half mile ahead of his cruiser.

By the time Payne got to the general vicinity of the crime, the rapidly evolving situation had put him and his partner on the wrong side of a freeway, one of California's famous multitude of multilane high-speed roads. Payne pulled to a stop, jumped out, and opened the cruiser's rear door. Argus's tail wagged in anticipation of work as Payne hooked his lead to the dog's collar. On command the K-9 jumped from the car and both members of the San Diego Police Department bolted across the freeway.

On the other side of the road an eight-foot-tall chain-link fence blocked the pair. Payne hunted along the fence until he found a weakness in the obstacle. He lifted up on the bottom, and he and Argus worked their way through.

A few minutes after clearing the fence the two found themselves on a jogging path. They almost immediately ran into a patrol officer who had been chasing one of the suspects. Payne already had sweat pouring from his body. He saw that the other officer was near exhaustion from his foot chase of the agile burglar. The officer told Payne that one of the suspects had stayed on the jogging path while the second had run into the immense woods of Balboa Park, which lay before them.

Payne decided it was time for Argus to be put to use. He shouted out the standard K-9 unit warning into the forest; if the man didn't surrender himself, a police dog would be set loose and the man would be bitten. Payne yelled the warning twice, then let Argus, who now understood what was going on around him, free of his lead. The dog ran up the canyon and into the woods, the two officers staying as close behind him as they could manage.

It wasn't long before the trio broke out of the trees and into one of the many open parks that dotted the area. People were sitting around, enjoying the fine weather and picnicking. Payne realized he couldn't keep Argus on the search mode with all the citizens about, so he called his partner back and reconnected the lead to his collar.

For nearly forty minutes the trio moved around the area, looking for the suspect. Coming to another chain-link fence, Payne had the other officer climb over and, once on the other side, stick his PR-24 (a side-handled nightstick) through one of the links a third of the way from the bottom. Payne, using the PR-24 as a step, called to Argus to jump into his arms, then put the dog over the other side. He immediately gave Argus the command to lie down. It was a fundamental rule—the team would never split up with a fence between them. The officer served to protect the dog and the dog was there to protect the officer.

Payne noted that Argus was getting more excited as they traveled, a clear indication that the odor trail the suspect was leaving was getting stronger. Three or four more fences later—Payne lost count—they came to the edge of the park and entered a residential area that opened out into a well-manicured yard.

Argus rushed to the top of the hill and began to bark at one large bush, but then soon jumped over it to a second. Payne, unsure what his partner was telling him, told the other officer to stay with the first bush while Payne checked out Argus's new interest. Carefully peering into the dense growth, Payne spotted a man's foot.

Aware from the initial description given of the two suspects that they were most likely Hispanic gang members, Payne radioed for a Spanish-speaking officer to respond to the scene.

Once the bilingual officer arrived, Payne directed him to give the standard K-9 unit warning to the suspect in Spanish. He had the officer do this four times. Payne hoped to take the man into custody with a minimum of fuss and didn't particularly relish the idea of having to do the paperwork involved when a police dog bit a person.

Payne was somewhat surprised when there was no response from the suspect. Most people, when they were aware a police dog was about to find them, had the good sense to surrender. Looking into the bush, Payne saw the man lying on his stomach, but his hands weren't visible. Did he have a weapon? Payne didn't know. He decided the only reasonable option left was to order Argus into the bush.

Argus moved in and Payne saw that the man had flipped over on his back; the dog was standing on his chest barking into his face. As Payne watched, the man slapped Argus hard in the face, at which point Argus bit him on the forearm. Since Argus was quite new to patrol, it was the very first time he had had to bite a person. It wasn't a bad bite, just a warning to the man to cut it out. Payne saw that, Argus had immediately let the man's arm go. With that, Payne watched as the man slugged Argus in the face. This time the dog bit him hard in the hand. Payne could see bone.

There wasn't a word from the bad guy. Payne called Argus back, not wanting to hurt the suspect too badly. He could see by now that the man held no weapons in his hands. Payne reached into the bush, grabbed the burglar's waistband, and began to yank him from his hiding place.

As the suspect came nearly clear of the bush, he kicked Argus in the head. That was a mistake. Argus grabbed the burglar above the knee and finished dragging him free for Payne.

Just as the man was secured by Payne and the other officers, a cry about half a mile away told them that the other K-9 team had secured the second suspect.

All the way down to the patrol car the suspect cursed at Argus. Payne marveled that it never occurred to the man that his problems were self-induced. If he hadn't committed the crime, he would never have been pursued. If he had surrendered when challenged, he would have gone unharmed, and if he had not struck Argus, he wouldn't have been bitten.

Some people never learn.

Inside a Chicken Coop

Ingo came to Payne as a contribution to the department from Mike Caputo. Dr. Caputo, who holds a doctorate in forensic medicine, is a highly knowledgeable aficionado of Schutzhund dog sports. Ingo was a finely trained dog, winning the United States tracking championship in 1987. His problem was that he was good at what he was doing and he knew it. That made him headstrong and arrogant. Smart as a whip, Ingo soon figured out that during sporting trials he wasn't corrected for doing what he wanted to do rather than what his handler wanted him to do. Ingo didn't know that when a competitor had to correct his dog he lost points, but then the dog really didn't care. He just knew that he could get away with a lot more than usual under those circumstances. In the contest of wills between Ingo and Dr. Caputo, Ingo was winning.

Ingo straightened out quickly when taken under Payne's wing. Here the rules were a lot different. There were no points to lose, just your life.

Payne, in addition to being responsible for patrol work, also served as an administrator. One summer day a few years ago he and Ingo were in the small K-9 unit office (they've since moved to a larger and more modern facility). Payne was shuffling pieces of paper while Ingo lay off to one side, sprawled out on his back, feet up, paws dangling in the air, fast asleep.

While he was in the office, a part of Payne's attention stayed with the always chattering police radio. One call caught his attention. A burglar had been spotted coming out of a residence by area neighbors. Officers from different sections of the city had started heading for the scene. There was only a single K-9 unit working the city that day, and Payne knew that the officer and his dog were too far from the area to respond. The K-9 unit office was barely five minutes from the burglary call.

A perimeter was in the process of being established by the

responding officers when the radio came alive with the report of a foot pursuit. To Payne it seemed that the situation was getting out of control and someone was likely to get hurt. He barked to his sleeping partner, "Ingo, here!" The dog bolted to his feet and both he and Payne, who was still fastening on his duty belt, dashed for the police cruiser.

The foot pursuit was headed in Payne's direction, and he reported over the police radio that he was less than five minutes from the site.

The crime had been committed in the Encanto area of San Diego. Made up of single-family homes on fairly large house lots, the 1950s-era buildings had seen better times. Payne thought their expansive front and back yards with their lush growth of weeds and tall grass gave the place a countrified look.

By the time Payne and Ingo arrived at the area's perimeter, there were fourteen or fifteen officers already involved in conducting a yard-by-yard search for the lone burglar. At the time the K-9 unit was only a few years old, and the patrol force was not in the habit of waiting for a dog to arrive before officers would begin to hunt for a suspect.

Payne asked the uniformed personnel around him where the suspect had last been seen. One of the men pointed to a field a block away and said that had been the direction where he had last been observed. Payne noted that aside from the noise being generated by a San Diego police helicopter orbiting overhead the area was fairly quiet. Except, Payne observed to himself, for a lone dog barking in a house just down the block. The officer wondered what that dog knew that everyone else didn't.

He and Ingo headed for the barking dog.

The dog Payne was interested in was inside an older house, behind which sat a couple of large—he estimated they were eighty to one hundred feet long—old chicken coops. Payne and his partner made their way to the rear of the house. One glance at the backyard's knee-deep grass made it obvious to Payne that it had been recently walked on.

Payne called for a backup officer. When he arrived a few

moments later, Payne informed him that Ingo was about to search the area because Payne found it suspicious. The officer replied, "Yeah, sure Sarge, I'll be here," a clear indication to Payne that the officer wasn't excited about being there. It was apparent that he'd rather be off with the other officers looking for the bad guy, not ditzing around with this K-9 sergeant and his dumb dog on what was obviously some wild-goose chase.

Seeing that the yard was fully contained so Ingo couldn't get out and perhaps inadvertently challenge an officer, Payne gave the standard give-up-or-get-bitten warning. He then released Ingo from his lead and ordered him to search the area.

In less than thirty seconds Ingo cleared the yard and headed for the entrance to one of the chicken coops. Seeing that his K-9 was on to something, Payne looked around for his backup officer and saw that the man had turned away and was slowly heading out of the yard. Payne called the officer back.

Walking up to the front of the dilapidated chicken coop, Payne noted that the disturbed dirt and ripped cobwebs at the entrance showed that the front door had been recently opened and closed.

The two officers, with their guns drawn and with Ingo in the lead, pushed in on the squeaking screen door and entered the coop. Once inside, the men had to stoop to clear the four-foot ceiling of the structure and were confronted with the sight of clutter brought on by years of accumulated trash and debris. A thick coating of soil, dried chicken droppings, and whatever else made up the floor of a chicken coop that had lain dormant for many years enveloped every object in the place. To describe the place as being filthy would have been an understatement.

Ingo wasn't deterred by the environment. Payne was heartened to see that the dog was highly excited—"electrified," to use his word. It was obvious to the experienced officer that his K-9 partner was on to something as the dog raced deep into the guts of the narrow building. Payne and the other officer managed to keep up with Ingo even though the men had to open small wire doors every ten or twelve feet that separated the various sections of the coop.

The K-9 took the two officers to the far end of the building. Up against the rear wall were about a dozen old mattresses. In the gloomy light Payne watched as Ingo barked and tore at the heap. Telling his cover officer to stand by, Payne pulled one mattress after another from its place, Ingo still very excited throughout the process. For ten minutes the pair worked, but to Payne's surprise no one was hiding within the heap. By this time his K-9 partner had become tired, so Payne ordered him to lie down. It would give the dog a chance to take a break and for Payne to figure out what was going on.

Seeing that the burglar was obviously not there, Payne reluctantly hooked Ingo's lead back on and decided it was time to leave. Pulling on the thick leather piece, Payne led his partner toward the small screen door.

At the doorway he stood and glanced down at Ingo, who returned his gaze with a clear look of anticipation. All at once the words of one of Payne's K-9 instructors came to him, "Tom, trust your dog."

Payne decided the suspect had to be in the room. He drew in a deep breath and called out the standard warning—in his frustration perhaps adding a few additional earthy words to the traditional phrase.

Without warning the suspect sat up, almost directly under the officer's feet. The surprise of seeing the burglar so close by caused Payne to nearly jump out of his uniform. It was now clear that all the while Payne and Ingo had been searching for the man, they had been walking on top of him! When the suspect had hidden in the chicken coop, he had dug himself into the dirt and debris, then covered himself over in trash and refuse.

The patrol officer, with weapon drawn, called over to the suspect to put up his hands. The man stood up and repeated in a calm, almost hypnotic tone of voice, "It's not me, it's not me," while he continued to move in the direction of the officers. Payne called out several times for the suspect to stop or he would be bitten. The man coolly continued his litany of denial and kept on coming.

When he came to within two feet of Payne, Ingo lunged. The K-9 grabbed the man right above the knee, taking the suspect down to the ground. Now the man decided to surrender. He called out, "I give! I give! I give!"

The ecstatic backup officer cuffed the suspect. As the three men and Ingo headed out of the chicken coop, Payne was pleased to see that the other officer now held a different opinion about working with some dumb dog.

Murder in Calexico

Calexico is a California town on the Mexican border, across from Mexicali, eighty plus miles to the southeast of San Diego. It's a sprawling, largely agricultural area. A number of years ago the town's chief of police was a retired San Diego police lieutenant, and he had a homicide on his hands.

It seemed that there had been a dispute between two men, migrant workers who toiled in the lettuce fields. One of them, a man smaller than most, had been picked on by a number of the other workers because of his short stature. He and a fellow laborer shared a cheap room in town, in a type of establishment often referred to as a flophouse.

The gentlemen had been drinking together one evening when the larger of the two began, or perhaps continued, to berate and ridicule his partner. The smaller man told his friend to leave him alone, which only seemed to encourage the larger bully to more vicious verbal taunts. The little man snapped and, using a machete-like tool called a lettuce knife, hacked his antagonist to death. He wielded the twelve-inch long, double-edged, thick-bladed implement with sufficient skill to carve the other man into pieces. During the attack the killer also badly cut his own hand.

After the crime the murderer fled town and headed toward Mexico. The Nuevo Rio (New River) ran near his rooming house and lay just beyond the town's border. To call that body of flowing liquid a river was less than accurate. In reality it had long served as a sewer for both toxic and human waste. Heedless of the foul-smelling liquid that flowed in the waterway, the killer had chosen its banks to flee the area.

It had become clear early on that the local police needed a tracking dog to find the suspect. The Calexico chief called the San Diego Police Department for the necessary assistance. At three in the morning Payne received the telephone call from his office, and by six o'clock he and Ingo left for the small town.

An hour and a half later Payne arrived at the Calexico police station. He was immediately assigned a local officer who escorted Payne to the crime scene. Forty people, law enforcement and otherwise, had congregated around the area where the homicide had taken place. Payne still remembers the distinct impression he had at the scene of a sea of cowboy hats arrayed before him. Cowboy hats and cowboy boots. Payne knew for sure he was now out in the country and such attire was the appropriate code of dress.

It was among this group that Payne first met Mexican Police Officer Roberto Aerolia and his K-9, Amore. Aerolia was also assisting the local police, a common practice in the area, where the border between the United States and Mexico is little more than a barbed-wire fence in the desert.

Aerolia asked Payne if he could come and watch. The Mexican officer said he was looking forward to watching the experienced American K-9 officer and his dog work and hoped to pick up some new tricks in the bargain. Payne replied it would be his pleasure for the other man and his K-9 to accompany him and Ingo.

Payne was shown the trail of blood and footprints that led from the hotel down to the chemical-filled river. Thinking this should be a piece of cake, Payne showed Ingo where the blood and footprints were and ordered him to find the suspect.

Ingo got right on it and ran for the river bottom. But as Payne watched, it soon became clear Ingo was having a problem. The odor of the chemicals in the water and along the river's banks was strong and corrosive. The dog began to blow air out of his nose to clear his nostrils of the noxious stuff. Soon the dog indicated to Payne that he wasn't about to sniff any more of that poison. Payne had two problems. The first was to find the suspect. The second was his wounded dignity. Here he was supposed to be this big-cheese K-9 cop from the city who was going to show this audience of country folk how it's done, and now his dog was telling him in no uncertain terms he was flat not going to do it.

Okay, Payne figured, he would try it another way. He turned the exercise into an evidence search for the blood spots. It worked. Ingo found blood on the leaves and in the sand and moved right along following the suspect's trail. Within half an hour the two K-9 officers and their dogs, with Payne and Ingo in the lead, came to a housing development. Coming up from the riverbank, Payne was surprised to find the same group of people he had seen at the homicide site standing around this cul de sac in the development.

Payne asked them how they had found this exact spot. He was informed that everyone had already known that this was where the killer's tracks and blood spots led; they all just naturally figured Payne wanted to start at the beginning of the trail!

The San Diego officer decided it would be best if he kept his thoughts to himself as he and Ingo again took up the search.

The trail led them to a paved area. The police chief asked Payne if Ingo could track on pavement. Payne was somewhat concerned, never having trained Ingo to track (trailing is the correct term when working on pavement) on that medium. He wasn't sure what his dog would do when directed to continue the hunt. The Mexican officer, listening to the conversation while standing off to the side, called out, "I can do that. My dog can do that."

Payne said, perhaps with some relief, sure, go for it. Aerolia brought his dog over and gave Amore the order to "find him," then both took off at a dead run. Payne, surprised by this turn of events, followed behind the other team, all the while wondering to himself what the heck was going on.

The group of four traveled about half a mile. By this time Amore had begun to tire. Aerolia asked if Ingo could take over. Payne figured, if those guys could do it, he and Ingo could do it. Payne ordered Ingo to "find him" and once more they went off at a run.

Unlike San Diego, where the temperature is moderated by the city's closeness to the ocean, Calexico can become very warm during the day. Although it was only eight-thirty, the temperature was already in the nineties. Payne, in his utility coveralls, was beginning to feel the heat.

They continued on for some distance. To Payne's pleasant surprise Ingo was doing just fine following the trail. After another mile they came upon a fence, which they followed to a house, then to a cinder-block wall. Payne had once more become concerned. Some time had passed since he had seen any sign of foot tracks or spots of blood. He didn't know what Ingo was following and was afraid that they might no longer be on the suspect's trail.

Payne, sure that they had lost track of the suspect, asked one of the local deputies standing by the cinder-block wall to call for a vehicle so that they could all go back to the command post. As the deputy was about to radio in Payne's request, two other deputies, who were on the other side of the barrier, called out that they could see blood spots on their side. Sure enough, when Payne walked the forty feet around the obstacle, drops of blood were clearly visible where the suspect had climbed over its top.

The search began anew. Ingo led a now-confident Payne to the shoulder of the highway. The sergeant could see that his dog was becoming tired, so he asked Aerolia to have Amore take the lead. With Amore once more at the head of the small posse, the group made their way across a road and into an irrigation ditch. Beyond the ditch Payne saw that before them lay a lettuce field, its earth freshly plowed. The suspect's footprints were clearly visible in the soft ground. Amore kept moving, first to a farm road, then to another lettuce field. Ingo and Amore began to switch positions as first one dog then the other tired.

By this time police vehicles had begun to move ahead of Payne and Aerolia. A hundred feet overhead, a search aircraft flew past the K-9 teams, the pilot using the direction Payne and Aerolia were taking to direct his line of flight.

The aircraft spotted the suspect in a ditch just ahead of the K-9 units. Cars rushed ahead of the two men and their dogs and captured the unarmed, unresisting suspect.

Payne calculated that he and Aerolia had traveled over two hours and more than five miles on the trail of the man. In the desert heat it had been a difficult job. Later, Payne learned that the suspect had no idea anyone was even searching for him. It seemed to him that one moment he had been sitting in a ditch, trying to clean the wound on his hand, the next instant a cordon of police were on top of him.

The suspect eventually pleaded guilty to the murder and was sentenced to prison.

Payne feels he learned a great deal from that incident. Mainly, it taught him not to doubt his dog. These animals know a great deal more about what is going on around them than their handlers do. Sometimes the handlers just have to listen extra hard to figure out what their K-9 partners are trying to tell them.

K-9s Troll and Beno with Police Officer Gene Oliver

Was that Cocaine I Saw?

Gene Oliver has served ten of his fifteen years in the San Diego Police Department with the K-9 unit. To date he has been assigned a number of canine partners; these include his first dog, Troll, and his second, Beno.

Some years ago he and Troll were out on patrol during an evening shift. At that time they were working the southeast division, a fairly busy area. A call came over the radio to Oliver, directing him to investigate a suspicious vehicle and driver at a local service station. The report also mentioned that there might be some narcotics activity involved.

Troll was cross-trained. Not only was the animal suitable as a patrol dog, but he was a narcotics-sniffing dog as well. That is, he could detect incredibly small amounts of various controlled substances by their odor. These included marijuana, cocaine, rock cocaine, hashish, methamphetamine, heroin, and tar heroin.

The station was some distance from where they had been patrolling, and it took Oliver nearly fifteen minutes to get to the place. By the time he arrived, Oliver saw that K-9 officer Dave Cookson, his dog Nero sitting next to him, was already on the scene. Oliver knew something was up when he saw Cookson's ear-to-ear grin.

The other officer could hardly contain his excitement. He called out, "Run your dog on this," gesturing toward a nearby car.

Oliver took Troll from the cruiser and led his dog to the vehicle. At the trunk the dog alerted aggressively, clawing, scratching, and biting at its metal surface.

Cookson smiled and informed Oliver that was exactly what Nero had done. Except that when Nero had alerted, in his excitement the dog had somehow managed to hit the protruding trunk release latch and the trunk had popped open. Inside he saw brick upon brick of cocaine. Then, in his flustered exhilaration at seeing all those narcotics, Cookson had slammed the trunk lid closed!

When the dog accidentally opened the trunk, the officer's inadvertent observation of the illicit material was absolutely legal. Had Cookson seized the cocaine then, there would have been no legal problem, since the drugs had been in plain view as the result of a purely fortuitous event. But then the officer had reclosed the trunk's lid. Once that happened the illegal material once more came under the protection of the United States Constitution.

At that point it was clear to both officers that to gain lawful entry into the vehicle's trunk a warrant would have to be obtained.

They contacted the narcotics unit and informed those investigators what had been discovered. Once another officer stood in place to guard the car, the two K-9 officers went to the nearest courthouse. Cookson made out an affidavit for his search warrant, detailing every aspect of the event, just as it had taken place.

When Cookson went before the judge, the man read the affidavit, looked down on the officer, and said dubiously, "I'm going to sign this warrant. But don't ever bring me one like it again with the same dog."

The two officers, Oliver amused, Cookson chastened, returned to the service station. Armed with their piece of paper, the trunk was once again opened. The weight of the drugs inside came to one hundred twenty kilograms (over two hundred pounds of cocaine).

Narcotics took over the case at that point and soon apprehended the vehicle's owner. Oliver figures next time Cookson won't be so quick to re-hide evidence his K-9 uncovers.

Kid with a Knife

It was only a summer ago, when Oliver was on patrol in the north division with K-9 Beno. That day, if he hadn't had his K-9 with him, Oliver is certain he would have had to kill a distraught, knife-wielding teenager in order to save his own life.

As on most San Diego days, the weather was fine, with temperatures in the seventies. Oliver had been out on patrol that particular evening shift for just under two hours when the call came over the radio of a "Fifty-one-fifty." The police dispatcher said something about an emotionally disturbed kid brandishing a knife and walking among the afternoon commuters in freeway traffic. Oliver listened carefully as the first cruiser arrived on the scene. That officer almost immediately called for additional units. Oliver learned later that the patrol officer, Scott Lawford, had pulled his cruiser up to the teenager and asked the young man what the problem was, only to be told by the five-foot-eleven-inch, one-hundred-eighty-pound, fourteen-year-old holding up a six-inch-long serrated-blade knife, "I'm gonna stuff this up your ass."

It was at that point that Officer Lawford decided it would be most prudent to get back into his cruiser and call for backup.

Numerous other police units, along with Oliver, responded to the request. Oliver had heard the urgent tone in Lawford's radio call and knew that speed was essential. But the first supervisor to reach the scene had closed off the freeway traffic, so what should have been a six-minute car ride for the K-9 officer lasted twenty. Halfway there, Oliver requested permission to go code three, that is, to use his flashing lights and siren, something only the patrol supervisor can authorize. The sergeant responsible for the district denied his request. Without lights and siren, Oliver could only drive as quickly as the flow of traffic and the traffic control lights would allow. In a few minutes, and while still some distance from the place where the teenager and officers had their standoff, traffic had stopped completely. The same sergeant who had refused permission for Oliver to go code three had also closed down the freeway in the direction the boy was headed. This was basically a good idea, as it precluded the young man from taking a hostage or putting other civilians—or himself—in further danger. However, Oliver soon found himself hopelessly stuck in traffic.

In a few minutes the sergeant called over on the radio and asked what was taking the K-9 unit so long. Oliver took a deep breath, picked up the microphone, and patiently explained that as he had not been authorized to use his emergency lights and siren, he was now unable to get past the vehicles stopped on the freeway.

The sergeant gave him permission to go code three.

By the time Oliver arrived, seven San Diego police cars were already there. The sergeant informed him that to prevent injury he wanted the emotionally disturbed teen to be taken down by Oliver's dog. The unspoken truth was, regardless of the danger the young person might have presented to officers, or the degree of risk that might have been involved in apprehending the youth, it was never a good thing for a police officer to have to shoot a teenager. Newspaper headlines after such an event always seem to be the same: "Cop Shoots Fourteen-Year-Old. Family Asks, Why?"

Understanding his mission, Oliver pulled around the other police cars and, along with a single backup unit, put himself in a position four hundred feet ahead of the teenager. As Oliver passed by the youth, he noted the young man aggressively flailing his arms about, the knife still in his right hand, ranting and raving against the world. Beyond the point where Oliver parked, the freeway ran alongside a park area. The K-9 officer knew he couldn't let the young man loose among the citizens there.

Oliver, once he had pulled off the freeway, let his K-9, Beno, out of the cruiser and attached his six-foot-long, heavy, brown leather leash to the animal's collar. With the lead held securely in his left hand, Oliver placed his pressurized container of oleoresin capsicum (OC, an antipersonnel spray) in his right hand. He noted that his backup officer also held a container of OC at the ready.

In a clear, commanding tone of voice, Oliver called out to the young man to drop the knife and lie down. The teenager continued walking toward the two officers, slashing the air with his arms and uttering words that Oliver couldn't make out. The K-9 officer yelled his orders again and again, to no avail. When the youngster was within ten feet, much too close to ensure the officer's personal safety, Oliver pushed the OC canister's button. A stream of pepper spray hit the teenager squarely in the face. The effect of the chemical didn't stop the youth. The teenager ran toward Oliver but around the cloud of OC spray lingering in the air. At that point Oliver released Beno. Without further command the big shepherd grabbed the boy on the left side and dragged him to the ground.

Quickly Oliver and his backup officer ran up to the teenager as Beno held the boy down by standing on his back. Oliver took the opportunity to kick the sharp knife out of the boy's right hand. At that point the boy decided he was going to fight the dog and struck Beno in the face. The K-9 bit into his arm. Oliver and the other officer now lunged on top of the big youth and finally subdued him, securing his arms behind his back with handcuffs.

The rest of the event was anticlimactic. The boy was taken to a local hospital, where the officers learned that an argument with a high school teacher had precipitated the nearly lethal confrontation. At the hospital the young man's father, a fire department captain, thanked the officers for not shooting his son. The boy, after calming down, admitted to his father that he had screwed up.

Oliver was glad he didn't have to hurt the boy; he was glad no one was injured in the incident. The officer was also aware that only a few years earlier, before K-9s were out on patrol, such an incident would probably have ended with a dead kid and newspaper headlines that screamed out, "Cop Shoots Fourteen-Year-Old. Family Asks, Why?"

Unhand That Lady!

While it's true that police dogs receive a good deal of training, the officers who handle them generally assume their dogs will respond to situations only as they've been taught. Most officers don't expect a great deal of reasoning on the part of the animals they work with. But sometimes the dogs can surprise their human partners and prove that K-9s can be pretty smart.

Oliver and his K-9, Troll, were out on patrol in the evening during the fall. The officer was aware that one of the most popular cars to be stolen in the area was the Mazda RX-7. So as a matter of routine, every time he saw that model car he would call in the plate. And on that evening, when he spotted a nice-looking RX-7 in front of him, he did just that. An immediate hit came back for the auto. It was stolen.

The driver of the Mazda decided that the lights flashing on the cruiser behind him were not a good sign. He mashed down on the accelerator and the chase was on. With lights and siren, Oliver followed close behind the stolen Mazda. After traveling some distance without losing his pursuer, the car thief pulled over to the wrong side of the two-way street they were driving down and jumped from the car.

Oliver immediately pulled his cruiser in behind the Mazda, and he and Troll leapt from the police car and headed after the car thief. Over the police radio Oliver had already called for backup and had given directions for responding units to set up a perimeter in the area.

Oliver didn't let himself get suckered into a foot chase but stopped just short of the alley through which the thief had disappeared. The officer continued to keep watch both up and down the street, which was lined with single-family houses. His professional patience was rewarded when he spotted the fleeing man coming back onto the same street Oliver was watching, obviously having planned to double back on his pursuer.

This time Oliver and Troll did run after the man. The team was slowed down by two fences that the lone man easily climbed over but that took Oliver and Troll a bit longer to negotiate.

By the time the K-9 and his handler made it to the main thoroughfare where the thief had fled, Oliver observed the man darting among the evening parade of pedestrians. Oliver decided to give Troll the voice command to capture the fleeing criminal. The car thief, seeing that he hadn't shaken his pursuers, made a terrible tactical error. He grabbed a woman on the street and attempted to use her as a hostage and shield against the officer and Troll.

For a moment Oliver was concerned. Troll had never received instructions on what to do in such a situation. The last thing the officer wanted was for the dog to bite an innocent civilian in the pursuit of a crook.

He needn't have been concerned. While the woman struggled with the thief and yelled for him to let her go, Troll lunged between her legs and grabbed onto the man. The unharmed woman was immediately released, as at that moment Troll was the only thing on the car thief's mind. With the K-9 dealing with the crook, it didn't take much additional effort for Oliver to place the man under arrest.

After the incident, Oliver recalled how pleased the woman had been with both him and Troll. She patted the dog, having decided that it was Troll who had saved her. As for the RX-7 thief, for the stunt of grabbing onto the woman as a shield and hostage, he received substantial jail time. Oliver is certain that, had the arrest been only for a stolen car, the man would have walked out of court before the officer had finished his paperwork.

As for Troll, well, Oliver figures that maybe dogs are, after all, a little smarter than we humans like to think they are.

Troll's Last Night on Patrol

Troll had been with Oliver as his patrol partner for several years. The K-9 was as sharp as ever, but a degenerative disease of the spine had been causing him physical problems for some time. Troll was to retire to the Oliver home, and the very next shift the officer worked was to be at the academy, training with a new dog named Beno.

Near midnight Oliver and Troll were dispatched to a burglary-in-progress call. A private security company, Sonitrol, reported that one of their alarms had been tripped. Unlike most burglar- and security-alarm companies, this one supplied their customers with a service that, once one of their alarms had been set off, permitted them to monitor sounds inside the protected structure. The company's security people notified the San Diego police dispatcher that not only did they have an activated alarm, but their staff could hear banging sounds and two people speaking inside the building, a single-story commercial structure that housed a number of retail stores.

Oliver and a two-officer unit pulled up to the address, an L-shaped structure, with their car lights switched off. The three officers quickly did a survey outside but were unable to locate the point where the burglars had entered. They decided that Oliver would cover the front of the place, a second officer would do the same at the rear, and the third officer would climb to the top of a hill that ran alongside the building so he could view the rooftop.

From the hill the burglar's point of entry became obvious. The officer's flashlight showed that a vent cover from one of the skylights had been pried open.

The officer put the information over his portable. This not only let Oliver and the officer's partner know what was going on, but also served to bring four or five additional San Diego police cruisers heading their way.

Oliver then put in a call to dispatch to request that the building's owner come down with a set of keys so the officers could gain entry.

The police dispatcher informed Oliver and the others that Sonitrol personnel were still monitoring the two burglars inside. The men now knew that the police were aware of their crime and were discussing among themselves how they would kill the first officer that came in after them. There was the sound of additional movement, more threats, then the two inside went quiet.

Oliver figured that either the pair had set up some sort of ambush for the incoming officers or were now attempting to hide.

Shortly thereafter the owner showed up. Using his key, the officers unlocked the front door and, with their guns drawn, pushed the door open. Oliver, Troll at his side, stuck his head in the store and gave the give-up-or-you'll-get-bitten warning. The two men inside responded with silence.

With no viable alternative left open to the officers, Troll was sent in to ferret out the two burglars.

The K-9 first worked the front of the store, moving quickly among the rows of shelving and around the counters. Troll found no one there, so Oliver ordered him to the rear of the establishment. The officer saw that as Troll moved to the back of the place his pace quickened. From his canine partner's body movement Oliver knew he was clearly on to something.

At the far end of the store Oliver saw what looked like a storage closet. Troll dived inside. Oliver and the other officers—by now there were several—shined their lights on the stockroom area. They heard loud crashes and sounds of fighting, and they could see boxes flying out the door. A few moments later Oliver watched as Troll, his teeth around the leg of one of the suspects, literally dragged the man out of the room. The burglar was flat on his back, screaming and fighting with the dog.

Even though Troll had the first suspect, the officers could still hear crashing and banging in the closet. It seemed that the other thief had tried to hide himself on the top of a tall shelf and the large shelving system had fallen down on top of him even as Troll was fighting with the first man.

Once officers took the first burglar into custody—Oliver noted that the man seemed to have lost any desire to kill police officers at this point—they entered the storage room. As they did so, the other crook, also demonstrating he had no wish to commit a homicide at that moment, called out, "Don't send the dog in! I give up! I give up! Don't send the dog in!"

As the officers called for the number-two man to come out, boxes and debris rolled off the suspect. Oliver thought it looked like water streaming off the burglar as if he'd just come out of a river, as the man tried to extricate himself from the tangle he'd made.

With both thieves in custody, the incident was over. If the two tough guys had had any firearms with them, none could be found in the disarray they had created. Oliver was pleased that no officers had been injured, that the worst that had happened was that one of the burglars had been bitten on the leg, and that Troll was okay.

Oliver figured that although it was not a major case, no homicide or robbery, it was nonetheless a most suitable way for a good police dog to end his working years.

A Game of Hide and Seek

San Diego K-9s can get called in to assist a number of different public safety agencies. In one particular case that Oliver remembers, a request came in from the State of California Department of Parole. Every time parole officers went looking for a particular wanted individual, a member of a violent street gang who had been convicted of assault with a deadly weapon and was now considered a parolee at large, he wasn't at home. Or rather, the parole officers would search the man's house but couldn't find him inside, even though they had strong reason to believe he was in there.

Oliver was working with Beno at the time, and they were just coming to the end of their day shift when he was directed to an address in the southern part of the city where he was to meet with the parole officers. That day a team of officers had once more gone to the man's home, in a neighborhood that bordered on the Mexican community of Tijuana. This time they had snuck up on the place and peeked in a window. Their suspect was seen sitting in a chair, smoking a cigarette. Now there was no debate, the man was definitely home.

The officers immediately set up a perimeter around the house, a detached, two-story structure. A number of agents knocked on the door, and after a delay the suspect's mother answered. She informed the parole officers that the man wasn't inside. With a perimeter of officers remaining in place around the residence, three officers entered and searched the location. Once more they couldn't find the man, but they did find an open window that led to a sort of balcony off of the second floor.

Somewhat perplexed over this turn of events, the parole officers decided to call in a K-9 unit.

Oliver and Beno, along with two of the parole officers, entered the home, which had already been cleared by the parole people of everyone but, they hoped, their suspect. Oliver yelled two warnings and then took Beno off lead and gave him the search command. The K-9 proceeded to check out the ground floor, with no results. The group made their way up the stairs to the second floor. Again, the K-9 didn't alert. At that point the parole officers assured Oliver that the man had to be somewhere in the house as it was certain that he hadn't gotten past their perimeter.

One of the officers pointed out the open balcony window to Oliver. The K-9 officer left Beno inside while he stepped through the opening. Oliver saw that there wasn't really a balcony out there, just a flat portion of the roof. But by the way the roof curved up from where he stood to a small vent opening about sixteen by sixteen inches in size, it was clear to him that a modest-size attic lay beyond that point.

Oliver stepped back into the house for a moment, explained what he had observed, and then took Beno and the cover officers back out on the roof with him. He carefully stepped over to the vent hatch, opened it up, and shined his flashlight inside. The place looked like the interior of a small A-frame home, its walls coming directly down to the floor at an angle. He saw that a person could stand in the middle of the space directly under the peak, but otherwise there wasn't much room to move around. He also noted what seemed to be a layer of blown-in insulation, a gray, powdery material, on the floor. Following procedure, the officer gave two verbal warnings to whoever was inside to give up or be bitten. Oliver neither expected nor received a response, so he hoisted Beno through the vent and into the small attic, then squirmed his way inside. As he worked himself into the enclosed space it occurred to him that Beno might have a problem if the ceiling wasn't well supported. The dog could possibly fall through to the floor below. On the other hand, this had to be the place the suspect was hiding, so if the wanted man was in there, the structure should be sufficiently sound for his K-9 to walk on.

Beno immediately dashed over to the far end of the attic, sinking into the insulation nearly up to his chest as he went. When the dog got to the other side of the room, he took a big sniff at a vent on the far wall, became excited, and ran back toward Oliver.

Four feet to the officer's right Beno dived into the insulation. The gray material exploded, Oliver heard a yell, "Ouch!" and saw Beno surface with his jaws around the suspect's upper thigh. The wanted man sat up, looking like a big gray snowman. The parolee submitted to arrest without further incident.

Once the situation had calmed down, Oliver reflected that while the suspect had been no more than four feet from him, he had remained invisible. Without his partner Beno on that job, they would never have found the parolee in that attic space.

K-9 Ajax (Ax)
with Police Officer Frank Pecoraro

Oh, for a Day Off

San Diego is just not a major location for winter sports enthusiasts. Not when everyone who lives there figures it's a cold day when the temperature drops to fifty degrees. But where there's a will there's a way. K-9 Officer Frank Pecoraro's two kids were interested in playing hockey, as were a bunch of other youngsters who lived nearby. Using in-line in lieu of ice skates, and with the aid of the local YMCA's asphalt rink, a hockey league was created.

Pecoraro reluctantly went off to work early on the Sunday scheduled to be the opening day's ceremonies for the new hockey teams. His eight- and six-year-olds were excited and wanted their dad to be there. Pecoraro told his kids not to worry. Although he had been unable to get the day off, he was certain that once at work, he would be able to talk his shift supervisor into letting him go in time to make the ceremony.

Shortly before six in the morning, Pecoraro and Ajax (he's called Ax by everyone) arrived at work. The officer slipped on his uniform and made his way to roll call. There he was pleased to see that eight other officers were in for the shift. He figured with so many other cops to cover the work load, getting some time off should be a piece of cake. However, instead of having to deal with a seasoned supervisor, he found that the officer in charge of the shift, an acting sergeant, was less than enthusiastic about Pecoraro's proposal. The acting sergeant turned the request down, telling Pecoraro he just couldn't authorize the day off. No amount of reasoning would sway the man, and in desperation—he had, after all, promised his kids he'd be at the ceremony—Pecoraro let the sergeant know he'd have to go to a higher authority, the watch commander, to attempt to overturn the acting supervisor's decision.

Pecoraro and Ax reluctantly took to their cruiser. To no one's surprise the shift was turning out to be as quiet as most early Sunday shifts. Time dragged on until Pecoraro glanced at his watch and, seeing that it was almost nine o'clock, figured he'd better head out to find the watch commander, a lieutenant, so he could plead his case.

As Pecoraro drove to meet with the lieutenant, a call came over the air—a four-seventeen, man displaying a weapon. The police dispatcher added it was a "hot call," that is, the dispatcher was on the telephone line with the victim, the man's girlfriend, and would remain on the line with the victim until the matter was resolved. The call wasn't Pecoraro's job; he could easily have continued to search for the lieutenant in hopes of getting the day off. Instead, the officer picked up the microphone and let the dispatcher know he and Ax would be backing up the cruiser already en route to the scene.

Three minutes later Pecoraro arrived at the block where the call had originated. He noted it was a rundown part of town; most of the small homes' lawns displayed grass that was just a little too long, the yards were unkempt, and trash lay about the sidewalk. It seemed to him to be an older, somewhat tired-looking neighborhood.

Just as Pecoraro's cruiser pulled up to the address, a second backup unit arrived. Before either officer had time to park his vehicle, the officer who had received the call, and who was already on the scene and inside the house, radioed, "He's in the back, he's in the back!" quickly adding that the man was armed with a small, blue metal pistol. Pecoraro put his car into reverse and backed up half a block, to an alley that led to the rear of the block of homes.

He jammed his cruiser's shift into drive and turned down the narrow path. The passageway rose to a crest ahead of him. Pecoraro couldn't see over it to the black Datsun 280Z that was headed right for him, driven by the man with the gun and being pursued by the second officer's vehicle. By the time the Datsun was on him, it was impossible to stop.

Pecoraro slammed on his brakes. The man in the Datsun managed to slow his car down to perhaps fifteen miles an hour when the two cars collided, nearly head on.

Pecoraro, unhurt, jumped from his police car and, using the cruiser as cover, inched his way over to the rear passenger compartment. He opened the door and grabbed hold of Ax's collar, taking him out. Ax, fortunately unfazed by the accident but without any idea as to what was going on or what was expected of him, stood patiently by the side of his human partner, who continued to ensure the cruiser stayed between them and the armed man.

Pecoraro heard the officer who had pursued the man yell "Stop!" several times, then call out "Gun!" to warn Pecoraro of the danger he was facing.

Still holding tightly to Ax's collar, the officer peeked over the hood of his car in time to see the armed suspect flee from the other officer and run along the opposite side of the police car, clearly unaware that Pecoraro and Ax were lying in wait. Pecoraro permitted the man to move beyond the rear of his cruiser, then ordered Ax to capture the suspect. Calling out "Paken" to his K-9, Pecoraro let go of the collar and Ax lunged for the running man. On hearing the shouted order, the suspect whirled and while still running extended his gun arm out in the direction of the attacking Ax. Pecoraro saw a muzzle flash and heard a *pop*. Ax yelped in surprise and pain. The man continued to run, then turned to face Pecoraro, aiming his handgun at the officer. There was an exchange of gunfire. Pecoraro let go with several rounds from his service pistol, as did the pursuing officer. The suspect went down, hit twice.

Ax, not knowing what the bullet impact meant and thinking that he had done something wrong, had by this time come back to Pecoraro. Pecoraro himself, although unaware of it, had also been struck in the leg by one of the suspect's rounds. Ax lay down next to the officer.

As other officers converged on the shooting scene, Pecoraro called out that the suspect's gun was underneath the man. He let the backup officers deal with the wounded man and turned to the injured Ax. He didn't like what he saw.

The dog was bleeding badly from the nasty wound. It looked as if the suspect's round had done a good deal of damage, entering the chest cavity and exiting at Ax's shoulder.

Pecoraro tried to get up to lift his dog and was surprised when he fell over. Now he realized he too had been wounded. Unable to stand, he dragged himself over to the rear passenger door, yanked it open, and told Ax to get in the police cruiser. The K-9 unsteadily complied with the officer's command. Pecoraro then pulled himself over to the front of the police car and called over the radio to the other officers to tell them where his dog was, just in case the ambulance got there for him before his dog was seen to.

The dispatcher working the run later told Pecoraro that she had been amazed how calm he sounded when he radioed for assistance after being in a gunfight and taking a bullet. The dispatcher did say that when Pecoraro requested assistance for Ax, his voice sounded more concerned than when he asked for an ambulance for himself.

Pecoraro wound up at the University of California San Diego Medical Center that night, while Ax was driven to the Emergency Animal Clinic. Both members of the San Diego Police Department did just fine and were back to work in a couple of months. As for the hockey ceremony, Pecoraro's wife, after visiting him outside the hospital's emergency room, had to stand in for him, but his kids understood.

Another Gun Battle

For several months after the gunfight in which these two members of the San Diego police force were wounded, the pair were out on line-of-duty (LOD) injury. To get themselves back into shape, Pecoraro and Ax went to Lake Chollas for rehabilitation. The officer would throw a floating toy into the lake, and Ax would delight in jumping into the water to retrieve the object and return it to his partner. His human co-worker figured it was a fun way for the K-9 to build up his muscle strength.

One time the pair was there when Pecoraro saw, some distance away, two young children running and playing alongside the bank of the lake. He noted that they were with a young woman and correctly surmised she was their mother. However, Pecoraro was concerned that the mother probably wasn't aware that the sides of the shore dropped off sharply and that if one of the children fell in the water, he could be in serious danger.

Pecoraro's fears were well founded. Hardly a moment after he noticed the three, one of the children tripped and fell in. As Pecoraro ran to their aid, he saw that the mother had instantly dived into the lake, clothes and all, to retrieve her son. The officer hurried on to the small family to see if he could still be of some help, and, grabbing her hand, pulled the woman and child from the water. The mother thanked the officer, and she assured him that, except for their wet clothes, there had been no damage done. Then the woman looked out at the lake and saw that her red slip-on shoes were thirty feet away from the shoreline and rapidly heading to the middle of the substantial-size lake. Clearly relieved that her child was unhurt, she simply commented to the officer that her shoes were gone, adding she would just have to drive home without them.

Pecoraro then asked, Would she like her shoes back? At first she was uncertain what he meant. Did he intend to swim out and get them? No, Pecoraro told her, his K-9, Ax, would do the honors.

Two quick leaps into the lake by Ax, and the woman was all smiles as her shoes were returned, wet but otherwise with no damage done. The pair might have been out on LOD, but that didn't stop them from helping people.

Some months after the lake incident, now fully recuperated and back to work, Pecoraro and Ax had their next brush with death. It was a clear night, and although it was nearly eleven, the temperature was pleasant enough for Pecoraro to work without wearing his jacket. Sergeant Dan Plein, out on patrol along with a local news cameraman as his passenger, reported a possible drive-by shooting. He radioed that he had heard a couple of shots and that he wasn't sure where they had come from. Then a 911 call came in and confirmed that shots had been fired nearby.

Pecoraro called in to the dispatcher, first giving his identification of twenty-nine-forty-two Nora and asked if the dispatcher would like him to respond. She would.

As he headed to the scene, additional information came in over the police frequency. A citizen reported that the officers should be looking for an older, light-colored, mid-sized sedan, occupied solely by the driver. No license plate number had been given by the caller.

The locale where the search was being concentrated was a combination residential and business district. Pecoraro knew the place well and was aware that there was heavy street-gang activity in the area. Each gang had its own territory. Should the member of one gang violate another's turf, then that person was subject to assault or worse. In addition, one of the customs that had sprung up among the gangs—not limited to San Diego by any means—was the drive-by shooting. Sometimes gang members would ride into the area of a rival gang and shoot at people they thought were affiliated with the other faction. It was of no matter to them that they were often wrong. Wholly innocent citizens were frequent victims of their mindless violence.

Pecoraro believed he was responding to the latter situation as he headed for the shooting scene. A moment later the sergeant radioed that he had the suspect vehicle in sight and was now in pursuit. With that Pecoraro went code three, flicking on his lights and siren. In the back of the cruiser Ax excitedly began to bark, as was his habit when his partner raced to the scene of an emergency. The K-9 knew that when he heard the police car's distinctive *whoop whoop* sound, action was at hand.

As Plein chased the fleeing suspect's car, he let the other officer know that it was running without its headlights on in an attempt to elude the police. The sergeant gave a running report on their location and ended up describing the suspect's auto going over an embankment at the end of a cul de sac and the driver jumping out and making his way down a hill to the street below.

By now Pecoraro was thirty seconds from where the vehicle had been abandoned. He heard the sergeant order another patrol car that had responded to the call, driven by Officer Troy Gibson, to head for the street where Plein believed their suspect was headed. Following the sergeant's orders, the officer found himself face to face with the fleeing armed man. As Gibson got out of his cruiser, the escaping suspect opened fire on him from one of the two handguns he was carrying. The officer unholstered his own firearm and returned fire.

From that point on events moved very quickly. Gibson radioed there had been an exchange of gunfire and let everyone know where it had taken place. Pecoraro pulled up thirty feet in front of Gibson's cruiser, unaware exactly where the gunman was hiding. He jumped from the police car and, grabbing hold of Ax by his collar, took his K-9 partner with him. Not only did Pecoraro want absolute control over Ax, but there was fairly heavy traffic on the street and he didn't want the K-9 to get hit by a passing car.

Pecoraro ran up to another officer, Buddy Johnson, who had also just arrived at the scene. Johnson, using a telephone pole as cover, held a twelve-gauge shotgun in his hands, but neither he nor the K-9 officer could see the suspect, who was hiding, crouched down, in thick brush. Angled forty-five degrees away from Pecoraro and Johnson was Gibson, still exchanging rounds with the suspect. Neither Pecoraro nor Johnson were able to see anything of the other shooter except his flashes of gunfire lighting up the center of the heavy brush. Without having a definite target, they felt they had no choice but to hold their fire.

Pecoraro decided to get down on his hands and knees in an attempt to peer into the dense growth. Even that change of position didn't help. Sergeant Plein had only a moment earlier run up to them. Pecoraro turned to him and told the supervisor that he was going to send Ax into the bushes after the suspect.

As was Pecoraro's habit, he called out his warning, in English and Spanish, that he was about to send in the dog. The man cried back in Spanish, "Kill me, kill me!"

Pecoraro gave the command, "Paken," and released Ax's collar. The K-9 dove headlong into the heavy growth. In an instant he was gone from sight. Hardly a second later the suspect began to scream.

Only Gibson was able to see what was happening in the thick vegetation. He called out, "He's biting the suspect's arm!" Gibson, still firing, then yelled out, "The guy's trying to reload!" and quickly added that the dog was being pistol whipped by the man.

Sergeant Plein, believing that too much time had already elapsed during which the wanted man had been permitted to shoot at the police, ordered Johnson, "I want two shotgun blasts into the bush, now!"

Pecoraro started to say, "Let me get my dog back first." The words never had time to leave his lips. Johnson's twelve gauge barked twice, *blam, blam.* Then there was silence. No screaming, no fighting, there was no sound at all coming from inside the bush. Pecoraro's heart sank. He thought, "Everybody in there is dead. I've lost my dog."

Then the bush rustled. Out came Ax, dragging the inanimate body of the suspect along the ground. In stunned silence the officers watched as the K-9 pulled the hundred-sixty-pound dead body out to the sidewalk.

Pecoraro, happy to see his partner was all right, ran up to the dog and called for his K-9 to let go. To his surprise he had to give the order more than once, an unusual event with the well-trained Ax. But Pecoraro could see that, as he put it, "The dog was one angry puppy." The officer then noticed the cuts on the K-9's face where the sharp edges of the man's pistol had dug into his flesh.

Even as Pecoraro held onto his collar, the powerful K-9 pawed at the sidewalk, as if trying to get back at the man. Pecoraro had never before seen his dog so incensed.

The later investigation found that the man had drugs in his body. The whole situation stemmed from an incident where the deceased had earlier, for reasons unknown, fired shots at the occupants of another vehicle. The result of those actions was his own death. Sometimes people do things without considering the consequences of their acts, and then the police wind up having to bring their actions to a halt. Pecoraro wondered who should ultimately be held responsible for the result, the person who initiated the confrontation or the police officers who are called in to end it?

What's That Stupid Dog Think He's Doing?

Sometimes crooks do stupid things and sometimes they do very stupid things. Robbing a bank located next to a police station comes under the latter category.

The town of La Mesa, to the east of San Diego and with a population of around 100,000 souls, has a police department of about seventy-five officers. One warm summer day a team of four men, armed with handguns, decided it would make sense to rob a bank during the busy noon lunch-break time—a bank situated only a hundred feet down from and on the same block as the La Mesa Police Department. To blend in with other citizens and look unobtrusive, each of the robbers wore black clothing topped off with a black hood.

Under the circumstances the robbery went as well as could be expected, fortunately with no loss of life, and the four men fled in a vehicle they had stolen for the job earlier in the day. It is fair to state that only moments after they departed the bank, the police were on their trail. In fact, officers' cruisers began chasing behind the four men's car as soon as it pulled out of the bank's parking lot. The chase was an extensive one, and the robbers ultimately abandoned their car and fled on foot. The location of the $180,000 dollars they had taken from the bank was unknown.

That day Pecoraro had just logged on to his cruiser's mobile data terminal (MDT), a device that looks like a laptop computer with a small television screen attached. It connects the officer to the dispatcher and permits back and forth information transfer without tying up the police frequency.

The dispatcher was aware that Ax had been trained to recover items used in a crime and inquired of the officer if he'd be available for an evidence search. As Pecoraro would explain to anyone asking how such a feat is possible, it is obvious that a K-9 can't distinguish a stolen item from something that hasn't been stolen. The dogs are trained to detect objects that don't belong or that are out of place in an area. For example, when a gun is tossed onto a lawn or under a bush by a fleeing criminal, the odor of the gun, the disrupted soil, and broken blades of grass are distinctive enough for a specially trained K-9 to detect. Should clothing or money be discarded where such objects are not normally found, here, too, the dogs are able to distinguish the anomalous odor and alert their handlers to the possible evidence.

Pecoraro tapped out his acknowledgement on his keyboard and then drove the seven miles to where the robbers' car had been abandoned. A La Mesa sergeant met him and briefed the San Diego officer on what had taken place. Pecoraro could see from the attractive homes that the neighborhood where Ax was to search was clearly upper middle class. The sergeant assured Pecoraro that the suspects had escaped the police pursuit and were long gone. However, the La Mesa Police Department could use some help in finding the missing loot.

Pecoraro called his K-9 partner from the cruiser and gave Ax the German command to find, "Such" (pronounced *suk*). The officer directed the dog to the top of the building lot they were standing closest to. Since its sides and front yard were covered with a heavy growth of pickle weed, a type of ivy, he reasoned that objects could easily lie hidden from view under the heavy growth. Ax headed for the crest of the lot and then began to work his way down.

La Mesa officers standing on the roadway below looked on with puzzled expressions. A couple of them called out, "What are you doing?" their tone of voice all but accusing Pecoraro of being an imbecile.

Pecoraro patiently explained that he was having Ax sweep

the area to see if he hit on anything. His words had hardly been uttered when Ax lay down, alerting his partner that he had located some object that shouldn't be there. One of the officers asked, "Why is he doing that? Is he tired?"

In his best I'll-try-to-explain-but-you'll-have-to-promise-to-listen-real-hard voice, Pecoraro responded that, no, Ax wasn't tired, he was doing what he was supposed to do when he found something. The officer made his way up the steep slippery slope and stooped down alongside the K-9. Next to the dog was a roll of quarters, part of the stolen bank money.

Pecoraro told Ax to continue the search. The K-9 went out a few more feet and alerted to another roll of quarters, this one split open. By now the La Mesa officers were closely watching the K-9 work, and no more wisecracks came from the audience.

Ax stopped for a few more quarters, and Pecoraro realized they could be out there finding pieces of silver for the next two days on that hill. He told the La Mesa officers to get a metal detector for the rest of the loose change and pulled his K-9 from the area, sending him to search a different path that he knew from his earlier briefing the robbers had taken.

Walking up a steep driveway, Ax, now on a lead, jumped up and placed his front paws on the top of a three-foot white stucco retaining wall. Pecoraro saw that his K-9 was interested in something on the other side. Peering over the wall, at first all the officer noted was that there was a ten-foot drop to the ground, and he was glad Ax hadn't leapt over the wall. Pecoraro then saw the dirty white pillowcase tangled in the brush. At first he thought that perhaps it contained personal belongings from some homeless person who might frequent the area.

Pecoraro told Ax to lie down, then reached over the wall and pulled open the mouth of the pillowcase. Inside were lots of green bills. He pulled his hand back and called out to the La Mesa officers below that Ax had found the money.

The total amount they counted in that sack came to $180,000, the amount stolen from the bank.

With that the La Mesa officers and detectives decided

they had found what they needed. They thanked the San Diego officer and took the money. Some days later Pecoraro received a letter of thanks for the work he and Ax had done.

Pecoraro was glad to have been of assistance and pleased that he and Ax had been so quick in finding what the other agency had been looking for. He figures that the next time a San Diego K-9 is called in to help in La Mesa, the officers will probably be just a bit less skeptical about what a trained K-9 and his handler can accomplish.

K-9s Flic and Iwo
with Police Officer Ken Fortier

Dog Stabbed

K-9 Officer Ken Fortier's partner, Flic, is a seventy-five-pound Belgian Malinois. This breed looks similar to the German shepherd but has a smaller and somewhat differently shaped head. These animals are known to be assertive and bold, although Fortier's description of Flic was that he's known around work and home as a big softy, who particularly enjoys roughhousing with Fortier's five-year-old son.

His canine partner loves to play and especially likes to toy with the orange traffic cones that lie strewn about the K-9 training field. If permitted to run loose, he enjoys grabbing one of the cones and chasing around the field with it in his mouth. He's even taught one of the other K-9s the same trick.

When Fortier first came into contact with Flic, the handler that introduced them explained that the name was French, a somewhat negative slang term for police officer. The handler thought that the officer might want it changed but Fortier said no, it would do just fine. Flic, now with several years on the street, is a veteran of the force and has the distinction of also having acquired a street name, just like a gang member. Fortier once overheard a couple of Hispanic gang members refer to his dog as *patas blancas,* or white paws, and the name has stuck with other members of the K-9 unit.

On one particular day shift, when Fortier was acting supervisor, he and Flic were in the area of Balboa Park when some patrol officers tried to deal with a derelict urinating on the side of a local store. The man turned on the officers and, brandishing a large knife, told them if he wasn't left alone he'd kill them. He then moved away from the officers, pushing a shopping cart loaded with his stuff.

Much later Fortier and the other officers discovered that the man had been out of a mental hospital for several weeks, after spending the previous ten years under psychiatric care. The reason he'd been held was that he had once stabbed a doctor several times, a physician who had attempted to treat him in a hospital emergency room. The explanation he gave was that the doctor had tried to cut off his penis.

Ten years later, when the case came up for review, the doctor was not available to testify. So based on the fact that it was now impossible to determine whether or not the physician had, ten years earlier, actually attempted to cut off the man's penis, the patient was released. It turned out to be an unwise decision.

For the past several weeks since he'd been discharged, the man had lived near the area where the officers found him. During this time he'd harassed the employees of local businesses. It was when he defecated on the hood of one of their cars that they decided to call the police.

Two patrol cars with three officers responded, and when threatened by the derelict, ordered the disturbed man to drop his knife. Upon his refusal they radioed dispatch that they had a "Four-fifteen, a man is refusing to drop a knife," and asked for K-9.

Less than a minute after getting the call Fortier was on the scene. Normally there would be time for him to be briefed before going into action. But in this case when he arrived, he saw the subject of the call screaming and rambling incoherently. Fortier could clearly see the knife in the man's hand and knew what he had to do.

The officer took Flic from the car, holding on to his collar. He saw that the K-9 had spotted the subject and had locked on to the man with his eyes. Flic, having been trained in France, had been taught to charge for a target's legs. In this case Fortier knew that would put his K-9 at a big disadvantage.

There were several officers between Fortier, Flic, and the subject. Fortier ran past them while continuing to hold on to his dog. Once beyond the last officer, seeing that the man had his back to the K-9, he gave the K-9 the bite command and released his collar.

The subject saw the dog coming just as Flic was let go and placed himself in a defensive crouch, the knife in his right hand. The K-9 lunged, hitting the man in the leg and knocking him on his back. Fortier saw the subject's right arm come up and then come down, again and again, the silver blade of the knife seemingly disappearing into Flic's back, the crazed man screaming all the while.

Fortier ran up to the pair. Unable to get too close because of the flailing blade, his first instinct was to do whatever was necessary to protect his dog. But he knew that there was no legal justification for him to use deadly physical force to shoot the suspect slashing at the K-9. Instead, Fortier decided to call Flic back before the K-9 was stabbed. Once the K-9 returned to Fortier, the man with the knife got up and began to run. Fortier once more commanded his dog to attack. The man, now cornered between a building and a ten-foot brick wall, was hit in the leg by Flic. Fortier watched as the crazed man reached down and grabbed the dog by the head and pulled him off. Flic then re-bit him on the left arm. At that the derelict raised the knife and Fortier clearly saw the blade thrust between Flic's shoulder blades. This time the steel found its mark. The K-9, having never before been stabbed and unsure what had happened, looked over at Fortier with a clearly confused expression on his face. It was obvious to Fortier that the K-9 was thinking that for some reason his partner had done that. Fortier, now sure that a police dog wouldn't be able to bring this matter to a conclusion successfully and fearful for Flic's well-being, called his partner back.

The subject was only twenty feet away from Fortier when he said, "I'm no longer a member of this earth." The next instant he charged at Fortier and the other officers. Fortier opened fire with his pistol as did the others and the man collapsed, dead.

While the other two officers dealt with the deceased, Fortier checked on Flic. Patting his K-9, he didn't see any wounds at first. The officer thought that perhaps the blade hadn't penetrated the dog's thick coat. When he took his hand away, however, it was covered with blood.

Fortier took a closer look at Flic and saw that the dog was breathing hard, his eyes wide, and he was clearly not himself. On closer examination the officer found that there were three deep stab wounds between Flic's shoulder blades.

Fortier had a serious problem. He'd just shot and killed a man. He couldn't leave the shooting scene. But if something wasn't done quickly for Flic, the dog would certainly die. He got on the police frequency, contacted the dispatcher, and told him to have Frank Pecoraro respond, code three.

When Pecoraro arrived a few minutes later he was unaware why he was needed, so when he jumped from his cruiser he had his K-9 with him. Fortier quickly explained the situation. Pecoraro put Flic in Fortier's police car and took him over to the Main Street Small Animal Hospital.

At the hospital the doctors quickly got to work on the police dog. Although one of the wounds went in three inches, the blade had fortunately missed all the vital organs. The K-9 was out with a line-of-duty injury for only three weeks.

Fortier doesn't claim to possess any special psychiatric knowledge. But in considering the whole affair, he has to wonder what the people who released the now dead mental patient had been thinking when they let go from their care an obviously disturbed individual, free to roam the streets, with no provision for supervision or care.

Iwo and the Cop Killer

Before Flic, Fortier had been partnered with Iwo *(Ivo)*. Unlike Flic, Iwo had the reputation of being a tough, no-nonsense working police dog. In fact, the two had been paired up when Iwo and his first owner clashed. According to Fortier, the dog wouldn't obey the officer initially assigned to him. As with virtually all police working dogs, Iwo was a dominant alpha male and his first partner was a woman officer. He simply would not listen to her. At the time Fortier had been assigned what the unit referred to as a push-button dog, meaning the K-9 would do exactly as ordered by its handler. A trade was made and Iwo and Fortier—after the officer and Iwo came to an understanding—became a working team.

K-9 officers, because they need to transport their dogs back and forth from work, take their cruisers home with them after their shifts. One morning, around five-thirty, Fortier and Iwo were headed in to their office when the radio came alive with the emergency call, "Eleven ninety-nine, officer down."

The morning fog was like pea soup, and Fortier drove as fast as he dared to the Paradise Valley Road and Meadow Brook intersection, to the apartment complex where the call had come from.

It took the officer fifteen minutes to get to the scene. Since it was a training day, Fortier was dressed only in blue jeans and casual civilian clothes. He did have his 9mm service handgun and other leather gear in his cruiser. Once at the scene he found some other officers and they told him the story. Two officers had gone to a report of a domestic dispute at the apartment complex. The woman complainant had given the officers a description of her husband but had not mentioned that the man possessed firearms. Shortly after the officers left her apartment, they spotted the man's vehicle and pulled it over with their cruiser. When the passenger officer, suspecting nothing but a simple domestic dispute situation, got out of the police car, the husband opened fire. The officer was killed. His partner opened fire on the fleeing man, who disappeared into the thick fog.

Within a relatively few minutes of the shooting, numerous officers had arrived to assist in looking for the killer. Normally such a search has only a single supervisor. In this case there were bosses from patrol, K-9, and SWAT on hand. Fortier thought that might be too much of a good thing, since no one would be able to take full command of the situation.

Fortier put on his full leather duty-rig and his bullet-resistant vest over his T-shirt. One K-9 was assigned to each team of five SWAT members. A good perimeter had been put in place around the area, and it was decided that each apartment in the complex—there were over one hundred—would be searched.

Fortier thought it would be productive to use K-9s to search the area around the building, but he was on the bottom of the decision-making food chain. The apartments were searched until well into the afternoon.

At about five o'clock the K-9 handlers and their charges were all taking a break in the complex's recreation room, now a temporary command post. Word had come down that the suspect had probably gone to relatives in Los Angeles. The officers were now just waiting to be released to go home, as the search was being called off.

A neighborhood woman called in to the police dispatcher and reported that she had seen someone in her backyard, which abutted the apartment complex parking lot. She claimed the man had jumped a fence and was between that fence and the lot's (there was a four-foot gap between the two). The call was one of over fifty received that day, but it had to be checked out. All the SWAT officers had their heavy gear off and everyone was tired, having been working since six in the morning. A sergeant came over to the seated K-9 officers and asked Fortier and two other dog handlers to go out to the parking lot and take a look before they went home.

Fortier and Ben Harris, who had Boomer, and Rick Widner, with K-9 Beno (not the same Beno as partnered with Gene Oliver), got up and walked out of the centrally located recreation center and headed for the parking lot. Another officer, normally assigned to motorcycle duty but for that day involved in the search, also went with the group.

The fence that the men came upon ran the length of the lot. Alongside was a row of parked cars, their tires butted up to flat concrete slabs, their front ends just a few feet away from the wood structure. At one part of the fence a few sections of wood were missing, making a hole large enough for a person to enter and exit. Peeking inside the opening the officers could see the gap between fences was filled with a good deal of debris and unkempt foliage, certainly a place where someone could hide. It was decided that Widner and Beno would go through to explore the other side while Harris and Boomer stayed to guard the parking lot entrance. Fortier and Iwo, along with the motorcycle officer, would walk the parking lot side of the fence, opposite Widner and Beno, in case whoever might be there tried to jump over the fence.

As Widner and Beno made their way along the inside of the fence, Beno began to growl at the wood structure. Seeing Fortier and his K-9 through cracks in the wood partition and thinking his K-9 was alerting to the officer and his dog, Widner called Beno off and ordered him to continue searching. While the K-9 teams were making their way down the line of cars, the motorcycle officer checked the space between the parked autos and the fence in case someone should be crouched there. At the place where Beno alerted, the officer attempted to look over the nearest car's hood, but its well-polished white surface caused the sun to glare in the man's eyes, blinding him. Unable to see, the officer simply moved on.

At the end of the fence line there was another gaping hole, and Widner and Beno stepped back into the lot. At that point, all the K-9 handlers and the motorcycle officer came together to discuss what, if anything, to do next.

The news media had been on the scene since the early morning hours, and they had been off to the side watching and videotaping this latest search attempt. One of the members of the press was approached by a local gang member, who commented, "Weren't those cops dumb? The guy they were looking for was behind the white car," indicating the vehicle Beno had alerted on only a minute earlier. He added that the man had been pointing a gun at the officers the whole time.

One of the cameramen, who didn't know the precise location the young man was talking about, looked over the row of cars and saw the suspect, with a pistol in his hand, its muzzle directed at the group of officers. He shouted, "Look out! The guy's in front of the white car!"

As soon as the cameraman yelled that warning, the suspect's .45 barked. The officers took what cover they could. Fortier, barely able to see the man, remembered a trick he'd been taught at the police academy. It seemed illogical, but by firing at the ground in front of a vehicle, he could make the bullets hit the hard surface and then race along near the ground, go under the car, and hit whoever was on the other side. Both he and Harris tried the tactic. It worked as advertised. The man with the .45 took numerous hits in his legs and went down.

A final round was heard from the .45, then all was calm.

Unsure what had happened, the officers decided to send a dog in. Widner ordered Beno to charge the suspect. The dog ran over and attacked the man, then, feeling no resistance, attempted to drag him from his hiding place. The K-9 was prevented from successfully doing this because the suspect's arm had caught around one of the cement tire bumpers. Officers ran up to the pair. The man was lying on his back, the .45 still in his hand. Because the dog was yanking on the body it gave the appearance of live motion. An officer ran up and kicked the gun from the suspect's hand, then handcuffed him. It took but a moment for the officers to see that their haste hadn't been necessary. The last round they'd heard from his .45 had been when the man had fired a bullet into his own head.

The K-9s had been on the scene for nearly twelve hours searching the apartments in the complex. The suspect had to have been hiding out in the general area during that period of time, since the perimeter securing the neighborhood had remained in place. The suspect couldn't escape, but then nobody was looking for him in the right spot. Had that woman not reported seeing the man when she did, the entire operation would have been shut down in only a few minutes and the shooter could have walked safely from the area.

Fate, chance, and circumstances. We don't often know how the three intermix to conspire for or against us.

Another Drive-By Shooting

Regardless of how much people pretend to be civilized and sophisticated creatures, police officers often take a different view of humanity, as they get to observe just how very strong the tribal animal in us cries out for release. Gang drive-by shootings are just one example of how the interaction of some members of our species brings them down to an almost primal level.

Two weeks before Fortier and Flic became involved in this situation, a brother of one gang member had been killed in just such an act of violence. The surviving sibling felt that it was necessary for blood to be spilled by a member of the other group. That he had no idea who had shot his brother, and that he was perfectly willing to simply shoot whoever had the bad luck to be opposite the muzzle of his gun when he pulled the trigger, did not seem at all illogical to the man.

On the day of the shooting, the brother of the first victim, along with another of his gang members, had driven down from Los Angeles to avenge the death. So while Fortier was chatting with a fellow K-9 officer, and as Flic frolicked about the open area opposite the K-9 unit's office, those two young men were out in San Diego determined to commit a murder.

That night, as was the standard practice, Fortier had been assigned to work one division while the other K-9 officer had been assigned an adjacent one. The second officer received a radio call assigning him to a drive-by shooting. He asked Fortier to give him a hand, which Fortier naturally agreed to do.

From the description that had been given of the assailants—shaved heads, long shirts worn outside and down to the knees of their baggy pants—the officers knew they wore the uniform of some gang. Gang members saw nothing incongruous in the fact that their clothing closely resembled clown's apparel.

The second victim of the shooting had been sitting in the passenger seat of a car. Unlike the man who had been in the driver's seat, who had been hit at point-blank range with the blast from a twelve-gauge shotgun, he had survived and gave police a description of the two assailants and the direction in which they fled, apparently on foot to the south.

The two K-9 officers headed for the shooting scene in their separate cruisers. The closer they got to the destination, the more police cars Fortier heard reporting their involvement in the search for the shooters. It was clear to him that the area would soon be saturated by officers, and it was also equally obvious to the experienced officer that the two shooters would be long gone from where everyone was now headed. Fortier decided it would be more productive for him to cover an area a half mile to the south of the shooting and slowly work his way back to where it had taken place.

When he got near where he wanted to begin looking, he pulled into the first major intersection, at Market Street. No sooner had he done so than he spotted two young men, dressed in the distinctive clothing described earlier by the police dispatcher. The pair were walking nonchalantly down the street, away from the officer's direction and across the nearby freeway overpass. Fortier saw that neither of the two was carrying anything in his hands.

The officer swung his cruiser in their direction and drove toward them. He wasn't even sure these were the right two individuals and held off reporting over the radio what he was up to. Once his cruiser got closer to the young men, one of them turned and saw the police car. He hit his partner on the shoulder to warn him and in a flash both took off running. At that point Fortier decided they were certainly worth checking out.

Because they were on the freeway overpass, the young men were locked into running in one direction. Fortier gunned his motor and pulled up on the sidewalk in front of the pair, blocking their exit, to stop them from scattering in the residential area on the other side of the overpass. He remained uncertain whether these were the men he sought, since he still hadn't seen a gun.

Fortier got out of the cruiser with his gun drawn and ordered the two to stop. The man nearest him reached behind his back and removed a pump-action twelve-gauge shotgun from its hiding place inside his baggy pants.

Fortier was about to open fire when two area youngsters, having seen the K-9 car—kids love the dogs—raced up from the rear of the suspect and headed for the cruiser. The officer held his fire.

Fortunately for both the children and the officer, the suspect didn't shoot but dropped his gun on the ground. The kids watching on the sidelines then left from the scene. Fortier had not had a chance to give a call over the police radio, which, at any rate, wasn't even switched to the correct frequency for the district he was in. The killer's shotgun still lay only a few feet from the man's hands. Now, with both suspects only yards from him, he didn't dare turn his back. Fortier pondered his next move. The pair chose that moment to run, each fleeing in a different direction.

Fortier popped open Flic's cruiser door, and, as the officer hoped, his K-9 lunged straight for the nearest running man. In an instant the dog was on him and the two began to battle. Fortier decided to let his partner handle that job while he ran after the second suspect. In short order he was gaining on his man. He heard the first man scream as Flic and he rolled around on the ground in the pickle weed. The image of the suspect taking out a gun and shooting Flic flashed in Fortier's mind. He broke off his pursuit and ran back to assist his partner.

While Fortier was dealing with his situation, a San Diego police helicopter (referred to as Able by officers) was overhead and had been watching the whole series of events unfold, relaying the information over the police frequency. In addition, one of the helicopter's pilots, Teresa Clark, who at that moment was acting as observer, called out to the second fleeing suspect over the helicopter public address system, "Where do you think you're going? Do you want to get bit just like your friend did? You get back there right now and put your hands up before you get hurt!"

Fortier, not fully aware of what was taking place overhead, had just finished cuffing the suspect nabbed by Flic when the second man arrived, hands in the air. Without a word he lay down on the ground!

After putting handcuffs on the second man Fortier decided it was time to switch his radio over to the correct frequency and let everybody know that both suspects were in custody and that he and Flic were okay.

After the dust had settled, Fortier was thankful for both Able's and Flic's help. It would be nice if all his arrests went down this smoothly.

SWAT Mission

Sometimes things aren't what they seem. Fortier's Sunday into Monday midnight shift had just begun, but it would end later than he expected. The situation started when patrol officers responded to a four-fifteen, noise complaint. Neighbors had called in to protest about the person living above them, who had been making excessive noise. They stated that the individual had been banging on the floor and had created a great deal of tumult in his apartment.

The officers knocked on the door of the person being complained about—they knew he was at home—but received no response. The resident soon came out on the balcony, a butcher knife in his hand, and, looking down on the officers on the street below, told them that if they tried to come into his home, he'd kill them.

The officers retreated and called for assistance.

Fortier and K-9 Officer Pete Mills were called by dispatch

to go to the scene. When the pair arrived they found that a sergeant was already there. As the officers stood around everyone present watched as the man in the top apartment stood by his window and barked like a dog. After tiring of that exercise he loudly sniffed the air, as if trying to get the officers' scent.

The sergeant explained that the neighbors had told him and the other officers that the man now baying at the moon had informed people that he was a karate expert, he had been a Navy SEAL, and he was a weapons expert.

The question that hung over the group was, what to do next?

Mills and Fortier made a suggestion to the sergeant. If the supervisor and the other officers would distract the man above, then the two K-9 officers would kick in the apartment door, and, if the gentleman declined to drop his knife and surrender, would have one of their dogs take him down.

The sergeant thought about their proposal for a moment, then decided he didn't want to provoke the man any more than he had to. He opted to call in a code ten, a SWAT alert. Now, supervisors do have a lot of responsibility. It's their watch and should anything go wrong they are held accountable by their department as well as being both civilly, and not infrequently, criminally liable for their decisions. Nevertheless, Fortier began to think that the little situation they now faced was about to turn into a three-ring circus.

When a code ten is radioed in, all police activity comes to a halt. Once the call for the SWAT assistance is made, officers at the scene simply maintain the status quo while the specialized troops suit up and get to them. Then the SWAT commander gets to the scene, determines what has to be done, formulates a plan, and puts it into action. Thus officers knew that when a code ten was invoked, whatever the initial problem was, everyone involved could be sure that their world would now go into slow motion.

SWAT members arrived by midnight. It wasn't until one in the morning that their commander, a lieutenant, got there. At that point diagrams of the apartment were procured. The lieutenant then spoke with other residents of the complex to gather as much information about the situation as he could.

Fortier and Flic, along with a patrol officer, wound up being assigned to the landing near the man's door, just in case he tried to get out. They watched as the resident alternated between barking from his window and scurrying back inside the apartment, leaving both officers wondering what he was up to.

During the evening Fortier had noticed, while the man was dancing around the apartment going through what were supposedly martial-arts exercises, that he had a flabby midsection. He was no Navy SEAL. In Fortier's mind, the guy inside was pulling everyone's chain. He was just after his fifteen minutes of fame.

Eventually the sergeant came up to Fortier and asked him to come downstairs to speak with the lieutenant. The SWAT commander explained that a plan had been formulated. What would Fortier think if they took down the door to the apartment and the K-9 officer gave a warning to the suspect to surrender and drop his knife. If he refused, the K-9 officer would order his dog to attack the man.

This plan sounded familiar to Fortier. He simply answered, "Sure."

A SWAT member was to throw a flash-bang grenade (very loud, very bright, and very distracting, but unless you're sitting on top of it, nonlethal) through the front window. This was supposed to draw the man's attention in that direction, perhaps even bring him to the window.

Other SWAT members, armed with a 9mm carbine and a twelve-gauge shotgun and wearing heavy bullet-resistant vests and Kevlar helmets, would be responsible for opening the door for Fortier. The K-9 officer did wonder why, if all those guys had all that great equipment, he'd be the first officer through the door. On second thought, it would be Flic going in first, and he had nothing on.

Life, clearly, is not fair.

Fortier heard the flash-bang go off, and with a tap of the "key to the city" (the SWAT team's battering ram), the apartment door flew open. Fortier stepped into the room.

The occupant had gone to the window just as planned, but now he turned to face the K-9 officer, the knife still in his hand. Without waiting for a formal introduction, Fortier ordered Flic to take the guy down. The K-9 jumped over a couch and as he leaped through the air Fortier saw the man's eyes grow to the size of silver dollars; both his mouth and the knife dropped at the same time.

It was just as Fortier thought, the man was no trained fighter. Flic hit him hard in the shoulder, driving him to the floor. The man began to scream in terror, so Fortier called off the dog, cuffed the wanna-be Ninja, and waved good-bye as he was headed out the door to the mental hospital.

Fortier glanced at his watch. It was four in the morning.

Well, he figured, at least the people downstairs would be able to get a couple of hours' sleep before heading off to work.

K-9s Maic, Fargo, and Eros with Police Officer Peter Mills

Man with a Knife

K-9 Officer Pete Mills had positioned his cruiser so the window of Officer John Tefft's police vehicle stood opposite his own. Maic (pronounced "Mike"), Mills' dog, lay quietly in the rear of the car. It had only been a few hours since their rather quiet midnight shift had begun, and the two men, police academy buddies, chatted about department gossip and traded rumors both knew deep down inside to be nonsense. But it was after midnight, the October evening was pleasantly warm, and nothing much else was going on at the moment.

In the middle of their conversation Tefft received an assignment, a four-fifteen, disturbance call. The dispatcher informed him that a man had destroyed some property and had threatened his roommate. Mills offered to back up his friend on the call. He knew that with any domestic dispute, what sounds at first like a fairly routine matter could easily escalate into a problem.

The two police cruisers took only a few minutes to arrive at the address. A number of two-story apartment buildings lay around a series of parking lots. The officers parked a couple of houses away from the place they had been sent to, a basic safety precaution, and with Tefft in the lead walked to the front of the building complex. For the moment Maic stayed in the cruiser.

Outside the building the two men were met by the apartment house manager. The man was visibly upset over the violence that had taken place there. Windows had been broken and the suspect had threatened to kill his roommate. Shortly after the officers' meeting with the manager, the roommate appeared. It was obvious by the marks and scratches on his face that he and his former friend had been in a battle.

While the four men were discussing the situation, from inside the victim's ground-floor apartment the stereo blared out a cacophony of music. Mills found that he nearly had to shout to be heard over the din.

The two officers decided they should first try to convince the person inside the apartment to come out. Mills walked over to one of the broken windows and shouted a warning, giving the man inside a chance to surrender. There was no response. Mills and Tefft then banged on the door. Again, there was no answer to their hail.

While Tefft waited by the apartment, Mills stepped out into the parking lot. He moved his hand to the rectangular plastic electronic device on his belt (it looked like a garage-door opener), pushed on a button, and called out a command to Maic at the same time. The K-9 jumped from the remotely opened door of the police cruiser and ran over to Mills. The officer put a lead on the dog and went back to Tefft.

Now there was nothing left to do but go in for the suspect. At the request of the officers, the manager unlocked the apartment's front door.

Mills, with Maic's lead in his hand, pushed the door to the wall, and he and the dog went in to search for the suspect. Inside, all the lights had been switched off. Except for the illumination that splashed in from the hallway and their flashlights, the apartment was pitch black. As they entered, the stereo blasted at the two officers with such force that it brought them to the edge of mental confusion. To Mills it seemed more like a scene from a grade-B thriller movie than a routine disturbance call. The officers moved forward carefully, staying behind the K-9. Mills, using his flashlight, saw that they were in a small living room. Tefft cautiously stepped over to the stereo and turned it off. The silence that followed was profound; Mills felt as if a great weight had been lifted from his shoulders. They found a light switch and it flicked on.

Without the deafening roar of the stereo, Mills decided to again announce the K-9 warning. He had a bad feeling about the dead silence that followed.

The three team members worked their way past the kitchen and down a narrow hall. Up ahead on the left was a bathroom; two bedrooms lay just beyond, the doors of which were closed. Good police tactics required that all the rooms be cleared.

Tefft took the bedrooms, Mills and Maic the bathroom.

Mills found that the bathroom was also without light. Using his flashlight to search the small room, he saw the shower curtain move. He called out a warning to Tefft, then shouted a command to the suspect, "Police department. Come out or I'll send in the dog." In his left hand the officer held both the dog's lead and his flashlight. In his right he held a Smith and Wesson .38 Special revolver.

The curtain parted and a man of average size stepped out. Mills sensed by the deliberate way he moved that he was under the influence of either alcohol or drugs. The officer shone his light on the man's hands and was relieved to see that they were empty. As the suspect started toward Mills, he passed the sink. On its surface lay a butcher knife that Mills had not noticed because of the poor light. The man reached out and picked up the knife, then put the tip of its point to his own chest.

People think that guns are the major safety concern most officers have on the street. That's not necessarily so. Experienced policemen, who witness dozens of human beings having been sliced, diced, and chopped up during their careers, frequently learn to fear blades more than bullets. Officers know that most criminals are lousy shots anyway and their firearms are frequently in poor condition. But a knife never needs reloading, and when a bad guy is close enough to use it, and for whatever emotional or psychological reason doesn't give a damn about the consequences, that's real danger.

Mills faced a serious dilemma. If the suspect wanted to lunge at him with the big knife, the officer was definitely in the kill zone. Was the man suicidal? Was this some sort of a ruse to bring him closer to the officer? Did the man even know what his own intentions were? In any case, close quarters made the situation terribly dangerous for the officer.

The hallway was only wide enough for Mills and Maic to back out toward the living room. Tefft was behind the suspect, just inside a bedroom. If the officers needed to fire their weapons, they threatened to shoot each other.

With the suspect still holding the blade to his chest, Mills slowly worked his way backward into the living room. He realized that the man could not be permitted to exit the apartment. He had threatened to kill his roommate and had demonstrated his propensity for violence.

The man had never uttered a sound from the moment he had gotten out of the bathtub and begun moving in Mills' direction. This only reinforced the officer's concern over the mental stability of the subject.

In desperation Mills called out, "Drop the knife or I'll shoot!" repeating the warning several times. The man didn't respond and the distance between them kept closing. By the time the man was three feet from Mills, the officer's problem had become a major one. Unable to take his eyes off the man, Mills knew there were obstacles somewhere behind him. As he stepped back one more time, with Maic to his rear, the backs of his legs hit the arm of a couch. Just as if someone had playfully tapped him behind his knees, Mills fell backward onto the couch and Maic bumped into the coffee table next to him. Mills was unable to order Maic to lunge because he was too close to the suspect. For a moment Mills felt like a turtle on its back, its belly exposed to some predator.

The man continued to move alongside Mills' prostrate body. The officer dropped Maic's lead and his flashlight at the same time and partially regained his balance. Seeing the suspect almost at the door, the officer took a chance and with his left hand pulled the man back from the apartment's exit.

The knife-wielding man was pulled backward, but Mills was now between the suspect and the door. The man moved toward Mills, taking the point of the blade from his chest and raising the knife above his head.

On many occasions Mills had seen what a butcher knife could do to the soft tissue of a human being. He wasn't about to be the victim of such bloody carnage. The officer fired two quick rounds from his .38. The man was slammed back against a closet door and then collapsed to the floor. Without a word from Mills, Maic automatically sprang to the attack. But, before the K-9 completed his lunge, Mills called the dog back.

No police officer enjoys having to use deadly force. In fiction, such a scene would end a movie or television show, but for the officer who, in the real world, has to pull the trigger on another human being, it is just the beginning. What lay ahead for Mills were endless hours of questioning by investigating officers and second-guessing by members of the district attorney's office.

Why didn't you—? Why couldn't you—? How come you didn't call—?

Most of the people who ask these questions have never had to face a man holding a butcher knife raised high above his head, ready to plunge it to the hilt into their chest. When cops are killed in the line of duty, they're heroes. It's when they choose to live that society likes to pillory them.

But in this case it was a good shooting, a clean shooting. No problem.

And best of all, Mills, Tefft, and Maic got to go home that night in one piece.

Score One for a K-9

Mills and Officer Pete Madrid had just finished eating their late-evening dinner at a local Mexican restaurant. Still savoring his meal of a carne asado burrito, Mills got back into his cruiser with the feeling that all was well with the world.

Madrid had just returned to his cruiser when he received a job from the dispatcher. He was to check out a hang-up 911 call. When an emergency 911 telephone call is made to a police agency, the address from which the call was made shows up on the dispatcher's console screen. If no one is on the other end of that call, a police car is automatically sent to find out why. Most of the time it's a mistake or a child has hit the wrong buttons. Sometimes there's a more serious reason why no one is on the other end of the line.

Mills offered to back up Madrid. As the two cruisers headed toward the hang-up call address, the dispatcher informed the officers that a report of a domestic dispute had now come in from the same location as the initial 911 call. The complainant had stated that her girlfriend had tried to kick in her apartment door and had made threats. The dispatcher gave the officers a description of the other woman and added that she was wearing a black leather jacket.

The cruisers soon approached the two-story apartment complex where the problem was reported to have been taking place. As the officers passed a Union 76 gas station Mills noted a young woman inside a telephone booth. She was wearing a black leather jacket.

At about that time another 911 call came in, this one from the manager of that same Union 76 gas station. He reported that, only minutes earlier, a woman in a black leather jacket had fired shots at a man who had tried to use the telephone booth.

Mills was not happy with the way the situation was unfolding. He and Madrid had just passed the station. They were at a tactical disadvantage if the presumably armed woman decided to open fire on them. Their two vehicles pulled over simultaneously, and Mills saw Madrid get out of his police car. The woman had by this time started to run in the direction of the apartment complex, but the two cruisers were between her and the building, and she was closing in on the officers fast.

Up to this time Mills had not seen a gun on the subject. Now, with his eyes focused on the woman, he saw her attempting to free a small, semiautomatic pistol from her waistband. Madrid must have seen the same thing, as both officers yelled warnings to each other at the same moment, "Gun!"

The woman kept on running in their direction. Mills mashed down on the button of the remote car-door-opener fastened to his belt, letting his K-9, Fargo, loose. At nearly the same moment he called out the bite command, "Fass" (German for grab). As Mills came up to Madrid's right side he heard his partner yell out to the woman, "Stop, police!" She replied, "Fuck you, pig!" and an instant later Mills heard the popping sounds of gunfire coming from the suspect's pistol. A second later Madrid opened up with his 9mm. Mills attempted to do the same, but Madrid still stood between him and the shooter. As Mills came up on Madrid's right side, he saw that one of his partner's bullets had found its mark. Hit in the leg, the woman fell to the ground. She was now on her back, but the gun remained in her hand. She aimed at the two men.

While the two officers engaged in a gun battle with the woman, Fargo sprang forward and lunged at the fallen shooter. The dog was almost on her when the woman pointed her pistol at Fargo. With her extended arm now his bite target, the K-9 grabbed her gun arm. At the same moment Fargo attacked, a muffled shot sounded from the woman's gun. The pistol dropped to the sidewalk, but Fargo continued to shake the woman's arm. Mills could see, though, that the dog wasn't really attacking her. It was almost as if the animal was confused about what was going on. Fargo soon let go of the arm and sniffed the woman's head. At that point the K-9 officer was sure that something was wrong.

Madrid, equally confused by the situation, called over to Mills to check Fargo, fearing that the dog had been struck by a bullet. The two officers, with their hand guns pointed at the suspect, carefully approached the scene. Fargo was sitting down near the prostrate body of the woman, barking, not certain what to do next. The woman's blue steel pistol lay on the sidewalk nearby.

When they came up to the woman, Mills could see blood on her leg where Madrid's bullet had struck her. She lay so still Mills suspected she had suffered some other injury. Looking more closely, he spotted the bullet hole in her head.

As with all police-related shootings in San Diego, the department's homicide detectives did a thorough investigation of the circumstances surrounding the woman's death. A forensic examination of the bullet lodged in the dead woman's skull showed that it had come from her own .380 caliber pistol, not from the 9mm service weapons of either Mills or Madrid. The shooting team investigators concluded that the woman had died of a self-inflicted gunshot wound to the head. A suicide.

Mills only knew what he saw. If the death was determined to be a suicide, that was okay by him. But he wondered: if Fargo could speak, what would his K-9 have to say about that ruling?

Another Shooting

It was just after midnight. His shift had only an hour remaining, and Mills was inside the police station, finishing up on his paperwork. In the middle of some mundane task he heard a call come in over the police radio reporting a residential robbery in progress. Dropping what he was doing, he immediately left the station and was headed across the parking lot to his cruiser when the voice of an excited police officer called over the radio that he was being shot at. Mills broke into a run for his car. Fargo had already been placed in the rear of the cruiser since earlier that night.

The two-officer unit on the scene continued with their

agitated report. The suspect, after jumping a fence, had been lost from sight. The officers requested that K-9 units respond. Nine K-9 units called in that they were on the way.

By the time Mills arrived, the general location was awash in police cruisers. It was clear to Mills, who was acting sergeant for the shift, that this was too much of a good thing. If he didn't get the situation organized, they'd probably lose the bad guy, or worse.

He ordered the patrol officers to form a perimeter around the area, a neighborhood made up of single-family homes. Then, using only K-9 officers and their dogs, he formed three officer teams, each being made up of a dog and handler, one police officer armed with a handgun, and one with a shotgun. The purpose of using only K-9 handlers wasn't a grandstand act on his part. The members of the unit routinely worked together during intensive training sessions. In addition, these men and women knew how to comport themselves around police service dogs under the very circumstances they would soon be in. It was a prudent and responsible decision on Mills' part.

The teams received their assignments. Mills, heading up his group, was their pistol man. Tom Andrews would handle his K-9, Jim; and Lee Norton had the shotgun. Fargo was going to have to sit this one out in the cruiser.

Mills' idea was to form a ring around the block, where the suspect was probably still hiding. The teams would work their way in to the center of the area, using the dogs to clear their way forward as they went and, they hoped, to find the suspect.

Perhaps it's memories from childhood of the imaginary monsters that lurked under the bed when the sun went down, but when an officer is looking for an armed man at night, shadows seem very, very dark and ominous. The teams slowly inched their way from bush to bush, garden to garden, house to house. There was little talk among them as they moved ahead in the night.

Mills' team found themselves making their way through a deeply overgrown lawn. Suddenly Andrews's dog Jim began to pull. The officer called out, "I have the suspect!"

Mills was on the opposite side of a combination shed and

garage from the spot where Andrews had yelled the warning. He ran around the small building and took up a position of cover against the shed. He could see Andrews down on one knee, holding onto Jim's collar. Lee Norton had his shotgun aimed at a dark mass on the ground by the side of the shed. Mills' eyes followed the barrel of Norton's gun to a spot only a couple of yards from where he stood. In the tall grass, his hands hidden by the vegetation, lay their man.

Mills didn't move. The only part of the officer that was exposed from behind the shed was his gun hand, flashlight, and as little of his face as he had to show.

Andrews was doing all the talking. He called out several times to the suspect, "Show your hands!" The man in the grass replied, "You're going to have to kill me!"

Mills knew this was not a great situation. The officers had cover and better equipment, but nobody knew what the suspect had in the way of firepower or what expertise he possessed on how to use it. And a man who has fired on the police, and who, after being challenged by other armed officers, yells out that they would have to kill him, has to be considered a very dangerous opponent.

For tactical reasons the three-man team had used their flashlights sparingly. But the lights and noise had attracted a lone uniformed officer. To Mills' horror the officer stepped up to a fence only a few feet behind the suspect and asked what was going on. Mills yelled for the officer to get out of there. Not only was the officer taking the team's attention away from the armed suspect, but his presence posed a terrible danger to all the officers concerned, since they would be in a crossfire.

The lone officer either didn't understand or ignored Mills' order to leave. Andrews, realizing that something had to be done soon, pulled out his canister of chemical spray, oleoresin capsicum. He blasted the contents of the can into the suspect's face. Although the chemical is virtually harmless, the stuff burns terribly when it first comes into contact with skin and especially if it gets in the eyes. Mills was startled to see the man twitch but otherwise appear unfazed.

The man started to raise his gun. Even though the other officer still stood opposite them, there was no other option now open to Mills and the other team members. Mills fired nine rounds into the suspect as Norton fired a blast from his twelve-gauge shotgun.

The man stopped moving.

Mills carefully made his way over to the now motionless body. As he came up to the dead man, the mist of residual OC hit him. He had to use all his willpower to ignore the burning sensation on his face as he bent down to take the man's gun from his lifeless hand. Fortunately, no one else had been injured during the shooting. As he did so, the officer reflected on the soon-to-come endless paperwork and probing questions he would have to face. It was part of the job for a busy cop like Mills; maybe someday he'd get used to it.

Anyway, Mills figured the man had been right after all. He wasn't going to be taken alive by the police.

Bomb!

Fargo is a bomb-detection dog. He can sniff out a large menu of explosive substances: dynamite, C-4, detonation cord, TNT, and a dozen other chemicals that are as unpronounceable as they are lethal. The Department of Defense makes up the training guide for these K-9s. To be a certified bomb dog, the K-9 has to be able to find and detect every compound listed in the manual.

A couple of hours into an otherwise normal afternoon shift, Mills was called by the dispatcher. There had been a request for a bomb dog, and he was to head for the job, code three—lights and siren.

The incident scene was twenty miles from where Mills took the call, but as Fargo was the only bomb dog working that particular shift, the dispatcher didn't have any choice but to give him the assignment. The officer found he had to fight his way through heavy midday traffic, even with his lights and siren going. He tried to stay on the freeway and ran along its center or, when necessary, the breakdown lane.

He arrived there as quickly as his racing police cruiser

could carry him. Fortunately his final destination was right off the freeway, in a business and commercial part of San Diego. As he pulled into the area, Mills was impressed by the number of emergency vehicles that lined the streets; there were fire trucks, ambulances, and patrol cars, each with their brightly twinkling rack lights on. Uniformed members of the various public safety units scurried about, and dazed civilians, many from the building Mills was headed for, wandered aimlessly along the street.

Two members of the San Diego fire department's Explosive and Ordnance Detail (EOD) met Mills outside the building where all the commotion was centered. They quickly briefed the officer. A disgruntled employee, recently terminated, had returned to settle the score. He had detonated two explosive devices, probably pipe bombs, and had then made his way up to his office. The twelve-gauge shotgun he had taken with him had been used to kill two people. Mills and Fargo were there because it was thought there were more bombs in the building, and they had to be found before anything else could be done. There was one last thing. The killer had been real slick. The bombs he planted had been set off by radio remote control. Since he had not been captured, he could be anywhere, certainly in radio range of the building, and he was most definitely capable of setting off any other devices he might have secreted within the structure. The EOD men also mentioned that even if the suspect no longer intended to deliberately set off any more bombs, since his devices were rigged to go off by a radio signal, any of the hundred or so cops, firemen, and news reporters running around outside the place with their five-watt portables could inadvertently accomplish the same thing with a stray radio transmission.

Mills nodded, considered the information for a moment, then opened his cruiser door and let Fargo out, hooking him up to his lead. It was time they went to work.

Mills, his K-9 partner, and the two EOD men entered the facility from a rear loading dock. The officer could smell the pungent odor of detonated explosive as they worked their way slowly into the building. They had only gone in a few feet when the team saw an unexploded bomb hidden by a stairway. The small antenna attached to the outside of its pipe casing showed clearly that the killer had indeed used a radio-triggered apparatus to detonate the bombs.

As Mills looked at the device he reflected that there was something morbidly fascinating about a bomb. It was so neutral. There it sat quietly, just a long pipe with a pound or so of chemicals inside and a few cents' worth of copper wire connecting it to the small radio receiver attached to its outside. One moment it hardly mattered, just a few bits of insignificant material. The next instant it could send everyone around it to a man-created hell. So neutral.

The team marked the site and moved on to another floor. As Mills made his way up the stairs it occurred to him that the suspect still had the power to trigger the device below, as well as any others that might still be lying about. But then again, he reflected, there wasn't much that could be done about that now. When they came to the second floor, he did take a moment to pick up a telephone (he certainly wasn't about to use his portable radio) and ask the dispatcher to have the police chopper overhead be on the lookout for a man standing on any of the other nearby building roofs who might be holding some sort of radio-transmitting device.

The structure's second floor was designed as a large modern office area. Cubicles were set up in the wall-free space for the privacy of employees. Other work areas, situated along the outside walls—Mills speculated they were reserved for higher-ranking staff—were separated from the rest of the room by their own glass partitions.

The officer didn't know why the killer was angry with the people in this company, but the first dead body Mills saw showed him just how far the man had been willing to go. One of the glass walls had taken at least one and perhaps more rounds of buckshot. The shooter's weapon of choice, a twelve-gauge shotgun, was capable of spewing out as many as a dozen pistol-ball-size lead pellets each time he pulled the trigger. At close range such rounds were devastatingly lethal. In the movies, after being hit by a blast from such a weapon, cartoonlike cars blow up and people defy the laws of physics as they are propelled twenty feet through the air. This was real carnage. The glass partition had pellet holes from floor to ceiling, shattering the wall and indicating that the shooter must have been firing at a fleeing target. The ounce and a half of lead that had found its mark had badly violated the first victim's body, which lay in the middle of a corridor. Blood had poured out from two dozen wounds. Mills' job was to locate more bombs, but he couldn't help looking at the victim. The man, lying in a reddish-purple pool of spreading blood, had been hit in the head and torso. Obviously, the shooter had wanted the man dead.

The team moved on, searching for bombs.

By one of the office cubicles they found the second dead man. This corpse had been hit once. By the size of the wound it appeared to Mills that the victim had taken the blast at point-blank range. His position within his cubicle made it look as if the man had been trying to use his desk as cover.

No additional explosives were found. The ordnance disposal people now had the problem of getting rid of the one device that had been discovered.

Mills was surprised to find that none of the public safety agencies in San Diego had a bomb-disposal robot. These machines, which have become fairly standard equipment for dealing with infernal devices, are rubber-tracked electric vehicles, guided from a safe distance by remote control. On-board television cameras permit the operator to know where the machine is going, and the machine's mechanical arms can perform delicate operations without endangering people.

The robots cost around $100,000, a lot less than a city would pay in medical bills, if an injured officer survived a close-up bomb blast.

Without such a machine, the EOD techs had to jury-rig a traffic cone so that by manipulating a rope and pulley combination the bomb was scooped inside its pliable plastic body. From there it was dropped into a bomb disposal bucket.

As Mills watched the operation, he decided it didn't take a rocket scientist to figure out that a robot would have been a heck of a lot more suitable to the task. Maybe in next year's budget.

With that bomb gone, Mills and the EOD techs resumed their search. Mills learned later that while he and the others were going through the building, the killer had driven over to the Riverside Sheriff's office and surrendered. Other officers had gone to his home and found a bomb-making factory in the man's garage.

Mills never did find out what drove the killer to do what he did. But, whatever the reason, the officer figured he must have been awfully angry.

Rape Suspect

It was lunchtime the day after Thanksgiving. Mills was just getting ready to eat his turkey sandwich when a call came over the air. A K-9 officer was being dispatched to the Torre Pines State Beach to assist other officers in a search for a rapist. Mills rewrapped his sandwich, stuffed it back in its brown sack, and headed for his cruiser.

The officer knew that Torre Pines is a rough area to search. The beach leads into an area where a series of hilly, undulating ravines branch out for miles. The natural rugged beauty of the place provides hundreds if not thousands of hiding places for a person fleeing the police.

As Mills made his way to the scene, the ongoing radio traffic gave him a picture of the situation he and Fargo would be facing. A lone woman had been sunbathing at a nude section of the park, Black's Beach. A transient (later discovered to have a history as a sexual predator), seeing the single female, had decided to take advantage of the situation. Another man, a jogger, observing the assault, had attempted to aid the woman. The rapist had turned on the good Samaritan and slashed at him with a large-bladed knife, fortunately not cutting him. But the distraction had been sufficient and the rapist had fled. Now it was up to the San Diego police to find the suspect.

The jogger reported to the arriving officers that the fleeing suspect had run up a ravine and had headed for some cliffs over half a mile away. The officers figured that the steepness of the cliffs might prevent the man from making good his escape. They decided to fan out in that direction.

Mills decided to bring his cruiser to the top of the cliff system so that he and Fargo could work their way down toward the beach. Not only would the going be easier, but they wouldn't cover ground already checked out by other officers.

By the time Mills arrived, the first K-9 to reach the scene had already searched that portion of the park. Mills' idea about going down from the cliffs to the beach was no longer a good one. He decided he'd be better off if Fargo attempted to track the rapist right from where the crime had taken place. There was a police helicopter flying overhead. Mills contacted the pilot and had the chopper land near him and his dog. The two got in the rear of the noisy machine and a couple of minutes later found themselves on the beach side of the park.

There officers told Mills which direction the suspect had headed, so Mills, Fargo, and one other San Diego officer began to track the man.

The trail was steep as it led up and away from the water line. There were three distinct ravines in front of them. For no particular reason they chose to start off down the middle one. Huffing and puffing their way along, the farther away the tracking team got from the beach, the more treacherous their route became.

As they moved up the sandy incline, Fargo broke from Mills and headed off to the right. Forcing their way through thick brush after the K-9, the officers soon located Fargo. He already had the suspect by the leg and was attempting to drag him from his hiding place in the brush.

Mills and the second officer worked their way to a position six feet above where the suspect and Fargo were fighting. Mills identified himself as a police officer and called out for the man to surrender. The suspect gave no indication he had heard him. Instead, the man rolled on his side, pinning Fargo in a headlock. To Mills' horror, the suspect then took out his butcher knife and began slashing at the dog.

The real world is not the movies. Not only are police officers very reluctant to use deadly force, but there are formidable legal restrictions against its use. Only if a human life is in the balance may an officer shoot at someone. And by the rules, although Fargo is a bona fide member of the San Diego Police Department and puts his life on the line every day he goes out on patrol with his partner, in the eyes of the law he's still only a dog.

To further complicate Mills' ethical and legal problems, a television video crew had found their way to the top of the cliffs and were taping the entire scene. Mills knew at that point that Fargo was on his own.

The K-9 officer watched in fascinated horror as the man and dog battled. Looking closely at the scene, he noted that Fargo wasn't yelping. Although the suspect was taking ferocious swipes with the big knife, the blade was glancing off Fargo's tough, thick fur coat. Stranger yet, to Mills it appeared that with each thrust the tip of the blade seemed to wind up striking the suspect.

Mills figured Fargo's luck wasn't going to hold much longer. The way the two were fighting, it was inevitable that the knife would find its way into the K-9's gut at any moment. The officer worked himself into a better tactical position to deal with the suspect, and he called Fargo back.

Mills and the second officer managed to position themselves within a reasonably safe distance from the man. From there, Mills' human partner sprayed a stream of oleoresin capsicum into the man's face in the hope of incapacitating him. The chemical had no effect.

Trying another tack, Mills opened a dialogue with the subject. The man, now seated, informed the officer he was a three-time loser and told Mills he couldn't give up. Mills, only six feet away from the man, wondered if the guy thought that the cops were going to leave because he said he couldn't give up. Anyway, the officer figured the guy should have thought of that before he raped the woman. So long as the suspect stayed seated, Mills wasn't going to shoot him. But he wasn't going to permit that butcher knife to wind up sticking out of his own gut.

The standoff between the officers and the suspect went

on for some time. The man eventually slid down from the thick brush and sat down on a rock, the butcher knife remaining firmly in his hand. Mills positioned himself fifteen feet away from the suspect, his 9mm pistol in his hand. For over an hour the two talked, and all the while the man refusing to surrender.

Mills realized that it wouldn't be long before he would have to face an additional predicament. The sun was going to set soon. He was not going to remain near this knife-wielding man when it got dark. Mills said as much to the suspect. In no uncertain terms the officer laid out the facts of life: the man had already attacked a woman on the beach with his knife and had also tried to slash the jogger who had come to her aid. He had attempted to kill Fargo as well. Mills would be mad to stay with him in the thick brush at night. The suspect had two options. He could drop the knife and surrender before it became dark, or Mills would have no choice but to shoot him.

Mills' words were no empty threat, but a statement of hard fact.

At dusk another officer started to make his way toward Mills and the suspect. Mills had a thought. He casually informed the man with the knife, "Okay, they brought this guy in to shoot you. I've been here long enough. He's come here for only one reason. He doesn't have a dog to get in the way. So he's coming down to shoot you."

Mills began to head away from the bushes and, before he had walked ten feet, the suspect surrendered.

To this day Mills is uncertain whether the man simply got tired of talking or if he really believed his make-believe story. Ultimately, the officer judged, it didn't really matter.

Another Man with a Knife

The dawn broke clear and beautiful, an end to what had been an uneventful midnight shift for Mills and Maic. The tour of duty had been his first day back at work after his involvement in a shooting, and he was looking forward to going home and getting some sleep.

He reflected that he and Maic had had some pretty eventful shifts over the past few months. Of course, the pair didn't automatically get into a situation every time they left the station. There was even one instance where he and his K-9 partner sort of screwed up, yet still managed to save the day.

They had been summoned to respond to a hostage call. A woman's husband was holding her at gunpoint. SWAT had set up a perimeter around the victim's home, and the armed man inside was still unaware the police were out there. Mills and Maic had been assigned to get close to the building's rear door, just in case the man made a run for it.

The two silently inched their way to their post, Mills holding on to Maic's collar to keep the K-9 close by him. The officer made sure he kept cars and buildings between them and the house so they wouldn't be seen. Just as he and Maic had quietly and painstakingly worked their way up to the home's carport, the officer pushed on his partner to better hide the K-9. The shove forced Maic's butt to jolt the suspect's car, setting off its alarm with a loud piercing squeal. So much for the silent approach, Mills figured, the only word that came to his mind at the moment being, "Swell."

The husband didn't have a clue that the police had surrounded the place and, fearing for his car's safety, he ran from the house. He ran right into Mills and Maic, and Mills made him an offer he couldn't refuse. The man had the good sense to surrender without a fuss.

No one was hurt and one suspect was taken into custody.

Then there was the time at a groundbreaking ceremony when Maic was a bit overenthusiastic in the digging part of the job and buried the chief's sparkling shined shoes in fresh dirt. But then, nobody's perfect.

Suddenly a call disrupted Mills's thoughts. The dispatcher came over the air reporting a situation not far from where the officer was driving. The dispatcher informed the police units there was a man threatening customers at a Shell gas station in the Old Town area. It was a part of the city that had gotten its name because, several hundred years ago, it was where San Diego had originally sprung up.

Mills picked up the call, and it took him only a few minutes to get to the scene. At the service station, off of freeway I-5, he spotted a group of excited people waving their arms to get his attention. To Mills that was the "investigative clue" that showed he was at the right place.

The agitated citizens told Mills that a bizarre man—he appeared to them to be a street person—had been seen by an employee of the station in the washroom going through somebody's backpack. The man, armed with a long-bladed military knife, had chased the employee out of the room. From there he had gone over to several customers who were pumping gasoline and chased them around the parking lot, still brandishing the knife. He had also gone after other employees as well, causing them to retreat behind the locked doors of the station. It was those last employees who had put in the call to the police.

With no one left to torment, the derelict then had walked over to the nearby freeway via a foot bridge.

Mills got back in his cruiser and drove around to Pacific Highway, the last-known place the knife-wielding man had been headed. It didn't take him long to find the suspect. Even in California, there just aren't that many erratic knife-flailing madmen walking the streets. The man's outfit also helped the officer make his identification. The description given to Mills by the witnesses matched the man to a T. The subject was wearing a knit beanie hat and flannel shirt and sported an unkempt beard. The guy's deportment looked to the officer like what a mythical bridge troll's ought to look like.

As Mills pulled near to the suspect he radioed for cover officers, reporting, "Man with a knife."

Mills drove behind the man and pulled off to the side of the freeway. The subject didn't seem to realize Mills was there. Leaving Maic in the car—the freeway would have been too dangerous for the K-9—Mills followed the man on foot. As he walked, the officer considered his problem. Although it was still early in the day and few people were out, he could not permit this obviously disturbed man to threaten other citizens. On the other hand, it was only a matter of time before they came to a more populated part of the city. The officer wondered how he would deal with this knife-waving crazy person using the minimum amount of force.

After walking about fifty feet, Mills called for the man to drop the knife. The man mumbled something incoherent back to Mills and told the officer to go away. He continued to flail about with the knife.

Mills put himself within ten feet in front of the man. At that point the man laid his knife on the ground. Okay, Mills figured, now we're getting someplace. As the officer stepped over to retrieve the knife, the derelict reached back down and picked it back up. This was not so good, Mills thought, as he backed away.

By now they were over fifty feet from the police cruiser. Mills had another thought. He hit the cruiser's door-release button using the electronic opener attached to his belt and called for Maic to come over. When the K-9 got to within twenty feet of the suspect, Mills ordered "platz," the command for Maic to get down. Mills could see that the derelict, still speaking gibberish to the officer, was unaware of the dog's presence.

The two men had slowly made their way an additional fifty feet. The man continued to play the baiting game of putting the knife down and picking it back up. Mills wanted to time a charge by Maic in such a way that the K-9 would be on the man before he had time to recover the weapon from the ground.

After laying down the weapon for the third or fourth time, the crazed man stood erect. Mills acted. He ordered "Fass" and Maic lunged to the attack.

The derelict saw the dog heading his way. He quickly reached down for the knife. As he attempted to stand up the K-9 hit. The force of eighty pounds of trained police dog smashing into him knocked the man off his feet and the knife flew some distance away and well out of reach.

With Maic firmly holding onto his wrist, the crazy man's tone changed. Mills observed that the result had been clearly therapeutic. From an out-of-control lunatic mouthing gibberish came the lucid words, "I give! I give! I'm sorry! I'm sorry!"

Mills quickly ran over to the now compliant man and cuffed him. With Maic following behind, the three headed back to the cruiser.

The officer reflected that only a few years earlier the situation he had just faced, a crazy person with a knife, would have certainly ended with shots being fired. There was Mills, with no backup officers on the scene, and a wild person flailing a deadly weapon around and refusing to surrender. The officer couldn't have let the man walk on much longer. He would have had to do something. But with a K-9, another world of options had opened, and what could have had a tragic ending turned into a simple and routine arrest.

Swamp Story

It was the summer of 1994 and Mills was working with a new K-9, Eros. The evening had been a tough one. One of Mills' sergeants had gotten into a gun battle with a rifle-carrying gang member. The sergeant had taken a round in the leg, but fortunately another officer involved in the shooting had managed to kill the man before anyone else had been hurt.

Mills spent most of that shift with Eros, clearing houses and looking for other gang members.

Now it was after eleven and the officer was ready to call it a night. Just as he neared his office another K-9 unit called over the air for all available K-9s to respond to the scene of a chase. Three armed men, a robbery team, had jumped from their car and fled into a large swampy area.

Mills knew the place. It was virtually impenetrable; hundreds of acres made up of six-foot razor grass, thick shrubs, gooey mud, and calf-deep pools of brackish water.

Mills picked up his microphone and informed the dispatcher that he was on the way.

When he arrived, there were two dozen officers already on the scene from several different departments. Five San Diego police K-9s had also shown up. Mills spoke to the sheriff's deputy, who had been at the initial crash scene. He informed Mills that the suspects had run into the marsh. The deputy pointed out the direction in which he had seen the men flee.

The K-9 units formed into teams of three—a shotgun officer, a pistol officer, and a K-9 handler. Already on site were Frank Pecoraro with Ax, Dean Davison with Al, and Carl Nielsen with Bern.

Mills, armed with a pump-action twelve-gauge shotgun, had left Eros in the cruiser and worked his way into the swamp in an attempt to find the suspects' trail. It was a slow, tedious, and tense process. In the dark there was no way for the officer to know whether or not any of the armed suspects were on top of him. He had to push his way through sections of tall, sharp-edged grass that cut at his hands. Sometimes the brush was so thick he'd have to go around; other times he and other officers would have to crawl under the tangled growth. It wasn't a pleasant place to walk around. Mills had planned to enter the swamp, assist the other K-9 officers, and eventually, when their dogs became tired, retrieve Eros and work with his K-9. Instead, circumstances kept Mills in the middle of the hostile environment from the start through to sunrise.

The first K-9 pair to go in to search was Pecoraro and Ax. That team soon met Mills, and Pecoraro gave Ax the order to find the wanted men. In what seemed like only a few minutes the dog returned with a man's boot. He was immediately sent back in again and this time he came out with a shirt. After going in a third time, Ax came back with a matching boot to the first. The officers figured the suspect who belonged to all this clothing was trying to get rid of his scent to throw the dog off.

After some discussion the team decided to work the area by breaking the swamp into imaginary grid lines. Still, they found it difficult to follow after the dog and at the same time keep track of their location. Often during that night they had no idea where they were.

The police helicopter on the scene proved extremely valuable. Equipped with Forward Looking Infra Red (FLIR), the copilot could tell the search team where they were as well as where they were in relation to their dog, who inevitably got out ahead of them.

After searching one section of the swamp for some time, Ax finally became tired. Pecoraro took his K-9 to the rear as Dean Davison brought in Al.

It wasn't long after Al was sent out to search that the team lost any idea where the K-9 had gone. They radioed the helicopter for assistance, and the copilot reported that their dog was fifty yards in front of them, adding that some other large animal, perhaps a deer, but it could be a person, was two hundred yards to their left. Mills figured no sane deer would live in this swamp and surmised that what the chopper was seeing was one of the suspects. At any rate, on one of his forays into the marsh, Al had brought a T-shirt back to the team. Mills reckoned that not many deer wear those.

Davison called Al back and put him on a leash, hoping the K-9 would lead the team to the location of the suspect. But the thickness of the brush made that impossible and Al was soon freed to move ahead on his own. The terrain was hard on the dog. The K-9 had to struggle up to his chest in thick mud and goo. Al pushed on, although by now it had become obvious to the team that the dog was getting tired.

The team kept Al with them and, with the aid of the overhead helicopter, headed to the suspect's location. When within a few yards of where the wanted man was supposed to be, Davison called out the standard "Give up or get bitten" warning twice. There was no reply, and he gave Al the order to capture the man who then let the dog go.

Soon the team heard screaming up ahead and rushed onward, fighting their way through the thick vegetation. Since the suspect was now aware of where they were coming from, the members had no hesitation in using their flashlights, which greatly aided them in making headway.

The officers came around a thick tree and spotted the suspect. Thirty feet of tree-root systems separated them and the wanted man. Half his body was lying in a stream. Al was on the man's leg, and Mills watched as the man grabbed the dog's head and, in an attempt to drown the K-9, shoved the dog under water. This treatment did not make Al happy.

The K-9 knew he was in a fight for his life. Al immediately released the man's leg, surfaced, and lunged for the suspect's armpit. He wound up with a mouthful of soft tissue. The K-9 proceeded to drag the suspect into the water, and he wasn't about to let go.

Davison called Al off and Mills handcuffed the defeated man. Now they had to walk back through the marsh to the nearest road. The linear distance was only around three hundred yards, but it was tough going, and the team had no way of knowing if any of the arrested man's friends were around. Mills made it clear to him that if anyone tried to take them on, the man would have a serious problem.

It took nearly an hour to make their way back from where they had made the arrest, even with the help of the overhead helicopter. Finally the team found the road, and members of the sheriff's office took custody of the robber.

Mills figured that the other suspects couldn't be much deeper in the swamp than the first man they had captured. For the next two hours the team moved through the area hoping to find the others. Al became completely exhausted. Davison took him out and the two were replaced by Carl Nielsen and Bern. Frank Pecoraro, without Ax, accompanied Nielsen in and became part of the search team.

Nielsen was somewhat concerned about Bern. His K-9 was fairly new, and the situation they faced was so unpredictable and unstable that the officer feared his dog would run out too far ahead of the team and either be of little value or simply get lost.

As Nielsen and Pecoraro fought their way into the brush after Bern, Mills found himself only twenty feet behind, yet unable to see either man or even catch a glimpse of their flashlights. Soon he thought he heard sounds indicating that the K-9 was on to something. He relayed his suspicions to the other two officers, who shouted out for the suspect to surrender. This capture was far less dramatic than the first, as the man quickly decided to give up the fight. He was cuffed, and with Mills covering him, they walked back to the waiting sheriff's deputies.

At four in the morning two trackers who worked with the Federal Border Patrol arrived. Mills had never worked with this group before and doubted that they could accomplish what the K-9s couldn't. He kept his opinion to himself.

The trackers went in with a sheriff's deputy and an hour later came back with one of the suspect's socks. One of the men described to Mills where they had found it. By this time, Mills had been in the swamp so long he actually recognized the place where they had been. It was about fifty yards beyond where they had found the second suspect. The trackers mentioned that the sock had been found near a cavelike depression in the root ball of a tree.

It was by now five in the morning, and K-9 Officers Gene Oliver and Mike Fowler, with his K-9 Uri, arrived. Daylight was starting to show, and to Mills' surprise, this made it more difficult to locate the places where he had been during the night. Mills had to ask one of the trackers to take him and the other K-9 officers to where the sock had been found. It took some doing, but they finally found the spot. As the team was searching, they noted that a fresh helicopter and crew had arrived on the scene. Mills asked the pilot to move along the tree line by the creek where they were now and follow it back to the ocean. Perhaps, he reasoned, their suspect had tried to make his way out that way.

The helicopter came down to tree-top level, much lower than Mills had anticipated. The JetRanger's whirling rotor blades kicked up a storm of loose debris as the pilot slowly advanced toward the sea. As soon as the machine flew by, the officers noticed that Uri began to sniff the air deeply, barking with excitement. The K-9 glanced first up in the trees, then around in the direction of the deep root bowl where the sock had been located. At first Mills figured that Uri, a new dog, had become confused by the scent of the four officers around him when the helicopter had churned up the surrounding air.

All at once Uri dove into the root ball and started digging. To everyone's amazement a voice was heard from inside the cave, "I give! I give!" From two feet under the ground, the suspect emerged, covered with marsh goop. The man was completely naked; he had been lying there for hours. One of the border patrol trackers had actually been standing on top of him at one point during the search that night.

The robber was fortunate to have surrendered when he did. He was hyperthermic, and Mills surmised he'd probably have died if he had stayed there much longer.

The search had taken nine hours and had involved nine K-9s and their handlers. Mills had been there for all three shifts. He believes it to be the longest search ever conducted by the San Diego Police Department.

As for the trio of robbers, they were convicted of their crimes, which included a series of armed robberies they had committed over the past several months.

Chapter 7

Seattle
Police Department
K-9 Unit

K-9 Rex
with Police Officer Kenneth Hooper

Rex and Police Officer (soon to be sergeant) Kenneth Hooper go back quite a while. The pair first came together over ten years ago, when Rex was just a six-month-old puppy. His K-9 training began only a few weeks later, and the K-9 hit the streets before he was a year old. So while Rex might be a veteran police K-9, he was raised in the Hooper family, grew up with the two Hooper kids and their friends around him, and in truth is a very mild-mannered patrol dog.

Because of the silvery mask on Rex's face and his unusually large ears and black head, Rex and Hooper's co-workers sometimes good-naturedly refer to the eighty-five-pound shepherd as a raccoon dog.

Along with the Hooper's children, the kids in the local school got to know this member of the Seattle Police Department very well. So when Rose, the officer's youngest child, graduated from the Silver Lake Elementary School, Rex and Rose attended the graduation ceremony together. Ken Hooper is proud to report that both Rex and his daughter were awarded diplomas; the officer escorted his partner up to the front of the auditorium to collect the sheepskin. As the officer likes to tell whoever will listen, it only took Rex eight years, but he did it!

When Hooper attended school functions with his partner—which was frequently—everyone asked about his dog. He figures not many people even knew his name, but Rex's was another matter. When there was a fund-raising auction at the school, one of the businesses donating goods made a gourmet doggy biscuit with Rex's name on it.

It's been a rewarding partnership between man and dog. Over the years Rex has been involved in solving many cases, and for two years in a row Hooper and Rex were recognized as the department's K-9 team of the year. Hooper is pleased to report that at ten years of age his Rex can still pound a beat with the best of them.

Three Escapees

Hooper and Rex were the only on-duty K-9 team working when the call came in. One of Seattle's other police officers had run a vehicle license plate over his Mobile Data Terminal (MDT), a computer in the police cruiser that is connected by radio to the data bank of information stored at headquarters. The MDT reported that the white Datsun with Oregon plates was reported as stolen. Dispatch immediately radioed the officer and confirmed the MDT hit. When the officer attempted to pull the small car over, the auto, which held four or five people, raced off.

Seattle is twenty-five miles long and no more than twenty miles wide. The little Datsun's driver took the officers on a tour of the compact city, eventually working his way out of town and into the more open suburbs. Thirty-five miles later, the vehicle, now in a neighboring unincorporated county, went out of control after striking the freeway side barriers. Hooper was thirty seconds behind the two chase cruisers when the crash occurred. By the time he and Rex arrived, two of the suspects had already been taken into custody. One was an unconscious fifteen-year-old girl, knocked out in the accident; the other was a young man. The others had run off. The two police had were local kids who had simply gone for a ride with the three young men in the Datsun.

While Hooper was getting Rex into his harness, his dog stood patiently in the back of the cruiser. Hooper yelled over to one of the officers, Ed Casey, saying, "Talk to me, Ed! Give me a description and a starting point where he [the driver] was last seen."

Casey was planning to join the K-9 Unit. He knew the drill and what information Hooper needed in order to start a search. He rattled off the facts the K-9 officer had to have.

Rex was now dressed in his K-9 working gear: a leather harness with the Seattle Police Department patch emblazoned on either side and a strobe light mounted on its top. He was ready to go.

The K-9 handler took Rex on a lead and both ran across the freeway. Once they were safely on the other side and over a four-foot-high fence, Hooper pushed in on the strobe light's operating button. The white flash it emitted told him it was working properly. Now when his dog ran out in front of him in search of the suspect, the officer could spot his location in the dark. Hooper ordered Rex, "Seek him out! Go find the bad guy!"

Rex immediately headed off into the thick woods. In an instant, strobe or not, Hooper lost sight of his dog, but he continued to hear the K-9 moving through the heavily wooded area. Hooper raced into the dense woods after his partner, using only the sound his dog made as a guide. As he moved through the thick growth, Hooper caught sight of the flashing lights of other police vehicles as they took up positions bordering the area he and Rex were in.

In the near distance the officer heard his dog barking. Hooper called after his K-9, "Take him, Rex! Take him!" both to encourage his dog and let him know that his human partner was not far behind.

Up ahead, through the heavy brush, Hooper spotted the strobe light. Seeing that his dog's head was down, the officer correctly assumed that he had someone at bay. Hooper put the beam of his flashlight on the suspect, a six-foot-tall, hundred-seventy-pound seventeen-year-old. The young man, who had tried in vain to hide in the root ball of a fallen tree, immediately gave up, wanting no more attention from the dog.

After Hooper handcuffed the now docile suspect, the three walked out to the edge of the woods. Ed Casey was already waiting there and put the young man in his cruiser.

Other police units, including a K-9 unit from a neighboring community, rounded up the other suspects. Once everyone was back at headquarters and the situation settled down, the officers ran the names of the three youths. To

Hooper's surprise he found that the three young men had only recently escaped from a detention facility in California.

During the breakout a guard was killed. He'd been beaten to death with a nightstick by the meek young man whom Hooper had caught. During the escape, that same youth had also tied up a female guard and raped her.

The two kids who had been in the car with the wanted men were not involved with the criminal activity of the other three. Hooper speculated that the trio invited the two youngsters into their car because they were interested in the female. He didn't know what would have happened if the officer who had first checked out the plate had not done so.

The three men didn't remain long in the custody of the Seattle police. They were soon returned to California to face trial for their crimes. Hooper can only hope that they remain in jail a bit longer this time around.

Rex the Wonder Dog

Summer nights in Seattle, as in any large American city, can be a busy time for officers. And some places can be a lot busier than others.

The Happy Valley bar was one of the more active spots in town. Quite a few of the patrons of this local watering hole were known to the police. It usually took three cars to respond to a call from that establishment.

So when the report of shots fired was broadcast over the police frequency, it not only got the attention of officers working the bar's patrol area, but it got them all headed in that direction.

One of the responding units was only a block away. When the cruiser pulled up to the bar's parking lot, the officer saw a man standing outside, arguing with another gentleman and firing a revolver into the air, a form of self-expression that is frowned upon in Seattle.

The patrol officer radioed, "Three Sam Four, we got an emergency! Man with a gun, Happy Valley lot!" There was an interminable moment of silence, then, "Three Sam Four, we're in pursuit!"

The Chevy Caprice the shooter had driven off in was being closely followed by Three Sam Four. Hooper soon came to the aid of the other officers and wound up as the second car in the chase. The vehicles weren't driving over fifty miles an hour, but the residential streets they were traveling through were narrow, and the fleeing car was ignoring traffic signals and signs.

Several minutes into the chase, the shooter came to an intersection and slammed on his brakes. Leaving his vehicle in drive, he bailed out of the auto and started to run around its front. As this was taking place the lead police cruiser veered off to the left. Hooper drove to the right. While Hooper began to get out of his car, positioning himself behind the door to protect himself against gunfire, Rex immediately jumped into the driver's-side seat, preparing to leap out. The suspect had only gone a few yards when Hooper saw the man's hand—with some object in it—come up to eye level. The officer then heard two pops.

Hooper dived below the doorsill of his cruiser, pulling a very upset Rex down with him. The instant the officer released his K-9 to go for his gun, his dog bolted after the suspect. The K-9 followed the man into the woods. Hooper, leaving the relative safety of his cruiser, followed close behind.

The dog was not wearing a strobe light, so all Hooper could do was head for the sound of Rex's growling and barking. It was clear from the noise that the dog and suspect were in a fight. Hooper, fearful that his partner would be shot, ignored his own safety and continued to run after Rex.

Afraid to turn on his flashlight, all Hooper could do was smash his way through the brush. Coming upon a footpath, Hooper followed it. Other officers soon took up the pursuit. Once out of the trees Hooper spotted his dog running down the street and focusing in on a house.

Hooper radioed for additional units, and in short order other patrol cars surrounded the block. The officer ran over to his dog, who he saw was attempting to work out a problem. He urged the K-9 on, asking him, "Find him! Seek him out! Where's the bad guy?"

Rex ran up to one particular home, returned to Hooper, then went back to this one house. The officer figured that would be a good place to look. Pointing his light on the ground, he saw footprints in the damp earth. Their trail led up to the door.

Hooper radioed that he wanted the block contained and that he had the suspect in a home.

Patrol officer Joe Bower arrived to back up Hooper. The two men, with Rex alongside, tried the front door, but it was locked. The door to the back of the house was ajar. The officers spotted a pile of dark clothes lying on the floor inside. Hooper told Bower to cover him so that Hooper could send Rex in and he would cover his dog. Rex and his partner stepped inside.

Hooper knew the house was occupied but had no way of knowing whether the suspect belonged there or had just burst in to hide.

Hooper, who is a SWAT trained officer, knew that he had to ensure each room of the home was cleared. Rex would do the actual searching, while the officers would cover him as well as each other.

Clearing the first room, Hooper repeatedly called out, "Seattle Police, come out and identify yourself!"

Rex's rigid body indicated that the dog sensed the suspect had been there. The K-9's ears pointed forward, his tail was down, and the animal was focused on what he was doing.

Hooper could hear people walking toward the officers. He called Rex back to his side. There was no way to tell whether it was the suspect or some innocent homeowner heading their way. The officers had to be extremely careful how they reacted, for the sake of their own safety and that of the civilians involved.

A fiftyish-year-old woman wearing nightclothes stepped out of the darkened rear of the home. Soon half a dozen youngsters appeared. Hooper estimated their ages as ranging from the early to late teens, along with one woman in her early twenties. The woman asked the officers what was going on. Hooper explained that they had chased a subject who had fired shots at them into her home and asked if it would be all right to look around.

She immediately gave her consent.

The officers inquired if there was anyone else in the house. The woman said no.

Hooper kept Rex by his side while other officers searched the house. When the officers returned, they reported that nobody else had been found.

Hooper asked the older woman once more if all the inhabitants of the house were in that room. Thinking the question over for a moment, the woman turned to her twenty-year-old daughter and asked where her boyfriend was. The younger woman replied that he was sleeping downstairs.

Hooper said he wished to take a look downstairs. In an instant the emotional atmosphere in the room changed from one of concern and cooperation on the part of the residents to open hostility. The young woman flatly stated to the officers that they couldn't search her room.

Hooper explained, as patiently as a person can who is looking for the man who just shot at him, that she didn't understand. Her boyfriend could be a hostage, he might well be the suspect they'd chased into the house, and he could even be hurt right at this moment.

She insisted that he was fine and was sleeping in the room downstairs and had been all night.

Hooper was adamant. He told her that room was going to be searched.

The officer gave Rex over to another handler and asked him to remove the K-9 from the house. There were too many people in a confined area, and Hooper didn't want to risk an incident involving his dog and some irate civilian.

Assigning two officers to watch the family, Hooper joined the two officers originally involved in the pursuit and went down to the room in question. After clearing the downstairs area they pounded on the door. Calling out the boyfriend's name, they ordered him to come out of the room with his hands where they could see them.

There was no response. Hooper opened the door and saw the suspect, lying in bed, feigning sleep. Hooper reached over and grabbed the blanket off the supposedly sleeping subject. On the blanket was blood from dog bites to his leg and injuries he had received to his hands during the chase. He was yanked out of bed, searched, and cuffed.

The man was taken away. When Hooper asked the mother for permission to search the room and the suspect's clothing for a weapon, both she and her daughter, using unladylike and colorful language, refused.

This did not present a major problem for the officers. The Seattle Police Department has a mobile precinct housed in a converted motor home. By this time it was on the scene. Hooper left the house, went inside the mobile precinct, and wrote out a request for a search warrant.

When it was completed the officers took the warrant over to Judge Goodmens, the on-call judge that night. She read the affidavit, asked if everyone involved in the gunplay was all right, and signed the piece of paper.

Now, with search warrant in hand, the men returned to the home to finish their job. In the room where the suspect had been arrested, they found the man's muddy clothing. The gray sweatshirt he had worn had puncture marks in its arms matching the wounds he had received in his battle with Rex. The same type of bite marks were also visible in the fabric of the muddy pants.

However, much to their disappointment, no gun was located.

While they were finishing their search of the room, Hooper pulled out his radio and informed Joe Bower that no firearm had been found. He asked the other officer to recheck the wooded area, especially along the path where the man had fled, to see if he could locate any evidence there.

Bower went back and, using his flashlight, found the hand gun. What was unusual about the scene was the fact that the revolver's cylinder was open. Both fresh and expended cartridges lay around the weapon. Clearly the suspect had tried to unload and reload his gun just as Rex pounced. The gun had gone flying, its cylinder open, and the bullets had scattered. The suspect then slid down the hill, hence the mud all over his clothing, got loose from Rex, and made his way back home.

So, in the dark, with a patrol K-9 on top of him, the shooter had had no chance to recover and use his weapon.

The officers soon discovered that this wasn't the man's first contact with the criminal justice system. He'd been convicted of burglary in the past. Because of the evidence the officers had secured against him, the suspect pleaded guilty to all charges. Hooper was considered a victim of attempted murder. This gave the officer the right to appear at sentencing and convey his thoughts to the judge. He made sure he was there for sentencing.

In anticipation of the proceeding, Hooper wrote to the trial judge, reminding him that the day after the incident an officer from a nearby municipality had been shot and killed. He asked that the court consider the fact that only the man's poor aim had prevented a similar tragedy from happening to Hooper. The officer asked that the judge consider putting the man behind bars for the maximum length of time permitted.

The judge acknowledged the letter in open court and sentenced the shooter to thirty months in prison.

Rex and the Slug

In the jargon of every police agency there is a word street officers use to describe the sociopathic, antisocial misfits they must deal with each day. The specific terms of art vary from region to region and are invariably colorful: scumbag, mope, dirtbag, skell. Whatever the word is, the meaning to the officers is clear. In Seattle such individuals are referred to as slugs.

These are the career criminals: burglars, purse snatchers, con artists, drug addicts, thieves. Sometimes they graduate to armed robbery and, not infrequently, murder. Such people exist on the edge of society, bleeding the system as much as they can for social services and money, while perpetrating mayhem in return. They have no conscience and they feel no remorse for their actions.

Police officers are trained to understand how people can be conditioned to act in such inappropriate ways, especially when raised in a dysfunctional environment. But after a sufficient number of encounters with slugs, and the destroyed lives and innocent victims they leave behind, officers lose whatever warm fuzzy feelings they might have once held for such persons.

Norman (not his real name) was a slug. He came from a long line of slugs, and by all accounts his family was a veritable slug convention. He was in his mid-forties and had spent a significant portion of his life behind bars. Larceny was his forte, but committing the occasional burglary was not beneath him. He is also a drug addict.

Hooper, on patrol with Rex, picked up his microphone when the radio dispatcher called, "K-9 twelve." He glanced at his watch—it was just after three in the morning. The dispatcher told the officer to respond to a burglary that had just taken place. Hooper knew the address was that of a housing project, a series of duplexes that had been mated together.

It only took him a few minutes to arrive, and as he pulled up he saw that officer Jay Wheeler was already there and speaking to the victim. The woman was telling the officer that she had heard a noise and, thinking her cat wanted to be let in, came out of her bedroom. In the living room she saw an arm snake its way through her ground-floor window, the disembodied hand reaching for her purse, which lay on a nearby table.

She screamed and slammed the window on the burglar's arm. The man, who was standing on a trash can placed under her window, didn't run away. She had to threaten to call the police to get him to flee. To the two officers that was a strong indication the person might be more than a bit aggressive. A person who remained on the scene after being caught in the act was bold and potentially dangerous.

Hooper decided he'd have Rex try to trail their man.

The officer had little hope that the effort would be successful. They were in a densely populated, highly traveled, concrete-surfaced area, and the odds of his K-9 partner locating their suspect's specific scent and staying with it were slim.

To the officer's surprise, Rex picked up a track immediately. The K-9 followed the scent over a quarter of a mile, to the end of the built-up area. There Rex moved under a power line, where the ground was made up of earth and vegetation, far superior for tracking purposes. Now the dog really had the man's scent. Both the officer and Rex soon came to another residential area. Following the invisible trail of odor molecules the burglar had left along his path of flight, the dog and officer scaled fences and moved through backyards, staying on the suspect's path all the while. Rex, with only a mild admonition from Hooper—"No dog!"— even had the intestinal fortitude to ignore being challenged by another canine, a resident of one of the yards he and Hooper had to trek through.

Just beyond the yard that held the territorial dog, Rex began to bark. Hooper came around the corner. Using his flashlight the officer spotted the suspect, Norman, hiding above them in a tree, his body pressed flat against the house in an unsuccessful attempt at camouflage. Hooper invited Norman down. But instead of simply climbing down from the tree and surrendering, the man jumped to ground level, then jumped once again to an underground garage below where Hooper and Rex were standing.

Hooper leapt down to Norman's level. The officer immediately placed the other man so he faced against the garage door. While doing so the officer ordered Rex to watch the suspect from his position above the two men. Norman decided that he would take this opportunity to run away. Using both arms he pushed off from the garage door, straight back into Hooper. The officer returned the shove. Even before Norman had a chance to bounce off the door, Rex was down and on top of him. It was at this stage in his life that Norman learned it was not prudent to assault a K-9 handler whose K-9 was on guard a couple of feet away.

Rex first grabbed Norman by a leg. The slug decided to fall down on his back and kick at Rex with the other leg. For an instant the tactic worked. Norman's kicks landed on Rex and the dog released the struggling man's leg. Norman then continued to kick at the unhappy Rex, another error in judgment. The slug missed on one of the kicks, giving the K-9 an opportunity to lunge at a less threatening part of the man's anatomy. The dog's jaws found their mark; his very sharp teeth clamped down hard on Norman's penis. Rex, just as he was trained to do, then began to tug.

Norman's demeanor immediately changed. Instead of spewing out curses and epithets, he let out a distinctive screech and stopped resisting.

Hooper quickly called his partner off. This time Norman chose to surrender meekly and was taken into custody. After Hooper completed some paperwork at the precinct, Norman was removed to Harbor View Hospital for patching up.

For all the bad things Norman had done in his life, Hooper suspects that that night's contact with Rex was probably the most punishment the man had ever received. But knowing Norman, he'll undoubtedly try and make up for it.

Serial Burglar

The officers of the South End district first began to suspect they had a serial burglar working their area when the number of nighttime reports of that crime began to increase.

Their district was predominantly middle class and composed of pleasant residential homes. First the police received reports of a peeping Tom. While frightening to their victims, as a general rule peeping Toms act out their fantasies without doing harm to anyone. But in this case the man's actions didn't end there.

Victims' stories made the police realize that the person had begun to enter homes. Items were taken, sometimes purses, sometimes cash, but often the man left with nothing but valueless trinkets. After several more weeks of frustrating attempts to capture this individual, the tales the homeowners told slowly began to change. The burglar was now boldly confronting women he came upon while he was in their homes. This man was no professional criminal; he was doing what he was doing because he enjoyed it. And it seemed to the police that he was now beginning to act out his more aggressive fantasies. During one of his latest break-ins, the police learned, the burglar had sat down on the bed of a thirteen-year-old girl, woke the sleeping child, and spoke to her, telling her how pretty she was. He left her room taking a pair of her shoes with him.

To the officers assigned to find the man, those actions could mean only one thing. It was only a matter of time before some innocent person would be badly hurt by their burglar.

The pattern had been evolving for nearly three months, and the sergeant of the sector had put together a plan. Whenever a burglary was called in to the area known to be frequented by their man, unless an officer was involved in an arrest in progress, he was to break away and set up a perimeter around the designated neighborhood. Whichever K-9 team was working would go in with the assigned officers and attempt to track the thief.

Over the weeks Hooper and his brother and sister K-9 officers had run several tracks on their man. But whether by craft or luck, the suspect had eluded them. The officers later discovered that one of the reasons they had such difficulty locating their suspect was that he lived within five blocks of all of his victims and was making it safely back home after each incident.

One June night when Hooper and Rex were working had been a slow one, undoubtedly partly because of the light drizzle that had fallen on and off over the course of the evening. Hooper and another K-9 team, that of officer Debie Myere and her four-legged partner P. D. Cody, had pulled off the road and were talking shop. Around two in the morning a call came over the air. Hooper knew it was their burglar; the area, timing, and description of the suspect were right on. In this case, the burglar came upon the woman of the house, who was dressed in nightclothes. He told her how appealing she was in her robe. The man then ran from the home, grabbing a computer terminal on the way out.

Hooper arrived at the house at about the same time as the officers assigned to the case. While the primary unit obtained information from the victim and began to broadcast the suspect's description, direction of travel, and whatever other bits of useful details they could come up with, the other police vehicles on duty in the area were at work setting up a tight perimeter. The officers hoped the numerous flashing cruiser dome lights would make the suspect feel the police pressure and that he would make a mistake.

The plan was a good one. It had been refined over the weeks, and with each new burglary, the area within the perimeter became tighter and tighter. Hooper and the others later learned that their encircling maneuver that night had blocked their burglar from returning to the safety of his home.

Armed with whatever information had just been gotten from the newest victim, Hooper now prepared his K-9 for the track. It was raining out—not great weather for such a mission—so the officer was not overly optimistic about the outcome. Nevertheless he decided to have Rex give it a try.

Starting at the back door of the home, he and Rex began their track, the K-9's bright strobe bouncing off building walls and windows as he moved forward. The team worked their way through several blocks of backyards and came out onto a main road, fortunately not heavily traveled at that time of the night. Surprising Hooper, Rex came to an abrupt stop and cut to the left. In an instant all Hooper could see was his partner's strobe light bouncing through thick bushes.

Pushing his way toward his K-9, he spotted Rex jumping up against a fence while shaking some object in his mouth. The officer took the object from his dog. It was a white cloth with the words "kitchen towel" embroidered on it. The officer felt the soft material. Clearly the towel was too dry to have been lying about outside for any length of time.

Hooper radioed to the officer on the scene, "Find out if the victim is missing any kind of towel."

A short time later the reply came back in the affirmative.

Now Hooper knew for sure that he and Rex were on the right track. The officer encouraged his K-9, "Seek him out, find the bad guy!"

Continuing through the overgrown lot, Hooper was hampered by the heavy vegetation and Rex was able to run out well ahead of the officer. Before Hooper could break clear, his dog had darted across the main road and was out of sight. All the handler could see was the glow from his dog's strobe as its light reflected off the walls of nearby homes.

Once out of the vacant lot, the officer ran over to where he thought his dog should be. By the time Hooper found Rex, his K-9 was already holding a suspect at bay.

Rex was put on a "down stay," and Hooper placed the man against a nearby wall and started to pat him down. The suspect had nothing on him except a book of postage stamps, with three of the stamps missing. Hooper asked the man what he was doing out on the street, and the suspect replied he was out for a walk and the next thing he knew a dog was chasing him.

Hooper glanced at his watch. It was two fifteen. Not all that many people go for walks at that hour of the morning, especially in the rain and while wearing an all-black outfit. Looking down at the man's pant legs, the officer noted that briars were stuck to the cloth. There was no doubt in Hooper's mind that this was the man Rex had just chased through the lot.

Once again Hooper got on his portable radio and asked the officer at the crime scene to have the victim look around and see if anything was missing. The only things the woman could be sure were gone were the computer terminal and the towel.

That was good enough for the officer. Hooper and another unit brought the man into the precinct, charging him with burglary. The next morning a search warrant was secured for the man's home. In his room were dozens of items taken from a multitude of burglaries. Articles of clothing, the thirteen-year-old girl's shoes, and many empty wallets and purses. The pattern of burglaries had been discovered only a few months earlier. Many of the objects found by the officers dated back to much earlier crimes.

Later that day the victim of the previous night's burglary reported to the officers that one other item had indeed been taken. It was a stamp book with three stamps missing.

The man pleaded guilty to burglary. Thanks to good police work, as well as Hooper's and Rex's efforts, he was sentenced to three years in jail. Hooper's hopes he finds another hobby when he's let free.

K-9s Alex, Topper, and Pounder with Police Officer Gary Kuenzi

Gary Kuenzi is the only officer assigned to the Seattle Police Department's K-9 unit who routinely goes on patrol with two dogs. Topper, a seventy-five-pound German shepherd, is a plain-vanilla patrol dog—sort of a canine grunt. Pounder, his golden retriever, is the technician of the team. He's been trained to sniff out drugs.

Pounder—he was paroled from a dog pound, hence the name—wasn't supposed to have started his police career working as a narc. He'd initially been slated for a job in the bomb squad of the Pierce County sheriff's office. But that agency's trainer heard that the Seattle police's bomb detection unit was looking for a good sniffer, and the deputy figured the young and energetic retriever fit the bill. Pounder was transferred. But he must have ticked off his new boss, because he soon got bounced into narcotics detection work with Kuenzi and Topper.

Not that Kuenzi minds having two dogs; it's just that sometimes Pounder gets confused about what he's supposed to be doing. That is what happened in the following two incidents.

But Can't I Play Also?

The overcast, forty-five-degree January day was considered fair weather by Seattle standards; that is, it wasn't raining. Kuenzi was working in plain clothes as he and Pounder had been assigned to do a job for the Drug Enforcement Agency Task Force. The situation, as Kuenzi understood it, was that the task force wanted to talk to some gentlemen involved in illicit activities that revolved around the sale and procurement of controlled substances (they were dealing dope). Pounder was needed to check out a couple of their cars.

The hotel the bad guys were staying at was a nice one. It was located across the street from the federal courthouse, which all the agents and police involved in the case thought most convenient. Kuenzi parked his marked cruiser, with Topper locked inside, among the other police cars over by the nearby court building. He and happy-go-lucky Pounder crossed over to the other side of the street and strolled into the parking garage of the hotel.

The lot went several floors below ground, and the officer and his four-legged partner had to walk down to the third level. Three task force people were already there and waiting by a shiny black Z-28 Camero.

Kuenzi directed Pounder to start his search by giving the command, "Find dope!" The K-9 began his work at the front of the vehicle. When the dog came to the driver's side door, he alerted as he had been taught to do, by sitting down (although Kuenzi noted that Pounder had recently added his own refinement to the procedure—he now also gave his paw).

Kuenzi turned to the agents and said, "I've got a good alert. The dog is indicating the presence of narcotics odor in the car."

The officer, K-9, and agents moved some distance away from the Camero, while keeping it in view. A short time later a man in his early twenties, accompanied by a young woman, came out of an elevator and walked over to the vehicle. The law officers stepped over to him and explained why they were there. One of the agents nodded in Pounder's direction and informed the man that, "The dog says there's dope in the car."

The suspect, surrounded by four beefy lawmen, chose not to argue the point. He raised his hands and told the agents he had a 9mm in his front jacket pocket, a small .22 in his rear pocket, and dope in his jacket pocket. He also told them there were some additional drugs in the backseat of the car.

Removing the guns and narcotics, the agents advised the man of his rights.

Meanwhile Pounder was now inside the vehicle, checking it out further. While Kuenzi and his K-9 were busy, the second man involved in the deal came down the walkway, two other DEA agents casually walking along nearby.

As soon as the second suspect saw the agents around the Camero, he figured out what was going on. He ran. Kuenzi instinctively called out to his K-9—who for a moment he thought was Topper—to "Take him." Pounder, having seen his brother K-9 in action on numerous occasions, rose to the challenge. Leaping from the car he raced past the pursuing DEA agents and up the ramp in pursuit of the fleeing man. Just before the suspect came to the street exit, the K-9 grabbed on to the running man's jacket.

Now, Kuenzi knew that Pounder would never bite anyone. This whole incident was just a big game to his friendly, outgoing golden retriever. So while the suspect desperately tried to rid himself of the seventy-pound Pounder, the dog's tail wagged furiously as he enjoyed the fun.

When Kuenzi and the other agents raced up to the struggling drug suspect, Pounder, unsure what he was supposed to do next, simply let go. It then took all three law officers to bring the struggling man down and handcuff him.

As they walked the cuffed drug dealer back down to the

Camero parked on the third level, Kuenzi had Pounder do a search of the area the suspect had just sprinted through. At parking level two, the K-9 found a wad of cocaine, securely wrapped in a Zip-loc plastic bag, lying next to the dumpster where the man had just tossed it.

Kuenzi and the other narcotics officers don't know whether the suspect would have gotten away without Pounder's intervention, but the intercession of the spirited K-9 sure helped.

A Pack of Police Dogs

The East Precinct in Seattle is composed of both commercial and residential-apartment complexes. While on patrol there one night with his K-9 partners, at around two in the morning Kuenzi received a call reporting a burglary in progress. Three police cruisers headed to the ongoing crime, but Kuenzi, who was right around the corner when the radio report came in, got there first.

Driving up slowly, without using his car's lights or siren, the officer saw a white van parked at a construction site, blocking the entrance. Kuenzi jotted down the plate and called it in. He spotted two men pushing equipment and goods into the open side doors of the van. They were rolling the heavy objects into the vehicle over some wooden planks.

At first the two burglars didn't see the officer. One of the men, whose name was Brown, apparently caught sight of Kuenzi while the pair were trying to wrestle an arc welder into his van. Without even saying "so long" to his partner, the man bolted down the road. The second suspect, finally understanding what caused his buddy to run, darted off in the opposite direction.

Kuenzi jumped from his car and tried yelling out the old standard, "Police, stop!" However, the experienced officer was neither disappointed nor surprised when that ploy didn't work. Kuenzi, his attention focused on Brown, yelled, "Take him!" to Topper. His trained K-9 sprang out of the driver's side window. First one blur went past the officer, then, much to his surprise, a second, lighter-colored blur followed. It was Pounder! The dog had been lying on the cruiser's front floorboard and when he saw his buddy jump out, he decided that duty called.

"Oh, not again," thought Kuenzi, whose plan had been for Topper to grab the first suspect while he went after the second. He had to quickly change his tactics. Fearful that the untrained—at least for street work—Pounder would get hurt, he headed off after his two K-9s.

By this time the suspect had made it across the street, running between two cars. Kuenzi didn't know whether to laugh or cry when he saw his two intrepid K-9s both try to get between the bumpers of the same parked vehicles at the same instant, jamming themselves together in the process. It was a scene that could well have come from a Keystone Cops comedy routine.

Unsticking themselves, the two dogs, Topper first, got between the cars and continued the chase. As he watched the scene, Kuenzi wondered whether some retraining for his partners might not be in order.

A block later the boys caught up with their suspect, Topper grabbing on to him while Pounder circled around the struggling duo, apparently wondering, How do I play this game?

The suspect tried a trick, calling "Out" to Topper. It worked, at least for the moment, as the dog let go. Kuenzi, on the run and almost there, ordered the dog back in. After that, no amount of yelling "Out!" by the burglar worked.

An instant later Kuenzi jumped on the suspect, finally securing him with a set of handcuffs.

With the prisoner now in custody, the officer began to radio in the arrest when the burglar, Brown, blurted out, "It's no big deal; I give up!"

As the two men and the dogs headed back to the cruiser, Brown complained to the officer about the "pack of dogs" that had been sent after him. Kuenzi tried to explain what happened, but the burglar remained unconvinced. He still figured he'd been double teamed.

K-9s Tali and Adam
with Police Officer Jon Emerick

An Old Dog

Officer Jon Emerick's first K-9 didn't work out. That happens sometimes. Dogs have personalities, just as humans do, and the probationary K-9 assigned the probationary K-9 handler just couldn't cut the mustard. He was simply neither sufficiently aggressive nor assertive enough. So instead of working the streets of Seattle, after months of training and effort he was turned out of the department to be assigned as someone's really well-schooled house pet.

Thus the K-9 unit had a dilemma. They now had a fully trained handler but no matching trained dog. Then someone remembered Tali. That K-9 had worked the road for ten years and was about to be retired. Still, there was nothing wrong with the animal. In fact he was an award-winning K-9. It was simply that ten years is a lot of years to be a working dog, and Tali had done his part.

In the end it was decided that another year on the street would work out okay for both the inexperienced human and the veteran police dog.

So it was that after a couple of weeks of bonding and training together the newly minted (sort of) K-9 team hit the bricks.

In the days when Emerick and Tali started out, the K-9 unit had officers working both day and evening shifts. So it was that the radio call that Emerick and his K-9 received, of a robbery in progress—a purse snatch—came in while it was still light out.

A young male-female team had run up behind their elderly woman victim. The girl had snatched the older woman's purse and knocked her down, then both younger people had run off. The girl was described as being around sixteen years of age and wearing lots of makeup.

A number of citizens saw what had taken place. One man had run after the two, grabbed the purse back from the girl, and captured the young man. Emerick was called to the scene by the responding police units, who had the young man in custody and now wanted the K-9 officer's help in locating his girlfriend.

When Emerick arrived, one of the officers informed him that the girl had been seen running into a nearby single-family home. Taking Tali out of his cruiser, Emerick put his dog on a lead and walked up to what he saw was an older, run-down property. He approached the place and spoke to one of the people from inside, a young woman. She claimed the house belonged to her grandmother and gave the officer permission to search the place.

While other officers stayed outside, Emerick and Tali entered the building. Inside, the officer saw that the place could only be charitably described as a dump. Debris and garbage lay all over the place. Paint was peeling from the walls, and from what Emerick observed, he wouldn't even consider letting his K-9 spend a night there.

First Emerick called out a general warning that a K-9 would be searching the building and the young woman should surrender now. Not surprised by the lack of response he and Tali began to methodically check out each room in the house.

Every closet was checked, each bed was looked under. Yet, he, or rather Tali, couldn't locate anyone.

Nevertheless, Tali was alerting. The dog was showing there was human scent around him. Emerick noted his K-9's body language change; his ears and tail were raised and he pranced about the place, telling Emerick that someone was indeed there. The officer and his K-9 stepped back outside, and Emerick again spoke to the young woman who belonged in the residence. After some questioning she admitted that the person they were seeking might be hiding in the basement. She pointed to a small door on the side of the home.

Emerick opened the door and saw that what the woman had referred to as a basement was little more than a crawl space, with an uneven dirt floor. At some spots in the place

Emerick could just about stand, but at others there was little more than a couple of feet of space between the ground and the home above.

Once more Emerick called out the standard K-9 warning. Using the beam of his powerful flashlight the officer illuminated what he could see of the apparently vacant space before him. The site looked empty. Yet, at the end of the lead his barking K-9 tugged strongly, showing every indication that he sensed strong human scent around them. The officer let the agitated dog loose.

Tali ran directly to the narrowest part of the crawl space and uncovered the hidden purse snatcher, who had buried herself in the earth. The bravery she had demonstrated in attacking an elderly woman failed the girl as the veteran K-9 grabbed hold of her arm. She let out a piercing scream as the dog attempted to pull her out.

Emerick called Tali back and told the girl to come over to him. Frightened by the K-9, the girl was yelling to Emerick to keep the dog away from her. When she got close to the officer, she jumped on him. Emerick knew that the girl was simply seeking his protection. However, Tali, while an intelligent and well-trained dog, couldn't read her mind. He reacted to what appeared to him to be an attack on his handler and reengaged the girl, grabbing her on the knee.

Once again the handler called his dog off. He took the girl from the crawl space and had the medical personnel already at the scene render first aid to her injuries.

The sixteen-year-old girl and her male companion were placed under arrest and led away. Going back into the home, which the officers learned was a drug-user hangout, they found a trapdoor in the bedroom that led from the main part of the house down to the crawl space below. Clearly, the occupants of the place had fled from the police before.

It was the first street action Emerick had been directly involved in since he had joined the K-9 unit. For some time after, he reflected on what had transpired that night. Both the power and ability of his dog, as well as the responsibility he now held, were impressed on him by what had taken place that evening.

Officer Shot

Emerick had now been on the K-9 unit for two years. Tali had been retired and Emerick's newest partner was Adam, a ninety-five-pound black and reddish tan, tall-eared shepherd. That particular evening had been a quiet one for the pair but was about to validate the police-officer maxim that their job was one of long periods of boredom interrupted by occasional moments of terror.

As Emerick drove along, he eyeballed another Seattle cruiser, which had stopped in the turn lane of the four-lane road they were both on. The officer noticed a tall blond-haired man approaching the other vehicle. Probably someone asking the officer for directions, Emerick figured, although he didn't see another car near the man and wondered why anyone would travel on foot in this mostly commercial northwest section of the Ballard district.

Emerick had turned a number of corners since seeing the other patrol car and was once again heading in the other officer's direction when a stressful but controlled voice came over the radio with, "Three boy two, I need some help. I've been shot."

The startled dispatcher asked the officer to repeat the message. Emerick had got it right the first time. Although he had no reason to believe the officer he had seen earlier was the one who had just called, his gut told him to head in that direction. As his foot pushed down on the accelerator pedal, the officer instinctively flicked on his overhead lights and cruiser's siren. An excited Adam stood erect behind his handler, aware only that lights and siren meant trouble was ahead. The K-9 barked in anticipation of the unknown danger that he'd soon be facing.

In less than a minute Emerick's cruiser came racing up behind that of the wounded officer. The civilians around the other car all pointed in the direction the shooter had taken. Before Emerick jumped from his vehicle, he first radioed in their exact location. The injured officer, Brad Thomas, had been off by two blocks. Thomas was slumped over, his upper body facing the driver's side window. He was conscious but in pain, having taken four slugs from the shooter's gun.

Emerick looked down at the man. Blood was everywhere. Emerick badly wanted to start after the assailant, but the sirens wailing in the distance informed him help would soon arrive, and common sense told him he'd have to wait until other officers got there so they could take charge of the injured Thomas, before he could go running off with Adam after the other man.

Thomas looked up at Emerick and, in response to the other officer's question, "Brad, do you know where you've been hit?" answered, "I don't know. I can't believe it." He then added, "I shot at the guy too, but I don't know if I hit him."

Seconds later one of the responding police cruisers came onto the scene. The rescue unit was not far behind. Emerick decided it was time to let others assist Thomas while he and Adam did what they got paid for.

The K-9 handler returned to his car, put Adam's harness on, and attached a lead. With Adam at his side he then approached the citizens who had witnessed the shooting. All agreed on the general direction of the shooter's flight. They told Emerick that they saw the man cut between some apartment buildings a few blocks away.

Before starting on the track, Emerick radioed the dispatcher. He told her to direct officers responding to the shooting to set up containment around the neighborhood he was headed for.

Emerick asked another officer to grab his shotgun and come with him and Adam. The K-9 team then started on their track.

Emerick was anxious about doing the job right, dreading the thought that he might lose the suspect. He knew Thomas well and wanted badly to catch the man who had shot his fellow officer. So, in his desire to succeed, he made a crucial mistake, one common to relatively new handlers. Instead of listening to his dog, he pushed him.

K-9 teams work as a unit. The bond between handler and dog is very strong. What the K-9s want most is to please their masters. But communication between the two species remains less than perfect. So when a K-9 finds himself in conflict between what he knows and what he's being told to do by his handler, he does what his handler wants him to do. And that can create a problem.

Emerick began the search with a preconceived notion that the shooter had run between two buildings. The witnesses, from their perspective, believed that was what they had seen, but they were wrong.

So, when Adam tried to take his partner across a yard, Emerick corrected his dog and told him to head in another direction.

It took ten minutes for the officer to figure out that he and Adam had lost the track. Emerick took a deep breath, brought Adam back to where they'd started, and this time resolved to trust his dog. He now let Adam determine where they'd go.

Emerick again told his K-9 to "Seek," then stood back and permitted the unleashed dog to work. The officer remained confident. There were so many police units now surrounding the area, it remained highly likely the shooter was still close by. The pair, working by themselves now, came up to the buildings the suspect was thought to have run between. This time Adam, not hindered by human assistance, moved away from that spot and around a fence. Emerick saw that Adam was becoming increasingly tense as the team worked the track. That fact only heightened the officer's sense that their man was nearby.

Traveling through a number of yards, Adam turned the corner of a private home that had distinctive fake-brick siding and disappeared from Emerick's sight.

Something told Emerick not to go any further. He doesn't recall any unusual sound, nor did Adam bark. But his sixth sense informed him that his man was just around the corner.

A moment later Emerick saw Adam pulling the silent suspect by his leg from out of the driveway where he had been hiding. The left side of the man's coveralls was soaked in blood. Thomas had indeed hit his assailant.

Emerick tried to put the now-protesting man on the ground. He worked on getting him to face down. While he and Adam were subduing him, the suspect blurted out, "He shot me!" Then, almost as an afterthought, he added, "But I shot him, too." Emerick knocked the still-resisting man fully to the ground. With his gun firmly screwed into the suspect's ear, the officer radioed for assistance with his portable. The transmitting location was poor and only one other officer managed to hear the garbled transmission clearly, but that was enough. The other officer relayed the information to the dispatcher. Soon it appeared to Emerick that half of the Seattle Police Department had arrived on the scene.

At that point the wounded suspect decided to thrash around, yelling and screaming that it was self-defense. With so many other officers around them, Emerick wanted Adam out of the fray. He spotted a rookie police officer and, calling Adam off the suspect, directed the young man to hold on to Adam's collar while Emerick continued to assist the other officers in subduing the struggling man.

The rookie was clearly unaware of how powerful a ninety-five-pound upset police dog can get when he sees his partner fighting with someone. Adam broke free of the rookie officer's grasp and reengaged the man, this time biting him in the only open space available, his crotch. It took Emerick's direct intervention to get the dog off.

Just as newsmen came up, the man was cuffed and hustled off in a cruiser, screaming to the news crew people that it was self-defense. An empty pocket pistol, its seven rounds having been fired at Thomas, had been taken from his pocket.

At Harbor View Hospital the man was treated for his injuries, none of which was life threatening. Emerick, concerned with Thomas's well-being, also went up to the hospital. He was told his friend had taken four slugs, one in each shoulder and one in each wrist. Since Emerick was already there, he checked on the suspect as well. In the hallway one of the nurses came up to him and complained to him that his dog had bitten the poor man, the man who had shot Thomas. Several appropriate rejoinders came to the officer's mind, but a department chaplain standing nearby came up to Emerick and quietly suggested that no response to the woman was necessary, nor would any be helpful.

Emerick agreed and simply walked away.

It took some investigation, but finally the motive behind the shooting came out. The man in question had had several run-ins with the police in Utah. On one occasion he had nearly managed to wrestle an officer's gun from its holster.

So, upset with Utah officers, he decided to take it out on a member of the Seattle Police Department. For some time prior to his encounter with Officer Thomas, he'd been living inside his car, under a drawbridge. Sort of a modern-day troll. But instead of having a disfigured body, he had a mind that was ugly.

Earlier on the evening of the shooting, just a bit farther along the same street where he'd meet Thomas, the suspect had approached another police car. Inside was a female officer. The man looked at her and said, "You're not the one." He then moved on.

When he finally came upon Thomas, the shooter pulled his pistol on the officer and told him to put the car in park and take his foot off the brake. He then told the officer that he wanted his money. Thomas, aware that he was dealing with an unstable individual, told the man that would be fine, and as he reached back with his right hand, he grabbed his handgun instead of his wallet. The two exchanged shots; seven from the suspect, four from Thomas' gun.

Thomas healed, was returned to duty, and is now working as a K-9 handler alongside Emerick.

As for the trial, that went quickly. There was little doubt as to the outcome, and the man was found guilty of attempted murder and sentenced to twenty years in prison.

Which is good, Emerick figures, because when he was being interviewed by the homicide detectives, the shooter made a point of telling them that he would shoot a police officer again. Emerick believes him and hopes to be retired before the guy gets out of jail and comes looking to try and kill another cop.

Chapter 8

Hampton, Virginia, Police Department
K-9 Unit

K-9 Rody
with Police Officer Glennell Fullman

It's not that Hampton, Virginia, is such a large town, but the fact that it sits next to one of the major cities in Virginia, Newport News, with its population of 180,000 people, can make it a busy place to work for a police officer. So some years ago the smaller department's chief decided that it would make sense to use K-9s to aid the Patrol Force. Soon after that determination was made, Patrol Officer Glennell Fullman was introduced to Rody, and she and the hundred-five-pound German shepherd became the first tracking K-9 team in the department.

Rody is gone now, having lived a long and full life. Fullman remembers her K-9 partner as being a sweet and loving creature. There was one incident, while she and her husband were tending their garden on the large piece of property where they live, when she saw Rody chasing after a stray cat. Just before she had a chance to yell for him to stop, the dog broke off his pursuit. Fullman thought nothing more of the matter and went back to work.

A few moments later Rody walked up to her, some object obviously in his mouth. Still bent down on her knees, Fullman reached a hand out and said, "Give it here," thinking that he had brought her a stick. Rody then gently placed a live baby rabbit in her open hand.

She was momentarily shocked by what her dog had done. With the tiny rabbit in her hand, she rose and walked over to where Rody had chased after the cat. In the grass lay three dead baby rabbits.

Fullman raised the little rabbit until it grew old enough to be released into the wild. Now, every time she sees a rabbit, she can't help but think of her Rody.

Fullman and her husband, Captain Charles Fullman of the same agency, have over twenty years on the force. That very special K-9, Rody, played a major part in the many successes Fullman has had during her police career.

You Can Run but You Can't Hide

Jesse Perron worked as a welder in the large, privately owned Newport News Shipbuilding and Drydock Company facility. His workplace was situated not more than five blocks from the neat, single-family home where he, his wife, Teresa, and their two children lived. It was a quiet, working-class neighborhood of older but well-kept homes situated on modest-size building lots. The Perrons must have been comfortable there, as they had plans to buy the place. By all accounts they were just an average American family trying to live their own lives.

But life holds many twists and turns. The Perrons' future would be changed by one person, someone whom neither Jesse nor Teresa knew, and who had his own plans for what lay in store for the family.

Something about Teresa must have fascinated this man, this person whom she didn't know. His desire for Teresa was sufficient to cause him to kill her husband, bashing his skull in with a crowbar as Jesse lay asleep next to his wife. Then the lust for the now-hysterical woman proved so strong that he repeatedly raped and sodomized her while they both lay next to Jesse's corpse.

Sometime before this tragedy occurred, although Teresa never mentioned it to her husband, for a number of days she noticed a sailor hanging around her neighborhood. Once she believed she saw him while out shopping. But Teresa hadn't thought much of it. She wasn't a paranoid person, and her life was busy, keeping up with the needs of her two children and husband as well as working at her home chores. It never occurred to her she might be in danger.

So it was that at five o'clock one winter's morning, the petite young woman awoke to see a maniac hovering over her husband, smashing the sleeping man in the head repeatedly with a crowbar. A small woman, not five feet tall, she was helpless in the face of the homicidal assault. With her husband dying on the bed next to them, the man she could only describe later as being in a white uniform raped and sodomized her.

The killer then took her downstairs to the living room, sexually assaulted her again, drank a Pepsi, then cleaned himself off with one of the children's diapers and robbed her of fourteen dollars. He left the house by the rear window, the same way he had entered.

Teresa called the police, but it was too late for Jesse.

The police arrived and, as is normal in any homicide investigation, they gathered the evidence and took it to the lab. Among the items were several the investigators thought might aid them in their search for the murderer. One was the diaper the killer had used to clean himself.

The woman also told the investigators that the killer had bitten her several times on the inside of the thigh when he was assaulting her. The Norfolk Medical Examiner was told of the marks and had the officers bring the woman to his office, where he took high-quality 35-mm photographs of the marks.

Using two of the more exotic tools of law enforcement, a tracking K-9 and a forensic odontologist, the police found both the diaper and the photos valuable in bringing the case to a successful conclusion.

It was five days later that Fullman and Rody were called in to the case. The detectives assigned to the investigation had called the chief of the Hampton Police Department and requested her and Rody's assistance. Fullman's chief in turn directed her to contact the detectives working on the murder. At the time Fullman's primary job was with the crime scene unit. She used Rody's services when a K-9 with tracking skills was required, and she and her four-legged partner were the only qualified team in the area. The pair went over to the neighboring city of Newport News, where Fullman drove her unmarked light blue Plymouth police car directly to the scene of the homicide and sexual assault, a twenty-minute ride.

Few serious crimes are solved by the work of one lone law

officer. In addition to the support given in this case to the investigators by crime scene unit people, they also depended on a number of other skilled enforcement specialists in order to conclude their complex investigation.

When Fullman arrived at the crime scene, two detectives, including Detective Charles "Chuck" Spinner, head investigator on the Perron murder, as well as crime scene personnel were waiting for her. Spinner showed Fullman the rooms where the events had taken place. The detective pointed out where the bloody crowbar had been found on the bedroom floor next to the blood-soaked bed. He took the officer down to the living room, showing her where the man had cleaned himself up and casually drunk a Pepsi.

Spinner also mentioned another fact that had been uncovered the day before. The reason Fullman had been asked to assist in the case was that a security guard who had been working at the gate to the large shipbuilding and repair facility near the Perron home had told investigators he remembered a sailor coming in on the same morning of the murder with blood on his uniform.

This was clearly a lead to be followed. Their problem was, the shipyard was enormous, with dozens of naval vessels based there in various stages of repair and refurbishment. The investigators needed to figure out which ship this possible suspect might have come from.

Many of the vessels in the yard were nuclear-powered, and the police department needed to get permission from the navy before they could set foot in the high-security area. At first the navy was skeptical about the claim that one of their personnel might have committed such a crime. It took some convincing, but permission had finally come down.

Fullman had told Spinner that she would need some scent material in order for Rody to start his track. What would be ideal would be the diaper the man had used to clean himself up with. Spinner had the evidence brought over to the crime scene from the police lab and placed it at Rody's disposal.

Fullman also made it clear that once Rody was on a track it would not be good to stop him because of some bureaucratic problem at the security gate. She was assured that the navy had given the necessary clearances for their mission to be carried out.

The neighborhood where the Perrons lived was fairly busy and consisted of a large number of homes built close together. Fullman wanted to begin Rody's track with as little disruption from the surrounding area as possible. She knew that their job was going to be a tough one no matter how she worked it—the scent trail was five days old, the area was heavily traveled, and the ground surfaces were mostly concrete and macadam, poor for holding on to the microscopic particles that make up the body-cell material Rody would be asked to follow.

Spinner showed the K-9 handler the plastic bag that held the diaper. Fullman asked the detective to have the bag placed, open, right by the window of entry and exit used by the killer.

While this was being done, Fullman, who had parked two blocks away from the home so that Rody wouldn't prematurely come into contact with the invisible track, prepared her partner. She went to the trunk of her cruiser and removed her K-9's heavy-duty leather harness. The piece of gear bore a silver-colored metal plate inscribed with the K-9's name. Rody wore it when he was tracking. Seeing the harness made her K-9 whirl in circles, tail wagging, dancing about in anticipation of doing what he liked best, working.

Opening Rody's car door, the officer secured the straps of the harness under his body and around his neck, at the same time telling him what they were going to do and asking him if he wanted to work. After she attached his bright blue, thirty-foot leash to his choke collar, Rody was ready.

The day was cloudy with the temperature in the mid-fifties, a good day to work. Fullman walked her partner over to the window. She had him sit, switching the lead from the chain collar to a ring located in the middle of the top of his harness. That way when he pulled, the pressure would be distributed over the animal's shoulders, chest, and back and not on his delicate and injury-prone neck.

She told Rody to "Such" ("suk," search in German) and at the same time permitted him to sniff the diaper in the plastic bag. Then Fullman stepped back about ten feet. Rody started by making four circles of the area, each one wider than the last, sniffing everything in sight. His nose went to nearby bushes, items of trash on the ground, whatever objects lay about. He then moved off at a fast walk. Heading toward the front of the home, he started for the sidewalk. With his nose to the ground, Rody pulled Fullman along, down the street and five blocks over to the gate of the shipyard.

The trackers were stopped by the tall chain-link fence and the security guard on duty. The detectives following behind Fullman and Rody quickly went up to the man and explained they had obtained permission to enter the premises. The guard knew nothing about it; he had to get authorization from higher management. This was the very problem Fullman had hoped to avoid, breaking off the search when her dog was hot on the trail.

It took thirty minutes for the snafu to be cleared up, and the officers and K-9 then were able to continue into the yard.

Once inside, Rody was once more permitted to sniff the diaper inside the plastic bag. Then the dog began to work his way past the heavy construction going on around him. Hundreds of people were working in the area, welding, riveting, laying electrical wire. The place was loud and disorienting, and smells of all sorts wafted around him from the various pools of liquid that covered almost all of the ground.

Rody went straight ahead for about a block. He made a right turn. On the left side of the dock they came to the U.S.S. *Carl Vinson,* a nuclear-powered aircraft carrier. The K-9 walked past the first gangplank, the one used by officers, and walked up the second, the entrance for enlisted personnel. The stairway was narrow, with gaps in its metal surface so that the ground below was clearly visible. The K-9 didn't hesitate for a moment. At its top, the law officers were stopped again by security personnel from continuing the track.

There was another twenty-minute wait until the ship's

captain came down and authorized the officers to continue. Rody rescented on the diaper and the track continued.

Five thousand people lived on the aircraft carrier. Many hundreds more worked on the vessel while it was in the yard for repair. The K-9 moved with deliberation, pulling Fullman hard through the body of the vessel. Sailors scattered upon seeing the big dog head their way. The team moved on through a number of large compartments until they came to an open metal door. To their right were stairs, really a ladder that went straight down. Rody went beyond the stairs about ten feet, stopped, and returned. He wanted to continue down the ladder.

Aircraft carriers are designed for humans, not dogs. There was no practical way to get Rody down that steep incline. The track was over. But it told the investigators what they wanted to know. Fullman assured the other investigators that whoever had killed Jesse Perron had gone onto the *Carl Vinson,* walked through the vessel, and gone down those steep stairs.

The question Spinner and the other detectives asked themselves was, how were they going to figure out which one of the five thousand crew members was the killer?

With Fullman and Rody's discovery, the navy changed its tune. They assigned a member of their own Naval Investigative Service to the homicide investigation team. The evidence that the investigators had to work with were the photos of bite marks taken from Teresa Perron's thigh.

Forensic odontology is a fairly new science. Its practitioners are dentists who have the skills necessary to identify individuals by the bite marks they leave on human flesh, generally at crime scenes and particularly at the scenes of sexual crimes or crimes of passion.

Teresa had observed her assailant only in the dark. Still, she was able to offer the police a general description of the man. She described him as being young and clean shaven, with sandy brown hair. Teresa also noticed black stripes on the man's white uniform. If he was in the navy, that would put him in the enlisted ranks.

The investigators used the woman's general description

to narrow down the suspects who were aboard the aircraft carrier at the time of the homicide. Members of the crew who were nonwhite, as well as all the females, were of course no concern. Although the suspect was probably an enlisted man, every non-excluded male would be looked at. The killer had a canine tooth that had grown in sideways. That anomaly would be sufficient to narrow down their suspects to a manageable handful of people. So the plan was for four dentists to examine the teeth of the 3,767 navy personnel assigned to the *Carl Vinson* who met the general description of the killer.

Fifteen men wound up on the short list. Impressions of their teeth were taken and sent to a local dentist to see if there was a match with the photographic bite marks taken of the victim's injuries.

The results were less than helpful. No match could be substantiated.

Then the investigators caught a lucky break. A confidential informant of Spinner's came forward and told the detective that a woman he knew had been bitten by a sailor during sex. The incident had so upset her that she had made a complaint about it to the police.

Spinner located the woman. She confirmed the informant's story. The couple had been seeing each other for a few months, and the man had gotten progressively rougher with her. On the day in question he had blackened her eyes and bitten her. This last incident had so distressed her that she had taken out a complaint of simple assault against the man. She told the detective the name of her former boyfriend, Keith Harward. His name was on the list of fifteen sailors garnered from the *Carl Vinson* part of the investigation.

Further inquiry turned up the fact that the man had been discharged from the navy several months earlier and was now living in a rural section of the western part of the state. Spinner checked out the man's name in the police files. He had never shown up for court on the assault charge, so there was a warrant out for his arrest. The detective decided to sit on that piece of intelligence for a moment.

Using their time wisely, Spinner and other investigators took the 35-mm evidence photos to New York City, along with the dental impressions that had been taken earlier of their suspect's teeth. There they met with Dr. Lowell Levine, a noted forensic odontologist. The doctor examined the material and told the men that their line of inquiry was worth pursuing, but it would take a few days for him to come to some conclusion.

Two days later, when Spinner was back in Newport News, Dr. Levine called. The doctor told the detective that with the preliminary work he'd done so far on the teeth, he couldn't tell the investigator the tooth match was one hundred percent. He could only say that in his opinion the match was 99.9 percent, and he suggested the investigators not bother to look at anyone else.

That was good enough for Spinner. It was also good enough for the navy. Dr. Levine, a captain in the naval reserve, was called in to active duty. He received orders to report to the navy facility near the Newport News boat dock for a two-week stint.

Using the modern facilities at the Norfolk navy laboratories, the doctor worked at putting together the necessary evidence to show conclusively that the bite marks made on Teresa Perron had come from one man, Keith Allen Harward, a twenty-seven-year-old who had just completed his service aboard the *Carl Vinson*. But the detective really needed a better mold of the man's teeth.

Harward lived in the western part of Virginia with his parents, who were in their seventies. Since he had been out of the navy for several months, he had no reason to believe he was a suspect in the Perron case.

Spinner and the other detectives decided to take a chance. The investigators knew Harward was due in court in Norfolk on the simple-assault case. On the day he was supposed to come before the judge, the detectives were there to greet him. After the hearing was over, they stepped up to Harward and spoke to him outside the courtroom. The detectives explained to the man that they were working on a murder case and asked if he would permit them to take him to a dentist for a mold to be made of his teeth. Just routine, you understand. They were investigating all the sailors aboard the *Carl Vinson*.

Harward agreed to the request. He was taken to a local dentist. After the simple procedure was accomplished, he was thanked and permitted to go home. The newly made impressions were rushed over to Dr. Levine. His examination was conclusive; only one man could have made the bite marks on Teresa Perron, and that person was Harward.

A warrant was obtained for the man's arrest. Armed with that legal document, Spinner and the other investigators went out to Harward's home, located out in the woods of Roanoke, and placed the man under arrest.

To the best of Spinner's knowledge, their suspect never made a statement to any law officer indicating his guilt. The detective remembered him as a quiet individual, really a loner, someone who hardly spoke at all unless another person spoke to him first. Harward's murder trial hinged on the bite-mark impressions from Teresa's thigh as well as the tracking of the killer onto the *Carl Vinson* by Rody. The two facts were weighed heavily by the jury. After due deliberation Harward was convicted of murder, rape, sodomy, burglary, and robbery.

So, because of a smart dog, dedicated investigators, and some solid police work, Harward will be spending the rest of his life in a Virginia penitentiary.

Murder in the Garden

Murders committed by strangers are fairly rare. Statistically, a person is far more likely to be killed by someone known to him or her. But then there are the exceptions. . . .

Debbie Dicus was a woman on the way up. A disk jockey for a locally popular country-western radio show, the thirty-one-year-old had a long and promising career ahead. She was also community minded. So when the town of Hampton set up an area for local people to plant gardens, Debbie decided to become involved in the project.

To get to the garden plots, which were located on Marcella Road, a person had to drive down a long dirt road. The area was not the best—why else would the town want the place spruced up?—just a vacant lot plowed over by the city. Now, though, instead of old tires and abandoned cars littering the place, there were a few dozen attractive garden plots tended by citizens.

On the day of her homicide, during the early afternoon, Debbie was working at her small piece of land. When she first arrived, a number of other people were tending their little rectangles of property.

Walking along on the outskirts of the area was a lone man carrying an air rifle and plinking at tin cans and birds. Several people noticed him, but he walked in such a way, with his head down, so that his face wasn't clearly visible. No one paid much attention to him.

The Hampton police received a telephone call from someone who claimed to have found a dead human body. The man's name was Ronald Earl Blanchard, and he called from the home where he lived with his young wife, their two-month-old baby, and his mother-in-law. A loner, Blanchard had dropped out of high school before finishing the tenth grade. The place where he and his family lived was on the top of a church building, and their stay there was made possible through the good auspices of the minister and congregation.

According to Blanchard, he had discovered the body and had immediately run home. His wife, coming down the stairs from their apartment, saw that her husband was upset. He blurted out, "I found a body." She observed that there was blood on his shirt and hands.

Blanchard's description of where the body lay was too vague for the police to follow. The garden area where it was situated was an out-of-the-way location. He agreed to meet the assigned officer at a nearby fire station to lead him to the scene.

When the officer arrived, he followed behind Blanchard's red-and-white Ford pickup truck. Blanchard drove his truck to the garden area, pulling up behind Debbie Dicus' small auto. Getting out of his truck, he pointed out to the officer where he had come upon the body. The first attempt by the policeman to locate the dead person was unsuccessful. The officer had to return to Blanchard and have him take him to the location, as the victim lay almost hidden from view behind thick brush.

With Blanchard's assistance, the officer finally spotted the partially nude corpse of Debbie Dicus and called for assistance.

Investigators soon came onto the crime scene and spoke to Blanchard. His story was that he was walking along, plinking at birds with his air rifle, when he spotted the dead woman. The investigators wondered how he could have seen the victim from the road, since the body was so well concealed from view from that location. One of the investigators then inquired if Blanchard had touched the body, as he had blood on his arm. The young man replied that all he had done was touch her hand to see if she had a pulse.

Asked if he was positive of that, Blanchard reiterated that he had only touched her hand to check for her pulse, that was it. He had then run home and called the police. When asked to account for the blood on his shirt, Blanchard stated that he had had to reach across the woman to touch her hands, thereby apparently smearing blood on his shirt.

That wouldn't be the last version of the explanation Blanchard gave of how he had come in contact with the dead woman.

The investigators moved their attention to the crime scene. Debbie lay half in a ditch. Her blouse and bra had been pulled off and her jeans and panties had been lowered below her crotch. She had apparently made a futile effort to grab for support, because her clenched fist held pieces of vegetation from the bank where she lay. The hoe that the woman had brought with her to use in her garden, and which turned out to be one of the weapons used to kill her, was lying under muddy water at the bottom of the ditch.

At that moment Blanchard wasn't a suspect. It appeared that he had found the victim, and while some of his explanations seemed strange, the investigators had to consider his level of sophistication when interpreting his responses to their questions.

At around nine o'clock Fullman and Rody were called in

on the case. As in most investigations, this was done when the majority of other leads had fizzled out. It was dusk by the time the officer and her K-9 arrived at the scene. She found cars parked all over the place. Many of them were department autos, but a large number belonged to local citizens, including members of the nearby church and of Blanchard's family. Fullman parked as far away from the crowd as she could, placing her cruiser behind the funeral home's hearse, then made her way over to the investigators.

The lead investigator, Detective John D. Spencer, walked her through the homicide scene. Stepping over the yellow crime-scene tape, the detective pointed out to Fullman the area where the struggle had taken place. To Fullman's trained eye, the story of what happened was clear. The dusty road held good impressions of the recent events. A woman's blue shirt, turned inside out, lay on the ground. Along with the shirt were car keys and two combs from Debbie's long hair, as well as cigarettes, some still in their pack, others loose and scattered about. Her Bic lighter, an iron garden rake, and a glove also lay on the ground. Blood was on the car, and its dusty surface showed rub marks where the bodies had moved against it as the victim and her killer struggled. Stepping away from the car, the officer could clearly see a trail of blood spots in the vegetation and dirt that led to the ditch where the body and broken hoe lay. Nothing had been touched yet by the investigators, although the crime scene unit people had already taken photos of everything.

Fullman asked the detective how the victim was killed. The investigator told her he wasn't sure yet. As there were deep long gashes visible on her back, one of the weapons used was probably some metal tool, perhaps a hoe—maybe the hoe lying under water at the bottom of the ditch.

Fullman didn't want to disturb the body, so she asked one of the forensic technicians to put on a pair of latex gloves and bring her the hoe. If that was a murder weapon, then the killer had handled it. It was just possible that Rody would be able to scent on it.

The man did as she requested, bringing the broken tool

up to the edge of the road and placing it on the grass. Meanwhile Fullman had returned to her car and put Rody in harness. It was about time for her partner to go to work.

She made sure everyone stayed back from her and her K-9. Taking Rody over to the hoe, Fullman had him sit by her side as she patted and talked to him for a few minutes. When she felt they were communicating, she pointed to the hoe and gave him the search command, "Such."

Rody stood up and stepped over to the object, smelling it all over. Fullman, at the other end of her partner's thirty-foot leash, just stood back and waited. The dog sniffed the ground, then began to walk in ever-widening circles. He then headed in the direction where all the cars were parked. Going past Debbie's small car, he stopped at the driver's door of Blanchard's pickup. Rody walked back and forth in the area around the truck, then headed straight for the crowd of people fifty yards away who stood silently watching him work.

Once by the large group of spectators, he sniffed around their periphery, then moved in among them. Fullman called out, "Nobody move! Stand still, the dog won't hurt you." As the officer was saying this, Rody made his way directly to where Blanchard, along with his wife and mother-in-law, stood.

When Rody came to Blanchard, the K-9 stopped by the young man and sniffed up and down his leg. Fullman, watching her partner work, realized that the track had just come to a successful conclusion. She gently pulled Rody back to her side and without comment returned to the investigating detectives.

She quietly told the lead detective, "Blanchard has held that hoe."

Now all the investigators had to do was prove the man had committed the murder. That meant collecting all the forensic evidence available and putting together their case.

While searching for more clues, Fullman's husband, who was also working at the scene, found a quarter-inch broken piece of black plastic sitting on top of the tread marks made in the dirt by Debbie's left rear tire. The object had fallen to the ground after the car's tire had made its impression. The object was retrieved and vouchered as evidence.

Blanchard was asked if the officers could look inside his truck. He said, "Sure." Inside the cab was his air rifle, which he permitted the investigators to remove so that they could examine it further.

That evening the detectives invited the man to come down to the police station with them to discuss the matter. That was the first of a number of meetings Blanchard had with investigators during the next few weeks.

Later, in the lab, the technicians found strands of hair and traces of blood on various parts of the rifle that matched the victim's. Also, a small bit of the gun's black plastic stock had chipped off. The piece of plastic Fullman's husband had discovered turned out to be a perfect match for the missing fragment.

The detectives' thorough investigation took some time. People around the area were interviewed. The officers reconstructed the evening of the homicide as best they could. They learned that one by one the gardeners had left the area. At around six in the evening some young boys on bicycles had passed by the place. When questioned later by the police, the youths told officers that the only two people they saw around them were the young woman tending her plot and a lone man carrying an air rifle.

With each interview Blanchard had with the police, the man changed his story to suit whatever new facts were presented to him. When they finally asked him about the hoe, he said that he had found the tool on top of the woman's body and had tossed it into the ditch before checking her pulse. The detectives weren't convinced. Blanchard's story became ever more convoluted the more he tried to talk himself out of complicity in the crime. It didn't help his case when the forensic lab came back with a report that the blood found on his shirt hadn't been smeared there, as he had claimed, but had splattered onto the cloth. Such splattering would occur when someone struck someone else with great force, breaking their skin in the process.

An autopsy showed that Debbie had suffered six major wounds to the head, neck, and back. The hoe and Blanchard's air rifle were shown to have been the striking implements used. The woman had died as a result of strangulation, partial drowning, and the blows to her head.

The evidence carefully gathered by the investigation team proved irrefutable. After a trial, Blanchard was convicted of first-degree murder, abduction, attempted rape, and the illegal use of a firearm. He is now serving two life terms plus twelve years in a Virginia penitentiary.

An Enterprising K-9

For nearly a month, Fullman had been trying to get to the police firing range to qualify, as required by state law and department regulations. Twice during the preceding four weeks she'd been scheduled to shoot, and both times the officer had been called away so that she and Rody could do their thing.

In fact, Fullman was an expert with a hand gun. During her police career she and her husband, who were both on the department's shooting team, won a Secret Service–sponsored police pistol competition in Maryland. So it wasn't for lack of desire that she hadn't gone out to requalify.

Fullman figured she would make it through her mandated training this time. The department's firearms instructor was already a half hour into his safety lecture to the fifteen officers present, and Fullman was determined to get the day's instruction over and done with.

Then the officer's pager went off. The message broadcast was, "Call headquarters." All Fullman could do was sigh "Not again" and excuse herself from the class to go and make the necessary telephone call. The sergeant giving the firearms safety lecture gave Fullman a withering look that said it all. He was never going to get this woman qualified.

At that time the range was situated behind the city's dump, and the nearest telephone was half a mile away. Fullman drove to the guard shack, used the phone there, and was told she and Rody were required to help investigate a burglary. Fullman hung up the receiver, returned to the sergeant, and told him, "I got to go."

The sergeant just shook his head, clearly less than thrilled that his hard-to-pin-down officer was leaving.

Wearing range attire—jeans and a T-shirt with a small .38 on her hip—Fullman didn't take the time to change into her uniform. She headed home, only a few miles away, to pick up Rody, who, on seeing his partner, began to jump up against the fence and run excitedly in circles. He knew that Mom didn't come home in the middle of the day for no reason.

Opening the gate, Fullman called out, "Let's go, gotta go to work, let's go." Rody didn't have to be told twice. Fitting his water bucket into its hole in the rear platform of the car, Fullman let Rody jump in and they headed to the crime scene.

The suspect had already been placed under arrest and was being held in a police cruiser parked at a car wash in a commercial district of town. The officers were there waiting for Fullman and her K-9. They knew they had a burglary. One of the victim's neighbors saw the man in custody coming out of a home, so there was plenty of reason to believe they had the burglar. What they needed to find was the evidence linking him to the crime. That's why Rody had been called in.

Among the K-9's talents was the ability (he had been trained for this) to find crime-scene evidence. The K-9 was able to search out anything that had an odor that didn't fit the surrounding location.

The suspect, a twenty-four-year-old wearing dark clothing, sat silently in the rear of the police cruiser. One of the officers walked over to Fullman and explained what was needed.

Fullman turned to Rody and connected his lead to his collar, not the harness. That meant to the K-9 they'd be looking for evidence. It was a task Rody was really good at. Once, during a training exercise conducted in an empty football stadium, Fullman gave another officer a two-inch square of plastic, the "evidence." She told him to go out into the open field and toss the little piece of plastic as hard as he could, while she and Rody waited behind the bleachers, out of sight.

Once the plastic piece was hidden, Fullman took Rody out from the bleachers and, because it was an enclosed area, unhooked his lead. She gave him the search command and timed him as he looked for the little square block. It took the dog eleven seconds to find the article in the empty football field. That even impressed Fullman.

This time it was antique gold and silver jewelry, a family's heirlooms, that Rody was searching for.

Fullman had one small problem. In order to find anything their suspect had stolen, she would have to do a reverse track on the man. Her K-9 wasn't permitted to come directly in contact with a live person in order to pick up a scent. She decided to try having the arresting officers roll down one of the rear windows of the cruiser where the burglar was seated so that Rody might then pick up his odor.

After the officers complied with her request, the K-9 handler brought her dog past the cruiser, and at the moment he went past the open window, Fullman gave Rody the evidence-search command.

Rody got the idea immediately. He began to circle the area, then headed to the rear of the car-wash building. He led Fullman to a ten-foot chain-link fence, which had a hole opened in it large enough for a person to get through. It didn't take a rocket scientist to figure out that their burglar had come this way before. She and her K-9 went through the hole.

Rody took his partner another twenty-five yards farther and down a ditch that ran parallel to the fence behind the commercial buildings. Trash and debris covered a good portion of the ground. Rody went directly over to some crumpled newspapers. When Fullman pulled on the papers, she saw that underneath lay all the antique jewelry stolen in the burglary.

Fullman congratulated her partner and notified the arresting officers. She stood by while the crime scene unit people were called in to take photos of the site.

With her and Rody's job done, she started back for the

hole in the fence, but Rody had other ideas. He refused to go. He tugged at his lead and looked in the opposite direction to where Fullman wanted to go, while he kept his nose to the ground.

Fullman was aware of only a single burglary, so she was unsure what her K-9 was trying to tell her. But she was also an experienced K-9 handler and wisely decided to listen to her dog.

She turned to a uniformed officer standing nearby and said, "Let's go see what he wants. Something's wrong."

Fullman unsnapped the lead from Rody's collar and fastened it to the top of his harness. With no other command, her dog took off. He headed fifteen yards farther down the ditch, then cut across and over to the other side. Fullman and the other officer found they were now in a residential area at the end of a cul-de-sac.

The two humans and the K-9 headed down the road. Rody stayed mostly on the sidewalk, but occasionally he wandered into the yards along the way. Making a right turn a few blocks from where they'd begun, he came to a handsome brick home and went around to the rear door, which Fullman and the other officer found ajar.

Concerned that there might be an injured person inside, the officer entered while Fullman and Rody stayed in the backyard. The place was empty, but it had been ransacked.

Once more uniformed personnel were called in to secure the location and the crime scene unit was advised to send someone down to dust for prints and take photos.

Fullman never permitted Rody to enter the home. She stayed in the yard with her partner during this entire time. While they were waiting for their support people to arrive, her dog continued to indicate to her he wanted to continue the track by pulling on his lead.

There was no second-guessing her K-9 now. As soon as she could get away from the crime scene, she and her dog continued on their search.

Rody took Fullman beyond the backyard they were in, over a four-foot fence, and onto the adjacent street. Traveling several more blocks, Rody again took his partner to the rear of a substantial residence. There she could see a broken window that was open several inches. The officer soon found that that house had also been burglarized.

With that last burglary uncovered, Rody stopped indicating to Fullman that he wished to go anyplace else. The track was indeed over.

While waiting for backup officers to arrive, Fullman contacted the first officers she'd dealt with. She asked about the swag Rody had first located. It turned out that not only was every piece of jewelry from the initial theft found, but there were additional pieces as well. It took some sorting out, but evidence from the other break-ins was eventually found among the recovered loot.

The evidence obtained through the remarkable work of Fullman and Rody was sufficient so that the burglar pleaded guilty to all the crimes. He was sentenced to six years in prison, with a minimum of four years to serve, a substantial sentence for a burglar to receive. All because of a smart and talented K-9 who had a handler who knew how to listen to her dog.

Chapter 9

Massachusetts State Police
K-9 Unit

K-9s Dan and Syros with Trooper Kathy (Kathleen) Barrett

"Dogs Don't Know How to Lie"

Kathy Barrett has been a member of the Massachusetts State Police since 1980. She recalls that back then women were just coming on to the force in numbers. While she might not have been the only female on the state police force, there still weren't many troopers of her gender listed on any troop's roster.

Her goal had always been to be a dog handler. Ever since she could remember, Barrett has liked dogs. When she was a child, strays seemed to be forever following her home. She first tried to get into the state police K-9 unit in 1985. It took her a few more years, but in 1987 Barrett graduated from the training program. Now Barrett is a veteran in the field and is a certified trainer for utility and working police dogs as well as cadaver-sniffing dogs.

Barrett's first K-9 partner was Syros. His name came from Greek mythology, referring to the god of the gates of heaven. She remembers him being a very special dog. Barrett purchased Syros with her own money. The state police K-9 program is changed now, and troopers aren't permitted to do that anymore. They took part in Schutzhund (the German word for a protection-trained dog) events, which involve statewide competitions. Syros was three when they teamed up and, as are all state police K-9s, he was an alpha dominant male. The pair worked together as partners for six years. Barrett remembers how Syros wound up with arthritis due to injuries he'd received on the job. As her partner grew older, she watched as the bone disease really slowed him down, but she proudly recalls that her dog's nose stayed sharp to the end. The hardest thing Barrett ever did in her life was to have the vet come over and put Syros down. The dog had been her friend and her patrol partner, and he had saved her life on many occasions. She recalls that she would talk to him as if he were a person, and she believes Syros could sense and understand her moods and wants.

But when the day came, in Barrett's heart she knew it was time. The trooper had seen that Syros's quality of life had become miserable. His arthritis had crippled him. Barrett is certain that if the two had changed places, Syros would have done the same for her.

The trooper buried Syros in her backyard.

Dan is Barrett's current K-9 partner and, like Syros, is a big shepherd. Oddly enough, his personality is the opposite of Syros'. Syros was an intelligent-looking dog and very methodical. When he tracked he put his nose to the ground and couldn't be distracted. And he loved kids. Barrett remembers how funny it was to watch her big, tough ninety-five-pound K-9 with a bunch of kids hanging all over him. On the other hand, Dan is, in her words, a "space-ball." Dan is hyperactive. That's just his personality. When he sees his tracking harness, he starts to whine like a baby. Dan likes to run when he tracks, with his partner hanging on to his lead for dear life. He came from Czechoslovakia, so Barrett figures (tongue in cheek) maybe that's just how Eastern Europeans are.

When Dan first arrived, Syros was still alive. Every day the three would go through obedience training. Syros, who was super sharp, would become visibly disgusted with Dan when Dan screwed up. When Dan didn't do what he was supposed to do, Syros would actually sigh. And when Dan heard Syros sigh, Barrett claims you could tell the younger dog realized he'd made a mistake.

Barrett feels that Dan is doing okay now, and she's sure he's going to work out fine.

Both dogs were imported. As with most of the handlers I've spoken to, Barrett found the American breed of shepherds were all too likely to suffer from bad hips. In the States dogs are raised for looks, in Europe for work. Syros and Dan were trained as utility-working police dogs as well as in handler protection. As are all Massachusetts State Police K-9s, both of her dogs were cross-trained. Dan is trained for search and rescue as well as for body recovery. Barrett likes to point out that not all police departments use cross-trained dogs. Some utility-work dogs, such as bloodhounds, are used only for tracking. Some are trained only for explosives, narcotics, or arson work; others just locate victims of disasters who are buried under tons of rubble.

Like Syros, Dan is a cadaver-sniffing dog. That is, he's been trained to alert to the scent of human blood, semen, and decaying human body parts (he's referred to as being crime-scene trained). Barrett claims that Dan is so good that even if a hundred people have been in an area, the trooper can show him an article of clothing from a specific person and he'll ignore everyone else's scent while looking for that particular individual. Dan also knows how to do building searches and will also do an article search, which means he can find anything with a human scent on it. He can even sit in a boat and tell you where a body is located under water, which, Barrett says, is something you have to see to believe.

According to Barrett, when a problem develops in the field, such as a disagreement between the K-9 and his human partner over whether anything of value is out there, most of the time it's the result of human error. After all, at three in the morning a person can't see, let alone smell, the human blood on the ground that the dog is trying to tell him is out there. Barrett argues that the dogs don't know how to lie. It's just that sometimes it's important for the handler to listen very closely.

If Dan could talk, the trooper figures she'd be unemployed, because he'd be driving the cruiser, answering the calls. Her bosses would love him, Barrett figures. He wouldn't know enough to talk back and would only cost some kibble and an occasional bone. Anyway, sometimes she thinks Dan would rather have her sticking her head out the back window while he was in the front, driving the cruiser.

Another Victim of the System

Dan is a big friendly dog, but he also knows how to protect both Barrett and himself. Recently the pair were working a night shift. It was a cold mid-January evening and the team was on the road working the Brockton area. The trooper's cruiser was sitting on a side street when a car, without its headlights on, started to come her way. Barrett swung the cruiser around, switched on the blue lights, and came up behind the other vehicle. The driver pulled over. As the trooper started to get out of her car, she made sure she had opened up the driver's side window for Dan. As the saying goes, you never know when you'll need a cop, and Dan is a damn good one.

As she moved closer to the man's car, Barrett sensed that something wasn't right. The driver was sitting with both hands on the steering wheel, his eyes staring straight ahead. The trooper ordered him to turn off the car's engine and roll down his window. He didn't budge or acknowledge her presence. Pulling open the car's door, she told the man once more to turn off his car's motor. For a few additional seconds the driver sat there like a zombie, then reached over for the glove compartment. As he did so the trooper saw something that made his leather jacket pocket swell out unnaturally. By this time Barrett was uncomfortable with the whole scene, and when she saw the bulge in the jacket, the image of a gun flashed through her mind. Barrett yelled for the driver to stop moving and thrust out her hand for his pocket just as the man did likewise. After a short tug of war, the trooper came away with two brown bags in her hand. Still uncertain what she had, she asked the driver if it was a gun. He said no, it was drugs, cocaine.

Now the man began to sweat profusely even though the January night was cold. In order to handcuff the suspect, who was now under arrest, Barrett ordered him to get out of the vehicle. That was a mistake. The next thing she knew, the man jumped from the car, shoved her into the oncoming traffic, then bolted down the road. A couple of cars came so close to her that their drivers had to swerve in order to avoid hitting her. By this time Dan was not a happy camper. He was just about to jump out of the troop-car window and into the traffic himself, when Barrett yelled for him to stay put. She wasn't about to risk Dan's life—he's her best friend after all—just to chase down some S.O.B.

She jumped back into her car. By this time the guy was racing down the street, and she radioed for backup. As Barrett kept her eyes on the running man, she watched him pull off his leather jacket and toss it away. Now he was wearing only jeans and sneakers, not even a shirt.

Barrett pulled the troop car off the road, and she and Dan got out to find the suspect. They trailed him for about half a mile along some railroad tracks. Dan and Barrett could hear him up ahead but couldn't see him in the dark (at least she couldn't; she doesn't know about Dan).

Finally the suspect came to a fence, jumped it, and headed into a residential area. Barrett radioed to other troopers and to the Brockton PD what was going on. In a matter of minutes she had five state and Brockton police cars surrounding the area's perimeter.

Dan and Barrett made it over the fence and found themselves in a backyard. All at once Dan nearly yanked the trooper off her feet as he headed toward a swimming pool. Looking under the pool's attached deck, she saw the suspect's legs within the wood structure. Three times the trooper yelled to the man to come out or she would send the dog in. Her flashlight beam was right on him, so she knew the suspect was aware the game was over. Barrett couldn't figure out why the guy didn't call it quits unless he had a gun and meant to keep her from taking him. Meanwhile Dan was barking, becoming more and more agitated.

Well, Barrett wasn't about to crawl under the deck to find out what this individual—who was still trying to move further away from her—had on his mind. That's what Dan gets paid for.

She released Dan, and her partner went right for the suspect. Dan grabbed the man by his leg and literally dragged him out from his hiding place. When she could see that the guy didn't have a gun in his hand, she ordered Dan to let him go.

By this time other officers were on the scene, and one of them cuffed the suspect. Barrett looked inside the brown bags taken from the man's jacket pocket and found what later weighed out to be fifty grams of cocaine. By the time they got back over to her cruiser, the suspect must have decided he needed a story. He blurted out, "You planted the stuff on me, just like they did O. J.!"

At that moment all Barrett could do was stand there and shake her head in wonder.

Three Tough Guys

Syros, her first K-9 partner, was pretty tough. Barrett remembers one incident among many when the pair were out working, also in Brockton. A call had been broadcast over the police radio alerting troopers to be on the lookout for three men who were wanted for an armed rape, a serious matter indeed. As luck would have it, the trooper spotted the suspects' car within a few minutes of receiving their vehicle's description and license plate number. She knew that she faced an immediate tactical problem as she pulled in behind the car. She could see that the vehicle's driver was keeping his eyes glued to her cruiser through his car's rearview mirror. If she turned on her roof lights, Barrett knew there'd be a chase, an event she wished to avoid. So she decided to try a ruse. After Barrett radioed in her location over the state police frequency, she got on her public address system and called out to the three men in the other vehicle that something was dangling from the bottom of their car. The trick worked. They waved to her and pulled over.

Once the two vehicles were stopped and safely on the side of the road, Barrett performed a felony stop. She leaped from her cruiser, her 9mm pistol in her hand, and ordered the three out of their car and over to the state police cruiser.

Syros had already obeyed her order to sit on the hood of the troop car.

She commanded the three to place their hands on the hood of her cruiser. To Syros she barked out the words, "Watch them!" He immediately began to move back and forth among the three, his face inches from theirs, barking and generally letting them know what was expected of them. The three men remained glued to the hood of the car. It was obvious to Barrett that no one in that trio had any doubt that Syros would take a piece out of the first man who tried to move.

With her partner covering the suspects, she moved back over to their vehicle. Through the passenger side window she saw the butt of a handgun jutting out from the rear bench seat. Barrett reached in, scooped it up, and waited for more officers to arrive. After a while, wondering what was taking her backup so long to get there, she turned away from watching the three suspects to see a swarm of cruisers sitting where a moment earlier her back had been turned. It seemed that her fellow officers had remained away because they were nearly as afraid of Syros as the bad guys were.

Calling her partner off, she let the other officers cuff the suspects. It was at this point that Barrett noted a foul odor coming from one of the individuals. It seemed that her partner had so unnerved the man that he had relieved himself right were he stood.

As the trio were being driven away Barrett thought: those three were pretty intimidating when they had a gun and were dealing with a lone woman. They didn't prove to be so tough when they had to face her partner.

Body, Body, Who's Got the Body?

Dan and Barrett were involved in an unusual homicide investigation not long ago. It began with a radio call over the state police frequency. The pair were headed for a work detail when Barrett was asked to swing by an address in the town of Plymouth. Members of the local department thought there was the possibility that a homicide had taken place. They did have one small problem—they couldn't locate the victim's body.

A day earlier a police operator had received a 911 call. On the other end of the telephone the police operator heard the sound of a woman screaming. Then the telephone went dead. The operator had the location's address, as it was automatically generated on a monitor by the emergency 911 system. Police were immediately dispatched to the scene. When officers arrived, they saw broken window glass and a good deal of blood splattered in front of the building—a long warehouse. A portion of the structure was rented out, but otherwise the inside was mostly unoccupied rooms full of assorted junk. A man met them inside and he had a story. He told the officers his name was Michael Kelly and he had cut himself on the broken glass they'd seen. Kelly told the police that he'd just called his wife and was leaving to get medical attention for his cut. The officers asked for and received permission from Kelly to search the building. A building search, particularly one with a large area that contained various-shaped pieces of debris, is a very difficult place for an officer to find evidence. The officers looked around but found nothing. For lack of any additional information, they too left the area.

Just a few hours later an officer from the same jurisdiction received a telephone call from a local family. Their nineteen-year-old daughter was missing. With a description of the missing woman's car, it didn't take officers long to find her vehicle behind the same building that the earlier 911 hang-up call had come from. More than a little suspicious of Kelly, the police ran a criminal-records check on the man. The officers discovered that Kelly had recently been released from the Massachusetts Correctional Institute at Bridgewater. Bridgewater, the officers knew, is where sexually dangerous criminals are incarcerated.

Yet, it wasn't until the next day that Barrett and Dan were called to the scene. The previous day, and well into the night, the police had painstakingly searched the warehouse as well as the building's surrounding area. Despite their efforts they had been unable to locate any trace of the probable victim.

While the search was taking place, other investigators had interviewed Kelly's wife. They learned she had married Kelly while he was still in prison. The officers also found out that her husband had not been home since the previous day. Based on this and other information, the police sought and received a warrant for Kelly's arrest. In addition, they put out a nationwide bulletin for the man's arrest.

By the time Barrett and her K-9 pulled up to the warehouse, a tired group of dispirited officers was standing at its entrance. Barrett released Dan from the cruiser, and the K-9 was promptly alerted to the blood that lay splashed around the front window. Almost immediately Dan broke away from the trooper and went tearing into the large warehouse structure, Barrett close behind. The trooper didn't have a clue about what was on Dan's mind, but she knew she had better stick with him.

By the time Barrett caught up with her partner, Dan had gotten to the warehouse's back door and was pulling vigorously on an old tarpaulin. On top of the cover was a heavy wood pallet, a bunch of cement, and a thick covering of some gritty material. It looked to Barrett as if the pile had been there for a long time, so the trooper couldn't figure out what Dan was doing. She speculated that perhaps some small object, like a bloody knife, had been tossed behind the mess and that was what her K-9 partner was excited about.

Barrett began to give Dan a hand at tearing into the material. Like all K-9 assigned troopers, she was dressed not in the spit-and-polish uniform of the Massachusetts State Police, but in a dark gray utility coverall adorned with the appropriate state police patches, a modified nylon duty belt cinched around her waist. Anyone who has ever watched Barrett while she's at work with Dan quickly realizes the reason the trooper is dressed the way she is. Being a K-9 officer can be both labor intensive and very dirty. Once the pair cleared away some of the material, Dan jumped behind the remaining rubble. Barrett climbed over the debris and looked down at the K-9. Next to him, on the side of a large cardboard container, she spotted a bloody handprint. Looking closer she could see a human toe jutting from inside that same box.

The handprint turned out to belong to Michael Kelly. The body was that of the missing nineteen-year-old.

Barrett returned to the officers who were still calmly standing by the front of the warehouse and informed them that she and Dan had just found a dead human body. For a moment there was stunned silence, and the officers stared at her in disbelief. After all, they had searched every inch of that warehouse for a day and a night.

Escorting the officers to the rear of the building, Barrett pointed out to them the cardboard box. The police now had body number one.

While the investigators were relieved to have found the victim, there was something else about the situation that bothered Barrett. The trooper knew that she and her partner had searched the same general area a few months earlier for another missing person, also a woman around twenty years of age. That person had never been located. And she had lived two doors down from the warehouse.

A few days went by. During this period the fleeing Kelly managed to get himself arrested in Florida—for drunk driving of all reasons. By this time his wife had started to become concerned that her husband had left other "things" lying around their home. She asked that the state police check both her yard and her parents' yard (they lived next door to each other), just to make sure.

Once again Barrett and Dan were called to the scene. The neighborhood consisted of middle-class homes on modest plots of land, one lot next to the other, indistinguishable from a hundred other Massachusetts suburbs. The K-9 team first went to the Kelly house and performed a search of the home and its crawl space without finding anything. Then they headed outside. Dan promptly went over to the rear of the yard where a substantial woodpile sat. He urgently began to pull at the pieces of wood. As always, Dan's partner came over and helped. Once the wood was removed, the pair found an old tire. Dan pulled on that.

Barrett moved it away, asking Dan, "What do you got buddy? What's down there?"

Dan ignored Barrett and kept on digging until he came to some large rocks. Again the trooper had to assist Dan in getting them out of the way. Barrett saw that the K-9 was still showing real excitement as he continued to vigorously dig into the soil. The layer beneath the unearthed rocks was composed of some bricks. Barrett could see that Dan's frustration level was getting high, and Dan began to make it clear that he knew he had found what he was supposed to and was expecting his reward. What Dan wanted Barrett to give him was the dirty old tennis ball she carried in a pouch on her duty belt. When Dan finds something they are looking for, the ball comes out. It's Dan's toy and his reward for a successful job. At that moment Dan was telling her, in very clear dog language, "It's here, we've got it, now give me the ball!" But all Barrett could see was more dirt. The trooper yanked out the layer of bricks and told Dan to keep at it.

The dog continued to paw at the ground until coming to a layer of kitty litter. Barrett knew that material had no business being so far under the earth. With that Dan put his head down, gave her a sideward glance, and growled, his way of saying, "Hey, stupid, I told you so. Now give me the damn ball." Lying under Dan's head was what they had both been seeking, human remains. It was the body of the missing young woman from a month earlier.

Kelly was brought back to Massachusetts and ultimately pleaded guilty to two counts of murder in the first degree. Barrett hopes that maybe he'll be kept in Bridgewater a little longer this time.

The Murder of Innocents

Barrett is an experienced, perhaps even hardened, state trooper. Her line of work demands that of a person. I've been there, I know. A few years back I served as a New York City homicide detective. When in the field, at a crime scene,

I'd tell myself that thing in front of me wasn't a dead human being, it was just a hunk of meat. I'd work hard at convincing myself it had never lived or loved or had hopes and dreams.

If you don't do that, you've got two options: find some other line of work or go crazy.

Barrett believes that so long as she can mentally disassociate herself from the victims she and her K-9 partner find, she can handle whatever comes her way. Except with kids. They're different. Most of the time it's okay, but other times there are images that don't want to fade away. There's at least one case Barrett spoke of, and which she didn't want me to write about, where the pictures in her head just won't disappear. But then there are the cases that simply rise to the level of being merely horrible. The next two stories are examples of those.

Baby Killer

The investigation began when a Lawrence police dispatcher received a 911 call from an upset woman. The person claimed that her boyfriend had killed her two children and buried them in the woods behind a local cemetery.

Gloria Pena, twenty, and David Alicea, twenty-four, lived together with their two children. The youngest was Alicea's. The two-year-old was the result of a liaison Pena had with another man. Neighbors of the couple thought nothing out of the ordinary when, during the fall, they stopped seeing first the baby and then a few weeks later the two-year-old around the neighborhood. When asked, Pena and Alicea stated that child-welfare people had taken their kids from them. Their explanation seemed logical to everyone around the couple and went unquestioned.

Barrett first heard of the matter late one afternoon while she was out on patrol with Dan. She claims he's like her American Express card, she doesn't leave home without him. In their cruiser was a video crew from the television show, *Real Stories from the Highway Patrol,* hoping to capture on tape some exciting action scenes for the viewing public's seemingly insatiable appetite for true police-adventure tales.

While driving along on what had been a routine day of work, the trooper received a radio call. She was to telephone the Middlesex County District Attorney's State Police CPAC unit. A few minutes later she was on the phone to State Police Sergeant Jack Garvin, who briefed Barrett on what he had. Pena's story was that her boyfriend had killed the two children and that she had helped bury their bodies on the grounds of a nearby cemetery. Was her story some twisted hoax? Would the police be able to bring the woman out to the cemetery to have her point out the places where the children were supposed to be buried? Those were questions to which the sergeant had no answer at the moment. They only thing he knew was, it would be dark soon, he already had a large number of state and local officers at the scene looking for grave sites, and he could certainly use Dan's ability to locate dead human beings, whether in the dark or at high noon.

Barrett rogered his request. Dropping off the protesting video crew—Barrett would be damned if she'd take them along to what might prove to be a fresh homicide scene—she and her partner headed out in the direction of the Lawrence Police Department.

The rush-hour traffic slowed her down, but once at the station house Barrett found Sergeant Garvin was already there, awaiting her arrival. He told her that everybody involved in the case was already out at the scene. After an additional short briefing, a Lawrence police cruiser was assigned to lead the trooper to the cemetery where a search was in progress at that very moment.

As Barrett and Dan's state police car turned onto the road that led into the Bellevue Cemetery, she discovered she had to hunt around for a place to park as other law officers' and medical examiners' vehicles were everywhere. Finding herself an open spot, the trooper saw that the crime-scene-unit people had bright floodlights set up on the grounds to assist the searchers. The unnaturally powerful white glare they emitted, which was blocked in places by rows of tombstones and by the dozen or so people moving about, cast eerie shadows on the snow-covered ground. The scene before her seemed to be just the right setting for conducting a search for two murdered children.

Barrett stepped from her car and walked over to a group of officers digging into the nearly frozen earth. She asked an investigator from the CPAC unit what they'd found and was told the body of the nine-month-old had just been uncovered.

The trooper went back to her cruiser and let Dan out, taking him fifty feet beyond the place where the dead infant lay. She was careful to position herself and Dan to ensure that the gentle early evening breeze wouldn't blow over the body and toward them. Showing her K-9 his thick nylon search collar—it let him know what was he was expected to do—she feigned excitement, asking him, "Do you want to go to work? Do you want to go to work?" her way of getting him in the right mood. Then she asked, "Where's your bally?" referring to an extra-large Kong ball she kept stuffed in the side pocket of her utility uniform. That ball would be Dan's reward when he uncovered something. It was designed to flop around on the ground rather than simply roll about, and Barrett would play with him and the ball for several minutes after a successful find.

The collar she slipped over Dan's neck instructed her K-9 that he'd be looking for a person, dead or alive, and that Dan was to be nonaggressive. That last instruction would have been particularly significant had the dog's mission been to locate a lost person who had emotional or mental problems. Barrett knew from experience that sometimes such people, when found by a rescue dog, may react in unpredictable ways. Sometimes such an individual will wave their arms and come at the dog to hug the animal. The K-9, surprised by such a move, would have no way of distinguishing that action from an attack. Thus the animals are taught to locate the subject of the search and then immediately return to their handler.

The trooper placed the collar over her K-9's head and let Dan go, ordering him to begin his search. As her dog began to move out, the trooper noticed that not far from where she stood she had an audience of fifteen people watching Dan work. She feared that their presence, since Dan does search and rescue when wearing that same collar, would be a big distraction for her K-9, but for the moment said nothing.

Only a few seconds after starting his search, Dan ran to a spot twenty feet from Barrett and began to paw a bit at the ground. He then stopped, looked back over to his partner, and headed her way. But instead of stopping by Barrett, which is what he should have done if he had found the scent of a dead person, he continued on to the crowd standing behind the trooper. He then headed back to Barrett and indicated to her that he wanted his ball. It was his way of saying that, after all, hadn't he just found a whole bunch of "lost people?"

Figuring her K-9 partner had just taken an easy out to get his reward, Barrett turned to the crowd and asked them to step back. She then took her partner off to the side by a big tree. Taking the search collar off she ordered him to lie down, then had a little talk with him.

She recalls that their one-way conversation went something like, "Settle down, Dan. Take it slow. Let's not do something silly here and piss off the old lady."

After a few minutes of keeping him away from the scene of his infraction, Barrett again put the special collar on Dan and directed him to resume searching. The K-9 headed straight back to the same place where he'd first pawed at the ground. Once there he began to dig but still looked back at the crowd of people not far away. Barrett had no idea what was in her partner's mind. Getting angry at Dan's apparent inability to focus on their task, she stalked over to him and began to ask him what he was up to. Starting off with, "Okay," and letting out a frustrated sigh, Barrett looked down at what her partner was doing. A white sheet, covered over by earth, was now visible under his paws.

Barrett went silent for a moment. Dan began to pull on the sheet. She then stopped him, aware of what he'd just uncovered. Calling to the CPAC investigators, "Over here!" she took her partner off to the side and got out the Kong ball. He had earned his reward.

After Dan had been sufficiently played with and fussed over, he was returned to their cruiser. Barrett was approached by a number of the officers. Their comments were "We could have been here all night, and even then it is unlikely we'd have found the body." Except, of course, for the fact that Barrett and Dan had done their job.

Those officers' comments had been right on target. Over the years, at dozens of crime scenes, Barrett and her canine partners had saved hundreds, if not more, officer hours by their skill and dedication.

The trooper made it look easy to the other people watching her in that cemetery on that cold January night. But she knew it had been a tough find. As a handler who respects her partner, she never wants to put her dog in a no win situation. And that evening's situation was close. The ground had been frozen and snow covered. There were people milling all about them who distracted Dan, plus one gravesite had just been uncovered, emitting a strong odor that her K-9 had been trained to key on. It had been a tough situation for a K-9 and handler to be in.

But Dan had come through, and David Alicea is in jail awaiting trial for murder. As to how the children had been killed, Alicea claims that the nine-month-old died of Sudden Infant Death Syndrome. He may find it more difficult to explain to a jury why his two-year-old died of rat poisoning.

A Church Deacon

Melissa Benoit and her family lived in Kingston, right on the town's Main Street, only a few hundred yards from the police station. Her proximity to all those officers would turn out to be of no help to the thirteen-year-old girl.

A year earlier the Benoit family had suffered a terrible and unexpected tragedy. Melissa's young father, George, had been stricken by a massive heart attack and died. He left his wife, Diane, and Melissa's eight-year-old sister, Erin, to go on with their lives.

It was Sunday, September 15, near the first anniversary of George Benoit's untimely death. Almost directly behind the family's home was the cemetery where the father had been buried, and Melissa was in the habit of visiting his grave daily. So, after spending some time with her cousin who lived nearby, Melissa left to go home. But first she went down the path behind her house that led to the Evergreen Cemetery to say hello to her father.

The little girl was never seen alive again, except by her murderer.

Diane Benoit first began to become concerned when her daughter, a punctual and responsible young lady, didn't come home for dinner. Calls to her brother's place, where the child had been playing much of that afternoon, only deepened the mystery. After a few more unsuccessful telephone inquiries Diane became deeply concerned. Before very long she called the police.

The Kingston police, after a brief investigation, initiated a search. Very soon hundreds of citizen volunteers were involved, as were dozens of law officers from around the area, fire department personnel, plus state police and FBI agents. For over a week the area around the Benoit home was scoured. People's permission was asked so that neighborhood homes and garages could be searched. On a hunch from the Kingston police chief, the grounds of the cemetery were gone over with a fine-tooth comb on three separate occasions.

In spite of the thousands of hours put into the search, for all anyone could discover, Melissa Benoit might as well have dropped off the face of the earth.

Three days into the search Barrett and Syros were called in to the investigation by the FBI. The bureau became involved because of their statutory authority in matters where a kidnapping is suspected.

At the Kingston police station Barrett was briefed by the chief and two lead investigators, Sergeant Jim Schillings and Detective Richard Arruda. There wasn't much of substance they could tell the trooper. The officers pointed out to Barrett that there were several people in the area they were interested in—people who either had a past history of sex offenses involving children, or whose behavior among youngsters was not normal. They also mentioned the fact that Bridgewater Hospital was located only two communities away, and that was the facility where sexually dangerous individuals were kept. And some of those people had been out on work release in the surrounding communities when Melissa disappeared.

It was only later in the investigation, when the officers reinterviewed Melissa's mother, that one particular individual came to their attention. Erin had recently told her mother that Melissa had confided to her that she didn't want to be alone with a neighbor, Henry Meinholtz. Meinholtz, a fifty-two-year-old married man, father of two daughters, was an upstanding citizen in the community, a deacon in the local church. He lived just next door to the Benoit family.

Meinholtz ultimately went on the list of names of people the police were looking at, individuals they would ask to take a polygraph test.

Unless one has ever been involved in this type of massive investigation, one involving multiple agencies and hundreds of civilian volunteers, it is difficult to imagine the degree of confusion such an activity engenders. The investigators are inundated with scores of theories and reports, each one more tempting than the other. Then there are the "sightings" of the victim, sometimes from all across the nation. A concerned citizen reported seeing Melissa in Halifax, walking along with an adult man. Other reports of sightings soon followed. Which of the hundreds, even thousands, of leads should investigators focus on?

In truth, there is no single answer to that question. Only after the investigation, when the facts come together, do the people with twenty-twenty hindsight—mostly from the media—begin their critique and tell the law officers how they should have run the case.

At the request of the police chief, Barrett worked Syros numerous times in and around the grounds of the Evergreen Cemetery. The chief had good reason for feeling strongly about that location. It was common knowledge in her neighborhood that the child visited her father's grave every day. Furthermore, it was the last place Melissa was headed to before she had disappeared. But strong hunches and reality sometimes don't match up. After the third meticulous search of the grounds, the trooper had to put her foot down. She told the other law officer, "I'm sorry, Chief, she's not here."

Emotion for all involved was beginning to run high.

The investigators did want the Halifax sighting checked out. Barrett told them that such a tracking job was beyond the capability of Syros. After all, it had been three days since the sighting, which was supposed to have been in a heavily traveled area. The trooper did recommend a bloodhound and handler she knew. It was arranged for the pillowcase from Melissa's bed—the object was loaded with the young girl's scent—to be bagged and used by the bloodhound.

Barrett went over to the house to get the pillowcase and was told it had already been brought over to the search and rescue people at their temporary search headquarters, which had been set up behind the police station. The trooper walked over to that location and was told by people there that the balding detective with the beard had taken the item. Barrett was confused. She didn't know any of the law officers involved who fit that description.

But soon enough she met a balding, bearded man. His name was Henry Meinholtz, a church deacon and concerned citizen. For it later turned out that Meinholtz had been all over the place, helping the searchers.

Barrett first met Meinholtz on the third day she was involved in the case. By that time it was decided that outbuildings—garages, sheds, equipment storage bins—surrounding the general vicinity of the Benoit home should be looked into. Barrett, for the moment without Syros, went along with some sheriff's deputies and their K-9. When they knocked on one home's side door, Henry Meinholtz stepped out to greet the officers. Asked if his garage could be searched, he replied, "Sure," mentioning that it had already been gone over once before. The officers explained they were re-searching all the buildings, just to make certain they hadn't missed anything. He assured the officers that he had checked the place himself and found nothing, but if they wished to look again, that was fine with him.

Meinholtz excused himself and stepped back into his house to get a key to unlock the building. Coming back out he and the law officers walked over to the two-car garage. Meinholtz unlocked the door for them. As soon as the door was opened, Barrett smelled a strong odor of wet paint. Glancing inside, the officers could see that part of the floor, as well as the metal support columns in the center of the structure, had recently been painted red. Meinholtz explained that his wife had trouble seeing, and the bright color was an attempt to assist her when she parked in the garage.

The sheriff's K-9 officers were concerned about bringing their dog into such a highly toxic environment. While Barrett stayed outside with Meinholtz and conversed with the man, a few of the investigators went inside and looked around. One of the bays was taken up by a small outboard motorboat, the other bay was empty. Finding nothing out of the ordinary, the sheriff's deputies came out.

During the time the deputies were busy inside, Meinholtz told the trooper what a nice girl Melissa was, how he'd been out looking for her with the other searchers, and how, when the Meinholtz and Benoit families had been to a wedding together, he had danced with Melissa.

Once the deputies stepped from the garage, its door was closed and again locked by Meinholtz. The man was thanked for his cooperation and the law officers went on with their search.

The days were long and tedious. Each started at six in the morning and ended with a debriefing at six in the evening. Barrett recalls that she searched miles of ground during that period. She and Syros even checked the Jones River by boat. Wherever somebody felt the missing girl might have wandered off to, Barrett looked there.

On Wednesday, September 26, the chief of police asked Barrett to bring along Syros so that she and her K-9 could assist his officers in conducting a consent search of a neighbor's house. The address they would go to was 255 Main Street. It was explained to Barrett that the man who lived in that home, Henry Meinholtz, had failed a lie-detector test. At that moment he was en route to take a second test.

The wife of Meinholtz, Jane, was asked if she'd mind if a search of the home was made. She said fine, and then commented, "By the way, you may want to bring a shovel."

Barrett, along with her partner and a large contingent of other officers, arrived at the home. Once inside Mrs. Meinholtz said to Barrett, "You probably want to check the cellar." She also mentioned there was a smell by the crawl space.

Barrett and Syros went down to the basement and headed first to the narrow crawl space. She called to one of the officers to assist her in moving some rocks blocking the small entryway. With that accomplished, Syros made his way in. After checking the area the K-9 returned, indicating to Barrett that nothing of interest was to be found there.

Syros stepped around some wood lying on the floor, past two lawn chairs, and made his over to the front of the oil burner. He immediately began to dig at the ground; then he began to bark. Syros only barked when he was on to something. It took only a few seconds for Barrett to see that her dog had uncovered a dead human body. It was then that she noticed the two lawn chairs; they had been arranged so that they faced where the body had been buried.

With Melissa's remains now uncovered, several things took place at once. The CPAC investigators secured the area, declared a crime scene, and initiated the procedure to procure a search warrant. As this was taking place, Barrett took out Syros' favorite ball and began to play with her dog. Her K-9 didn't work for overtime, days off, or medals. The only thing that mattered to Syros was to be rewarded with the attention of his handler when he found what they'd been looking for. After romping with her K-9, Barrett let Syros keep his toy ball.

The trooper came up from the basement with her dog and headed out the back door. Across the way, sitting on their rear deck, were members of the Benoit family. A large number of reporters from various news-media organizations had staked out the Meinholtz home and lined the end of the driveway. As soon as Barrett and Syros came outside, someone among the media people yelled out, "They've got her! The dog's got the ball!"

To Barrett's regret, she watched as the Benoit family members silently rose and stepped back inside their home.

Barrett thinks that's a hell of a way to find out the body of your child was inside the home of a neighbor. To this day she doesn't know who yelled out those words, but she'd very much like to have a little talk with that person.

After putting Syros back in their cruiser, Barrett returned to the Meinholtz home. For the next three hours she had to sit with Jane Meinholtz, ensuring the protection of the scene while waiting for the search warrant to arrive.

During this time Jane Meinholtz told Barrett what a fine man her husband was. She explained how at three in the morning he'd go out to help wayward girls, and even on Christmas Eve he'd leave the house to try and help kids.

Without commenting to the other woman, Barrett wondered to herself about a dead girl found during the early morning hours one day in the nearby town of Plymouth, and another girl found dead on Christmas day. Both were unsolved homicides. Who knows?

When a local youngster watched the evening news the day Henry Meinholtz was arrested and saw his picture flash on the screen, she became hysterical. She recognized him as the man who, the Friday before Melissa had turned up missing, had tried to abduct her, chasing her when she was at her school bus stop. She had described his pickup truck and plate number to her father after the incident. The family had every intention of going to the police with that information the following Monday but put it off when they saw how much effort the police were putting into their search for Melissa, figuring the officers had enough on their plate at the moment.

Barrett saw the young lady testify during Meinholtz's trial. In Barret's opinion she and Melissa could have passed for sisters.

When the search warrant arrived, the officers began to

look for additional evidence. While Melissa's body was being dug up down in the basement, Syros was taken back to the garage. There he became highly excited by the boat, actually biting at its wooden sides. The K-9 also alerted to a patch of earth under a workbench. There he dug up a brown paper bag containing a pair of female panties. No one has ever determined who they belonged to.

The investigators eventually established, through forensic evidence, that Melissa had been murdered in that boat. Using sophisticated equipment, it was evident that after the crime the body had been dropped from the boat onto the garage floor, dragged over to the door, across the yard, and then somehow gotten down the stairway and into the Meinholtz basement.

One mystery Barrett cannot explain is how Meinholtz could have accomplished all this by himself. Not a powerful man, he had the additional problem of having a very bad back. Who, she has asked herself many times, might have been the person who helped him in his attempt to hide Melissa's body?

Then again, why did Jane Meinholtz tell the investigators to bring a shovel?

Barrett is certain that if the police hadn't launched their search immediately after being notified the child was missing, Melissa's body would have been dumped in the ocean. For it was later determined that around the time Melissa was first discovered to be missing Meinholtz had called a friend with an offer to go fishing. But Barrett is sure the large numbers of officers in and around his home stopped him from carrying out that plan. No one knows for sure how long the body had lain at the bottom of his boat, but it couldn't have been too long after he murdered Melissa that she was buried in the man's basement.

At his trial Meinholtz testified that, yes, he raped and murdered Melissa, but his defense was that he was insane. He was careful to let the jury know, in graphic detail, how much he had enjoyed what he'd done. He stated that he had grabbed Melissa while she was coming back from visiting her father's grave, a pattern he'd been watching for quite a while.

Upon sentencing Meinholtz to life imprisonment without parole, the judge commented that it was unfortunate that the man couldn't be taken from the courtroom and hung.

The attorney for Meinholtz has never permitted any law officer to speak with his client. Nor has he released the ninety minutes of tape recording done when Meinholtz was interviewed by him when his client was under the influence of sodium Pentothal. It irks Barrett to think that there are families out there who have suffered the agony of having their children disappear who might well want to know what was on that tape.

A Typical Christmas Eve

Barrett comes from a large, Irish Catholic family. The church's rituals, as well as her connection to family, are important parts of life to her. Which is why Christmas Eve can be a time of such mixed emotions for the trooper. On one hand, Barrett enjoys all the good feeling and spiritual warmth that day and season bring. Yet, in her experience as a law officer, she finds that for many other people the heightened expectation of love and belonging only brings disappointment. There are a lot of suicides on Christmas Eve.

The Barrett family has a Christmas holiday tradition. On the evening before Christmas, each person exchanges a single present. The next morning the remaining gifts are opened.

A few years ago, when her son, Sean, was sixteen, Barrett was concerned because, although her son had an after-school job, he always seemed out of money. She would ask him what he was doing with his earnings, only to get vague responses. Based on his actions and answers to her questions, the only thing she could think was that Sean was throwing his money away.

So it was that on this particular Christmas Eve that the mother and son handed each other the presents they wished opened that night. Just as Barrett was getting the gift wrapping clear from the small box in her hands, her beeper went off.

Using a few choice words that perhaps were inappropriate for that holy night, she put down her present and turned to pick up the telephone. Sean stopped her and begged her to open her present before calling in to work.

Whenever a conflict arose between work and family, especially when it came to her son, Barrett believed she had only one option. She picked up the half-opened box and continued working to release whatever was inside. With the small lid off, Barrett saw the sparkle of gems. Taking out the piece of jewelry, she found that her son had bought her a diamond tennis bracelet. She then realized why he'd had so little money during the last few months.

After kissing Sean, Barrett, bracelet on her wrist, picked up the telephone and called the Middleboro Barracks. Lieutenant Jeff Taylor answered her call; he was celebrating the holiday while doing desk duty. His words were to the point. "Hey, Squirter (his nickname for Barrett; the two had known each other since she'd started on the force), you got a call."

Barrett replied with a good-natured, albeit somewhat obscene, rejoinder to that bit of information. The lieutenant, ignoring Barrett's observation, went on to explain that a woman in her early twenties was missing from Pocasset Hospital, a mental health facility, and had been since early afternoon. It was cold out. He explained that if she wasn't found soon, they'd be out looking for a dead body.

On hanging up the telephone, Barrett faced a dilemma. There was no question that she and Syros were going on that call. But she'd have to leave her son alone at home on Christmas Eve. She pondered her options for a moment. Aware that the situation she'd be dealing with was nonviolent, she made a mother's decision. Sean would come along with her and Syros. Anyway, her son had never seen his mom at work. It'd be a learning experience.

Pocasset, situated on Cape Cod and not far from Barrett's home, took them only an hour to get to. So it was around eight-thirty when she knocked on the hospital's door. As she stood outside, waiting for someone to let her in, she took in the cold, clear night air. She reflected that it was a perfect night for a lightly dressed person to suffer hypothermia.

A staff person from the facility opened the door and in a few moments briefed Barrett on all that was known about the situation. The young woman patient suffered from depression. She had gone off wearing a sweatshirt and slacks. It had been hours since anyone had seen her.

Barrett reflected that in her experience some facilities don't contact the authorities when one of their charges is missing until a week or more has gone by. At least here she had a chance of locating the person alive.

Barrett, along with Sean and Syros, headed out to the back of the property. Beyond that point it was heavily wooded. Taking out Syros' search-and-rescue collar, the one that let her K-9 know that the job ahead didn't require any aggressive behavior, she slipped it over her dog's neck and gave the command, "Go find her!" Almost immediately the dog's head snapped around to a specific direction, a clear indication to the trooper that he was on to something. In a flash he took off.

With Sean at her side, the two watched as the K-9 went bounding off into the expanse of dense Cape Cod woods that lay behind the hospital. They had trouble keeping the beams of their flashlights on the quickly moving dog as they ran after him.

With the senior Barrett in the lead, the two humans entered the forest. The dense growth made it nearly impossible to keep Syros in view. However, the trooper could hear her K-9 up ahead. She stopped looking for Syros and used her light to keep from crashing into the thick vegetation. When her canine partner stopped short, she kept on going, almost falling over him.

Syros looked down at the ground and began to bark. Barrett put her light on the spot he was interested in, but for the life of her she couldn't see anything but a forest floor covered with dead leaves. But she knew that Syros only barked when he had something. She commanded him, "Show Me!"

At once the big shepherd began to dig. From under him came the yell, "Ow!" a call so loud that Barrett was startled.

Syros, of course, had found the missing woman. Cold, she'd covered herself with leaves and had fallen asleep. Barrett knew that if she and Syros had not been called out to look for her, whoever eventually did find her would have found her frozen body right where they were.

Leaving Sean to keep an eye on the young woman, Barrett returned to the hospital and secured help. An ambulance was soon on the scene, and the woman was taken to an area hospital for observation.

When the woman was taken away, Sean asked his mother, "What does she do for Christmas?"

No answer was possible, nor was one forthcoming. The night had indeed been a learning experience for her son.

With the search over, Sean, his mother, and Syros returned to their car. Now that they wouldn't be running through the woods anymore that night, Barrett took her son's gift, the diamond tennis bracelet, from her pocket and carefully put it on.

After all, it was Christmas Eve.

Afterword

I thought I knew all about dogs before writing this book. After all, hadn't I owned, at various times and in packs of varying size (from one to four, plus cats), a dozen or so of these creatures over the years? I was wrong. I underestimated the intelligence, loyalty, and perseverance these animals can possess.

Humans and canines have coexisted for thousands of years. Why the other species wanted to put in with us in the first place is something of a mystery to me, especially considering how we as a group have treated them.

One exception that I found to the sometimes shabby history of human-canine collaboration is the relationship between law officers and their four-legged partners. The key here is co-dependence. Humans, without their trained dog's superior senses, are far more vulnerable to danger, as well as being much less effective while performing their difficult tasks. Animals, without their human partners and the direction they provide, are in even more dangerous straits. The symbiosis of the two species makes for a whole greater than the sum of the parts.

Almost without exception, when the handlers spoke of their canine partners, there was reflected pride, affection, and respect for their dogs. None of the officers I spoke with ever voiced doubt that their dogs would lay down their lives for them. Such feelings make for a strong bond.

On more than one occasion handlers told me the reason they wished to be interviewed was because they wanted the accomplishments performed by their K-9s—a number of whom were getting old, and some of whom had died—told to the world. I hope I have met their expectations. Both they and their K-9 partners deserve no less.